Focus on GRAMMAR 4A

FOURTH EDITION

Marjorie Fuchs
Margaret Bonner

ALWAYS LEARNING

To the memory of my parents, Edith and Joseph Fuchs—MF
To my parents, Marie and Joseph Maus, and to my son, Luke Frances—MB

FOCUS ON GRAMMAR 4A: An Integrated Skills Approach, Fourth Edition

Copyright © 2012, 2006, 2000, 1995 by Pearson Education, Inc.
All rights reserved.

Pearson Education, 10 Bank Street, White Plains, NY 10606

Staff credits: The people who made up the *Focus on Grammar 4A, Fourth Edition*
team, representing editorial, production, design, and manufacturing, are Elizabeth Carlson,
Tracey Cataldo, Aerin Csigay, Dave Dickey, Christine Edmonds, Nancy Flaggman, Ann France,
Françoise Leffler, Lise Minovitz, Barbara Perez, Robert Ruvo, and Debbie Sistino.

Cover image: Shutterstock.com
Text composition: ElectraGraphics, Inc.
Text font: New Aster

PEARSON LONGMAN ON THE **WEB**

Pearsonlongman.com offers online
resources for teachers and students. Access
our Companion Websites, our online catalog,
and our local offices around the world.

Visit us at **pearsonlongman.com**.

Printed in the United States of America

ISBN 10: 0-13-216937-1
ISBN 13: 978-0-13-216937-0

8   16

ISBN 10: 0-13-216939-8 (with MyLab)
ISBN 13: 978-0-13-216939-4 (with MyLab)

4 5 6 7 8 9 10—V082—16

CONTENTS

WELCOME TO *FOCUS ON GRAMMAR*

Now in a new edition, the popular five-level *Focus on Grammar* course continues to provide an integrated-skills approach to help students understand and practice English grammar. Centered on thematic instruction, *Focus on Grammar* combines controlled and communicative practice with critical thinking skills and ongoing assessment. Students gain the confidence they need to speak and write English accurately and fluently.

NEW for the FOURTH EDITION

VOCABULARY

Key vocabulary is highlighted, practiced, and recycled throughout the unit.

PRONUNCIATION

Now, in every unit, pronunciation points and activities help students improve spoken accuracy and fluency.

LISTENING

Expanded listening tasks allow students to develop a range of listening skills.

UPDATED CHARTS and NOTES

Target structures are presented in a clear, easy-to-read format.

NEW READINGS

High-interest readings, updated or completely new, in a variety of genres integrate grammar and vocabulary in natural contexts.

NEW UNIT REVIEWS

Students can check their understanding and monitor their progress after completing each unit.

MyFocusOnGrammarLab

An easy-to-use online learning and assessment program offers online homework and individualized instruction anywhere, anytime.

Teacher's Resource Pack   One compact resource includes:

THE TEACHER'S MANUAL: General Teaching Notes, Unit Teaching Notes, the Student Book Audioscript, and the Student Book Answer Key.

TEACHER'S RESOURCE DISC: Bound into the Resource Pack, this CD-ROM contains reproducible Placement, Part, and Unit Tests, as well as customizable Test-Generating Software. It also includes reproducible Internet Activities and PowerPoint® Grammar Presentations.

THE *FOCUS ON GRAMMAR* APPROACH

The new edition follows the same successful four-step approach of previous editions. The books provide an abundance of both controlled and communicative exercises so that students can bridge the gap between identifying grammatical structures and using them. The many communicative activities in each Student Book provide opportunities for critical thinking while enabling students to personalize what they have learned.

- **STEP 1: GRAMMAR IN CONTEXT** highlights the target structures in realistic contexts, such as conversations, magazine articles, and blog posts.
- **STEP 2: GRAMMAR PRESENTATION** presents the structures in clear and accessible grammar charts and notes with multiple examples of form and usage.
- **STEP 3: FOCUSED PRACTICE** provides numerous and varied controlled exercises for both the form and meaning of the new structures.
- **STEP 4: COMMUNICATION PRACTICE** includes listening and pronunciation and allows students to use the new structures freely and creatively in motivating, open-ended speaking and writing activities.

Recycling

Underpinning the scope and sequence of the *Focus on Grammar* series is the belief that students need to use target structures and vocabulary many times, in different contexts. New grammar and vocabulary are recycled throughout the book. Students have maximum exposure and become confident using the language in speech and in writing.

Assessment

Extensive testing informs instruction and allows teachers and students to measure progress.

- **Unit Reviews** at the end of every Student Book unit assess students' understanding of the grammar and allow students to monitor their own progress.
- Easy to administer and score, **Part and Unit Tests** provide teachers with a valid and reliable means to determine how well students know the material they are about to study and to assess students' mastery after they complete the material. These tests can be found on MyFocusOnGrammarLab, where they include immediate feedback and remediation, and as reproducible tests on the Teacher's Resource Disc.
- **Test-Generating Software** on the Teacher's Resource Disc includes a bank of *additional* test items teachers can use to create customized tests.
- A reproducible **Placement Test** on the Teacher's Resource Disc is designed to help teachers place students into one of the five levels of the *Focus on Grammar* course.

COMPONENTS

In addition to the Student Books, Teacher's Resource Packs, and MyLabs, the complete *Focus on Grammar* course includes:

Workbooks Contain additional contextualized exercises appropriate for self-study.

Audio Program Includes all of the listening and pronunciation exercises and opening passages from the Student Book. Some Student Books are packaged with the complete audio program (mp3 files). Alternatively, the audio program is available on a classroom set of CDs and on the MyLab.

THE *FOCUS ON GRAMMAR* UNIT

Focus on Grammar introduces grammar structures in the context of unified themes. All units follow a **four-step approach**, taking learners from grammar in context to communicative practice.

STEP 1 GRAMMAR IN CONTEXT

This section presents the target structure(s) in a natural context. As students read the **high-interest texts**, they encounter the form, meaning, and use of the grammar. **Before You Read** activities create interest and elicit students' knowledge about the topic. **After You Read** activities build students' reading vocabulary and comprehension.

Vocabulary exercises improve students' command of English. Vocabulary is **recycled** throughout the unit.

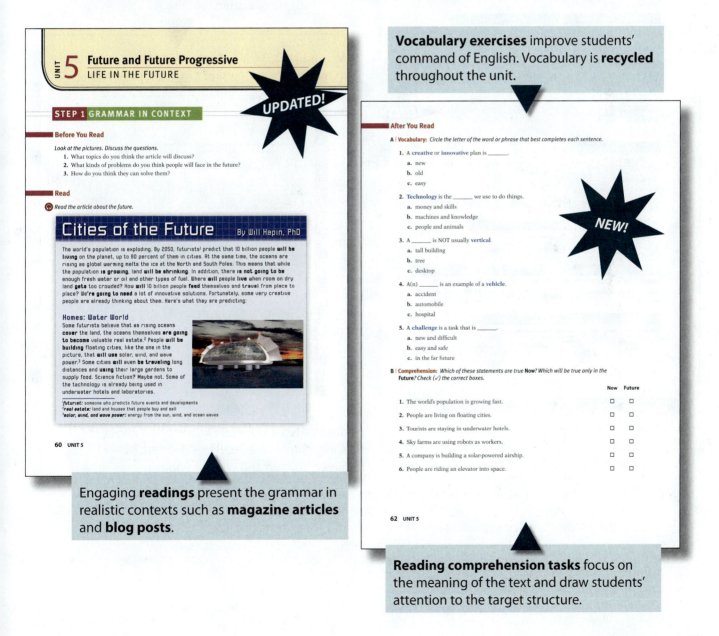

Engaging **readings** present the grammar in realistic contexts such as **magazine articles** and **blog posts**.

Reading comprehension tasks focus on the meaning of the text and draw students' attention to the target structure.

This section gives students a comprehensive and explicit overview of the grammar with detailed **Grammar Charts** and **Grammar Notes** that present the form, meaning, and use of the structure(s).

Grammar Charts present the structure in a clear, easy-to-read format.

Grammar Notes give concise, simple **explanations** and **examples** to ensure students' understanding.

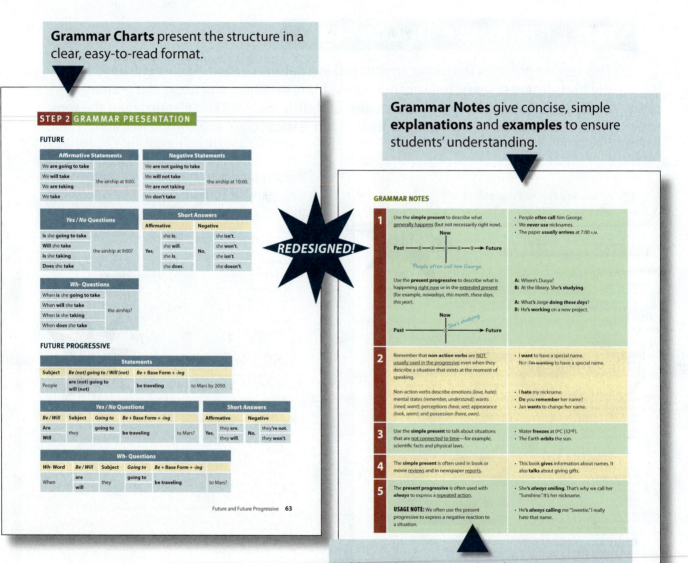

Additional **Notes** provide information about spelling, common errors, and differences between spoken and written English.

STEP 3 FOCUSED PRACTICE

Controlled practice activities in this section lead students to master form, meaning, and use of the target grammar.

STEP 3 FOCUSED PRACTICE

EXERCISE 1: Discover the Grammar

Match the facts with the speculations and conclusions.

Facts

___e___ 1. The original title of *Chariots of the Gods?* was *Erinnerungen an die Zukunft*.

_____ 2. Erich von Däniken visited every place he described in his book.

_____ 3. In 1973, he wrote *In Search of Ancient Gods*.

_____ 4. He doesn't have a degree in archeology.

_____ 5. *Chariots of the Gods?* was published the same year as the Apollo moon landing.

_____ 6. In the 1900s, writer Annie Besant said beings from Venus helped develop culture on Earth.

_____ 7. Von Däniken's books sold millions of copies.

_____ 8. As soon as von Däniken published his book, scientists attacked his theories.

Speculations and Conclusions

a. He must have made a lot of money.

b. He may have known about her unusual ideas.

c. He could have learned about the subject on his own.

d. He must have traveled a lot.

e. He must have written his book in German.

f. This great event had to have increased sales of the book.

g. He must not have had scientific evidence for his beliefs.

h. He might have written some other books too.

Discover the Grammar activities develop students' recognition and understanding of the target structure before they are asked to produce it.

EXERCISE 2: Questions and Statements

(Grammar Notes 1–4)

Circle the correct words to complete the review of Erich von Däniken's book, Chariots of the Gods?

Who could have make / **made** the Nazca lines? Who
                              1.
could have carve / carved the Easter Island statues?
                 2.
According to Erich von Däniken, ancient achievements
like these are mysteries because our ancestors could not
have / had created these things on their own. His
3.
conclusion: They must / couldn't have gotten help from
                       4.
space visitors.

Von Däniken's readers may not realize that experiments
have contributed to our understanding of some of these
"mysteries." Von Däniken asks: How may / could the Nazcans have planned the lines from
                                           5.
the ground? Archeologists now speculate that this civilization might have / has developed flight.
                                                                            6.
They think ancient Nazcans may draw / have drawn pictures of hot-air balloons on pottery. To test
                                            7.

"Here comes another one."

(continued on next page)

Speculations and Conclusions About the Past **275**

An **Editing** exercise ends every Focused Practice section and teaches students to find and correct typical mistakes.

EXERCISE 6: Editing

Read this article about cars of the future. There are ten mistakes in the use of the future and future progressive. The first mistake is already corrected. Find and correct nine more.

Flying Cars

Your class starts in 10 minutes, but you're stuck in traffic. Don't panic. With just a press of a button, your car will ~~lifts~~ *lift* off the ground, and you'll be on your way to school. No bad roads, no stop signs, no worries!

The SkyCar

Welcome to the future! It seems like science fiction, but it isn't. Engineers have been working on flying cars for decades, and they have already solved many of the big challenges. They predict that we'll all be use these amazing vehicles one day.

According to *Car Trends Magazine*, one model, part car and part plane, is going be on the market in the not-so-distant future. It will look like a regular car when it's on the road, but its wings will unfold when the driver will decide to take to the skies. It will runs on the same fuel for both land and air travel, and you'll be able to keep it in your garage. (But you're still going need an airport to take off and land.)

A better model will be a vertical takeoff and landing vehicle (VTOL). You won't need to go to the airport anymore, and all controls will being automatic. Imagine this: You'll be doing your homework while your car will be getting you to school safely and on time.

And what does this future dream car cost? Well, fasten your seatbelts—the price will going to be sky-high. At first it will be about a million dollars, but after a few years, you'll be able to buy one for "only" $60,000. Don't throw away your old driver's license just yet!

A **variety of exercise types** engage students and guide them from recognition and understanding to accurate production of the grammar structures.

Future and Future Progressive **71**

This section provides practice with the structure in **listening** and **pronunciation** exercises as well as in communicative, open-ended **speaking** and **writing** activities that move students toward fluency.

Listening activities allow students to hear the grammar in natural contexts and to practice a range of listening skills.

EXERCISE 7: Listening

A | *Some friends are at a high school reunion. They haven't seen one another for 25 years. Read the statements. Then listen to the conversation. Listen again and circle the correct words to complete the statements.*

1. People at the reunion have / haven't changed a lot.

2. Ann is wearing a lot of jewelry / a scarf.

3. It's the man / woman who first recognizes Kado.

4. Bob and Pat are the students who worked on the school paper / ran for class president.

5. Asha is looking at a photo / Bob.

6. Asha is the woman who married Pete Rizzo / Raza Gupta.

7. The man and woman know / don't know who is sitting between Asha and Pat.

B | *Look at the picture. Then listen again to the conversation and write the correct name next to each person.*

Ann   Asha   Bob   Kado   Pat   Pete

evil: a bad thing

EXPANDED!

EXERCISE 12: Writing

A | *Write a two-paragraph essay about a friend. You may want to begin your essay with one of the quotations from Exercise 11. Use adjective clauses with subject relative pronouns. You can use the essay in Exercise 6 as a model.*

EXAMPLE: Do friends have to be people who have the same interests or personality? I don't think so. My friend Richie and I are best friends who are complete opposites. He's an extrovert who can walk into a room that is full of strangers with no problem. In an hour, they'll all be new friends. I'm an introvert who . . .

B | *Check your work. Use the Editing Checklist.*

Editing Checklist

Did you use . . . ?

☐ *who* or *that* for people
☐ *which* or *that* for places and things
☐ *whose* to show possession or relationship
☐ the correct verb form in adjective clauses
☐ identifying adjective clauses to identify a noun
☐ nonidentifying adjective clauses to give more information about a noun
☐ commas to separate nonidentifying adjective clauses

NEW!

219

Pronunciation Notes and **exercises** improve students' spoken fluency and accuracy.

EXERCISE 8: Pronunciation

A | *Read and listen to the Pronunciation Note.*

Pronunciation Note

In **writing**, we use **commas** around **nonidentifying adjective clauses**.
In **speaking**, we **pause** briefly **before and after** nonidentifying adjective clauses.
EXAMPLE: Marta, who lives across from me, has become a good friend. →
"Marta [PAUSE] who lives across from me [PAUSE] has become a good friend."

NEW!

B | *Listen to the sentences. Add commas if you hear pauses around the adjective clauses.*

1. My neighbor who is an introvert called me today.

2. My neighbor who is an introvert called me today.

3. My brother who is one year older than me is an extrovert.

4. My sister who lives in Toronto visits us every summer.

5. My friend who is in the same class as me lent me a book.

6. The book which is about personality types is really interesting.

7. The article that won a prize is in today's newspaper.

8. My boyfriend who hates parties actually agreed to go to one with me.

C | *Listen again and repeat the sentences.*

EXERCISE 9: Discussion

A | *Take the quiz in Exercise 2.*

B | *Work with a partner. Discuss your answers to the quiz. What do you think your answers show about your personality?*

EXAMPLE: **A:** Question 1. People who talk a lot tire me. That's true.
B: I think that means you're probably an introvert. It wasn't true for me. I myself talk a lot, and I enjoy people who talk a lot too.

Speaking activities help students synthesize the grammar through discussions, debates, games, and problem-solving tasks, developing their fluency.

Writing activities encourage students to produce meaningful writing that integrates the grammar structure.

An **Editing Checklist** teaches students to correct their mistakes and revise their work.

Unit Reviews give students the opportunity to check their understanding of the target structure. **Answers** at the back of the book allow students to monitor their own progress.

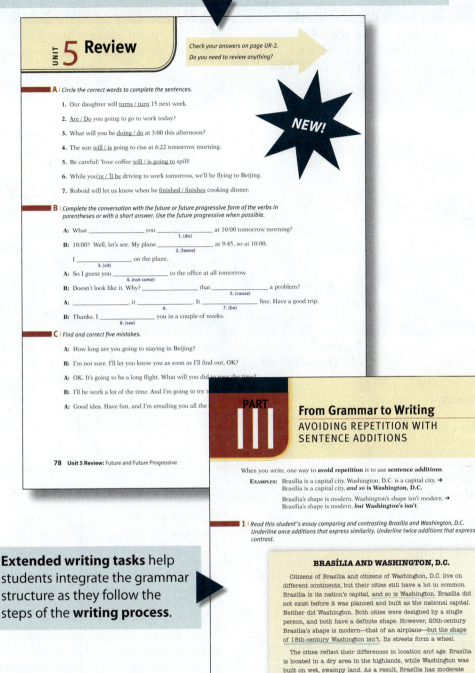

UNIT **5** **Review**

Check your answers on page UR-2.
Do you need to review anything?

NEW!

A | *Circle the correct words to complete the sentences.*

1. Our daughter will turns / turn 15 next week.

2. Are / Do you going to go to work today?

3. What will you be doing / do at 3:00 this afternoon?

4. The sun will / is going to rise at 6:22 tomorrow morning.

5. Be careful! Your coffee will / is going to spill!

6. While you're / 'll be driving to work tomorrow, we'll be flying to Beijing.

7. Roboid will let us know when he finished / finishes cooking dinner.

B | *Complete the conversation with the future or future progressive form of the verbs in parentheses or with a short answer. Use the future progressive when possible.*

A: What _____ you _____ at 10:00 tomorrow morning?
 1. (do)

B: 10:00? Well, let's see. My plane _____ at 9:45, so at 10:00,
 2. (leave)

 I _____ on the plane.
 3. (sit)

A: So I guess you _____ to the office at all tomorrow.
 4. (not come)

B: Doesn't look like it. Why? _____ that _____ a problem?
 5. (cause)

A: _____, it _____. It _____ fine. Have a good trip.
 6. 7. (be)

B: Thanks. I _____ you in a couple of weeks.
 8. (see)

C | *Find and correct five mistakes.*

A: How long are you going to staying in Beijing?

B: I'm not sure. I'll let you know you as soon as I'll find out, OK?

A: OK. It's going to be a long flight. What will you did to pass the time?

B: I'll be work a lot of the time. And I'm going to try t

A: Good idea. Have fun, and I'm emailing you all the

78 Unit 5 Review: Future and Future Progressive

PART **III**

From Grammar to Writing
AVOIDING REPETITION WITH SENTENCE ADDITIONS

When you write, one way to **avoid repetition** is to use **sentence additions**.

EXAMPLES: Brasília is a capital city. Washington, D.C. is a capital city. →
Brasília is a capital city, *and so* is **Washington, D.C.**

Brasília's shape is modern. Washington's shape isn't modern. →
Brasília's shape is modern, *but* **Washington's isn't.**

1 | *Read this student's essay comparing and contrasting Brasília and Washington, D.C. Underline once additions that express similarity. Underline twice additions that express contrast.*

BRASÍLIA AND WASHINGTON, D.C.

Citizens of Brasília and citizens of Washington, D.C. live on different continents, but their cities still have a lot in common. Brasília is its nation's capital, and so is Washington. Brasília did not exist before it was planned and built as the national capital. Neither did Washington. Both cities were designed by a single person, and both have a definite shape. However, 20th-century Brasília's shape is modern—that of an airplane—but the shape of 18th-century Washington isn't. Its streets form a wheel.

The cities reflect their differences in location and age. Brasília is located in a dry area in the highlands, while Washington was built on wet, swampy land. As a result, Brasília has moderate temperatures all year, but Washington doesn't. Washington is famous for its cold winters and hot, humid summers. Brasília was built 600 miles from the Atlantic coast in order to attract people to an unpopulated area. Washington, near the Atlantic coast, includes old towns that had already existed. Brasília is home to many famous theaters and museums, and so is the city of Washington. However, as a new city, Brasília has not yet become its nation's real cultural center. Washington hasn't either. Washington is its country's capital, but it is not its country's most popular city. Neither is Brasília. Many people still prefer the excitement of Rio and New York.

Extended writing tasks help students integrate the grammar structure as they follow the steps of the **writing process**.

134 PART III

The *Focus on Grammar* Unit **xi**

SCOPE AND SEQUENCE

SPEAKING	PRONUNCIATION	VOCABULARY	
Find Someone Who . . .	Stressing contrasting or new information	actually convince* institute*	style* (n) title
What About You? The first time you met someone who became influential in your life *Ask and Answer:* Important events in your life	Intonation and pauses in sentences with time clauses	couple* cover (v) influential	opponent recover* research* (n)
What About You? Talk about your hobbies and interests *Ask and Answer:* What did you plan to accomplish last week?	Reduction of *has he* ("hazee") and *did he* ("didee") *have you* ("havya") and *did you* ("didja")	celebrate engaged extreme	fantastic historic introduce
What About You? Compare your day yesterday with a classmate's *Conversation:* Talk about things you had never done before . . . *Game:* Find the Differences	Pronunciation of the contraction of *had* ('d) after pronouns and nouns	conduct* (v) contract* (n) enthusiastic	ethnic* participate* transform*
Reaching Agreement: Finding a time to get together *Discussion:* Which activities will robots be doing and not doing? *Information Gap:* Dr. Eon's Calendar	Stress for contrasting information	challenge* (n) creative* innovative*	technology* vehicle* vertical
Conversation: What will some of the people in your life have achieved by the end of this year, month, or week? *What About You?* Three goals you would like to achieve in the next five years	Reduction of *have* ("of") in the future perfect and future perfect progressive	budget (n) credit* (n) debt	minimum* purchase* (n) statistics*

* = AWL (Academic Word List) items

UNIT	READING	WRITING	LISTENING
7 page 100 **Grammar:** Negative *Yes / No* Questions and Tag Questions **Theme:** Places to Live	On-the-street interviews: *It's a Great Place to Live, Isn't It?*	An interview of a classmate about his or her city	Short conversations asking for information or looking for agreement
8 page 118 **Grammar:** Additions and Responses: *So, Too, Neither, Not either,* and *But* **Theme:** Similarities and Differences	An article: *The Twin Question: Nature or Nurture?*	Two paragraphs about two people who are close	A couple talking about their similarities and differences

PART III From Grammar to Writing, page 134
Avoiding Repetition with Sentence Additions: Write an essay of comparison and contrast.

9 page 138 **Grammar:** Gerunds and Infinitives: Review and Expansion **Theme:** Fast Food	An article: *McWorld*	A short editorial about a social issue involving food	Two college students discussing their responses to a food service survey
10 page 156 **Grammar:** *Make, Have, Let, Help,* and *Get* **Theme:** Zoos and Water Parks	An article: *That's Entertainment?*	A three-paragraph essay for and against keeping animals in zoos and water parks	A student and teacher talking about a writing assignment

PART IV From Grammar to Writing, page 168
Using Parallel Forms: Gerunds and Infinitives: Write a summary of a movie, TV show, or story.

SPEAKING	PRONUNCIATION	VOCABULARY	
Information Gap: London and Vancouver *Conversation:* How well do you know your classmates?	Rising or falling intonation in tag questions	adjustment* attract bother	originally provide structure* (n)
Discussion: Are the man and woman a good match? *Picture Discussion:* Imagine the conversations of reunited twins *Find Someone Who . . .* *Compare and Contrast:* Look at pictures of a pair of twins and find their similarities and differences *What Do You Think?* Which is more important, nature or nurture?	Stress in additions and short responses of similarity and difference	coincidence* despite* factor*	identical* image* outgoing
Information Gap: The Right Job? *Questionnaire:* Compare your answers on a fast-food questionnaire with your partner's *Cross-Cultural Comparison:* Describe a food from your culture. Then choose foods to include in an international food festival. *Problem Solving:* Solutions to social problems	Intonation to express sincerity or sarcasm	appealing consequence* globe*	objection region* reliability*
Discussion: Who helped you learn something? *For or Against:* Keeping animals captive	Reductions and linking of pronouns: *let her* ("let'er"), *made him* ("made'im"), *got them* ("got'em")	complicated former humane	physical* punishment reward (n)

* = AWL (Academic Word List) items

UNIT	READING	WRITING	LISTENING
11 page 172 **Grammar:** Phrasal Verbs: Review **Theme:** Feng Shui	An article: *Wind and Water*	Two paragraphs about how you feel in your home, office, dorm, or classroom	A couple talking about their home
12 page 186 **Grammar:** Phrasal Verbs: Separable and Inseparable **Theme:** Telemarketing	An article: *Welcome Home!*	A paragraph about an experience you have had on the phone	A telemarketing call

PART V   From Grammar to Writing, page 200
Using the Appropriate Level of Formality: Write a letter to a landlord about problems in a building lobby.

UNIT	READING	WRITING	LISTENING
13 page 206 **Grammar:** Adjective Clauses with Subject Relative Pronouns **Theme:** Friends and Personality Types	An article: *Extroverts and Introverts*	A two-paragraph essay about a friend	A conversation between classmates at a high school reunion
14 page 221 **Grammar:** Adjective Clauses with Object Relative Pronouns or *When* and *Where* **Theme:** The Immigrant Experience	Two book reviews: *Torn Between Two Worlds*	One or two paragraphs about a place you remember from your childhood	An author describing her childhood room

PART VI   From Grammar to Writing, page 237
Adding Details with Adjective Clauses: Write an essay about a famous person.

UNIT	READING	WRITING	LISTENING
15 page 240 **Grammar:** Modals and Similar Expressions: Review **Theme:** Social Networking	An article: *Facebook or Face Time? The Pros and Cons of Social Networking*	A blog post about your plans for the week	Two friends discussing Facebook

SPEAKING	PRONUNCIATION	VOCABULARY	
Problem Solving: How would you like to change your classroom or your school? *Compare and Contrast:* Describe the differences in Before and After pictures of a room	Linking final consonant sounds to beginning vowel sounds in phrasal verbs	complex* consultant* environment*	harmful theory*
For or Against: Telemarketing calls *Discussion:* What do you think about an ad, a piece of junk mail, spam, or an Internet offer?	Stress in separable phrasal verbs	authorities* constantly* eliminate*	equivalent* identify* tactic
Discussion: What do your answers on a personality quiz mean? *Questionnaire:* A friend is someone who . . . *Quotable Quotes:* Friends and personality types	Pausing before and after nonidentifying adjective clauses	contradict* define* personality	require* sensitive unique*
What About You? Share photos of people and places with your classmates. *Quotable Quotes:* Home	Breaking long sentences into thought groups	connection generation* immigrant*	issue* poverty translation
Discussion: What do you think of a student's profile on a social networking site? *Reaching Agreement:* Designing a class website *Problem Solving:* What would you do to survive on a desert island? *For or Against:* The advantages and disadvantages of online social networking	Reductions of: *have to* ("hafta"), *have got to* ("have gotta"), *ought to* ("oughta"), *be able to* ("be able ta")	comment* (n) content (n) involved*	network* (v) privacy resource*

* = AWL (Academic Word List) items

UNIT	READING	WRITING	LISTENING
16 page 257 **Grammar:** Advisability in the Past **Theme:** Regrets	An article: *Useless Regrets*	Three paragraphs about a dilemma that you have faced	A woman recording her regrets at the end of the day
17 page 270 **Grammar:** Speculations and Conclusions About the Past **Theme:** Unsolved Mysteries	An article: *Close Encounters*	A paragraph speculating about an event	Archeology students speculating about objects they have found

PART VII From Grammar to Writing, page 285
Organizing Ideas from Freewriting: Write a letter to a person you had a problem with.

UNIT	READING	WRITING	LISTENING
18 page 290 **Grammar:** The Passive: Overview **Theme:** Geography	An article: *Geography: The Best Subject on Earth*	An essay about a country you know well	Short conversations between two travel writers
19 page 308 **Grammar:** The Passive with Modals and Similar Expressions **Theme:** The International Space Station	An article: *Close Quarters*	Two paragraphs about your neighborhood, your school, or your workplace	Conversations from a science fiction movie
20 page 323 **Grammar:** The Passive Causative **Theme:** Personal Services	An article: *Body Art*	An email describing what you have recently done or have had done	A college student talking to her father about her new apartment

PART VIII   From Grammar to Writing, page 337
Changing the Focus with the Passive: Write a research report about a famous building.

SPEAKING	PRONUNCIATION	VOCABULARY	
Game: Find the Problems *Survey:* Sense of Obligation *Problem Solving:* What should the people have done in these situations?	Reductions of *have* in past modals: *should have* ("shoulda"), *could have* ("coulda"), *might have* ("mighta"), *ought to have* ("oughta of")	process* (n) psychology* ruined	strategy* technique* unrealistic
Picture Discussion: Speculate on what ancient objects are and how people might have used them *For or Against:* Do you agree or disagree with Erich von Däniken's theories?	Reductions of *have* in past modals: *could have* ("could of"), *may have* ("may of"), *couldn't have* ("couldn't of")	conclusion* contribute* encounter* (n)	estimate* (v) evidence* speculate*
Quotable Quotes: International proverbs *Information Gap:* The Philippines *Game:* Trivia Quiz	Stressing corrected information	decade* edition* explorer	inhabitant mission publication*
Reaching Agreement: What rules should be made for living in close quarters? *Problem Solving:* What things must be done to get a student lounge in order? *For or Against:* Spending money on space projects	Dropping the final "t" in *must be, mustn't be, couldn't be,* and *shouldn't be*	assemble* benefit* (v) cooperate*	period* perspective* undertaking*
Making Plans: A car trip to another country *Compare and Contrast:* Describe what a model had done to change her appearance *Cross-Cultural Comparison:* The types of things people do or get done to change their appearance	Contrast: Contractions of *have* in the present perfect (*She's cut her hair.*) and Uncontracted use of *have* in the passive causative (*She has her hair cut.*)	appearance event option*	permanent remove* risk (n)

* = AWL (Academic Word List) items

SPEAKING	PRONUNCIATION	VOCABULARY	
Reaching Agreement: Ordering T-shirts from a store's website *Cross-Cultural Comparison:* Shopping *Discussion:* What do you do when you want to make an important purchase? *For or Against:* Shopping in a "store with doors" and shopping online	Intonation and pauses in conditional statements	consumer* dispute (v) policy*	precaution secure* (adj) site*
Problem Solving: What are possible solutions to everyday problems? *Cross-Cultural Comparison:* Superstitions about luck	Intonation in conditional *yes / no* and *wh-* questions	anticipate* attitude* confident	insight* percent* widespread*
What About You? What would you do if . . . ? *Problem Solving:* Giving Advice *Discussion:* What three wishes would you make?	Contractions of *would* ("d") Dropping the final "t" after *wouldn't*	consent* (v) embarrassed enchanted	furious grant* (v) respond*
What About You? How a single decision or event changed your life or the life of someone you know *Problem Solving:* What would you have done in certain situations? *Discussion:* What is a situation in your life that you regret?	Reduction of *have* ("of") Contractions for: *had* ("d"), *had not* ("hadn't"), *would not* ("wouldn't"), *could not* ("couldn't")	alternate* (adj) intelligent* occur*	outcome* parallel* (adj) version*
Discussion: Is it OK to lie in certain circumstances? *Questionnaire:* Honesty *Game:* To Tell the Truth *Quotable Quotes:* Lying and telling the truth	Stress and intonation to express belief and disbelief about what someone said	average (adj) aware* justify*	majority* reveal*

* = AWL (Academic Word List) items

UNIT	READING	WRITING	LISTENING
26 page 417 **Grammar:** Indirect Speech: Tense Changes **Theme:** Extreme Weather	A news article: *The Flood of the Century*	A paragraph reporting someone else's experience with extreme weather	A winter storm warning
27 page 432 **Grammar:** Indirect Instructions, Commands, Requests, and Invitations **Theme:** Health Problems and Remedies	A radio interview: *Here's to Your Health: The Snooze News*	A paragraph about a dream	A conversation about treatment at a headache clinic
28 page 445 **Grammar:** Indirect Questions **Theme:** Job Interviews	An article: *The Stress Interview*	A report of an interview with someone working in a job that might interest you	A job interview
29 page 461 **Grammar:** Embedded Questions **Theme:** Travel Tips	An interview: *The Tip: Who? When? and How Much?*	A paragraph about a situation that confused or surprised you	A call-in radio program about tipping

PART X   **From Grammar to Writing,** page 478
Using Direct and Indirect Speech: Write a letter of complaint.

SPEAKING	PRONUNCIATION	VOCABULARY	
Game: Telephone *Interview:* Experiences with severe weather conditions	Stress on content words	bear (v) collapse* (v) damage (n)	evacuate optimistic restore*
Problem Solving: What advice would you give for some minor health problems? *Picture Discussion:* Which instructions did Jeff follow?	Stress in affirmative and negative indirect instructions, commands, requests, and invitations	astonishing fatigue (n) interfere	monitor* (v) persist* remedy (n)
Role Play: A Job Interview *Questionnaire:* Work Values *What About You?* A personal experience with a school or job interview	Intonation in direct and indirect *yes / no* questions	appropriate* (adj) candidate evaluation*	handle (v) potential* (adj) pressure (n)
Information Gap: Eating Out *Discussion:* What is your opinion about tipping? *What About You?* The problems you had when you did something for the first time *Role Play:* Information Please!	Intonation in direct and embedded *wh-* questions	clarify* custom depend on	logical* ordinary ultimate*

* = AWL (Academic Word List) items

ABOUT THE AUTHORS

Marjorie Fuchs has taught ESL at New York City Technical College and LaGuardia Community College of the City University of New York and EFL at the Sprach Studio Lingua Nova in Munich, Germany. She has a master's degree in Applied English Linguistics and a certificate in TESOL from the University of Wisconsin-Madison. She has authored and co-authored many widely used books and multimedia materials, notably *Crossroads, Top Twenty ESL Word Games: Beginning Vocabulary Development, Families: Ten Card Games for Language Learners, Focus on Grammar 3: An Integrated Skills Approach, Focus on Grammar 3 CD-ROM, Focus on Grammar 4 CD-ROM, Longman English Interactive 3* and *4, Grammar Express Basic, Grammar Express Basic CD-ROM, Grammar Express Intermediate, Future 1: English for Results,* and workbooks for *The Oxford Picture Dictionary High Beginning* and *Low Intermediate, Focus on Grammar 3* and *4,* and *Grammar Express Basic.*

Margaret Bonner has taught ESL at Hunter College and the Borough of Manhattan Community College of the City University of New York, at Taiwan National University in Taipei, and at Virginia Commonwealth University in Richmond. She holds a master's degree in library science from Columbia University, and she has done work toward a PhD in English literature at the Graduate Center of the City University of New York. She has authored and co-authored numerous ESL and EFL print and multimedia materials, including textbooks for the national school system of Oman, *Step into Writing: A Basic Writing Text, Focus on Grammar 3: An Integrated Skills Approach, Focus on Grammar 4 Workbook, Grammar Express Basic, Grammar Express Basic CD-ROM, Grammar Express Basic Workbook, Grammar Express Intermediate, Focus on Grammar 3 CD-ROM, Focus on Grammar 4 CD-ROM, Longman English Interactive 4,* and *The Oxford Picture Dictionary Low-Intermediate Workbook.*

ACKNOWLEDGMENTS

Before acknowledging the many people who have contributed to the fourth edition of *Focus on Grammar,* we wish to express our gratitude to those who worked on the first, second, and third editions, and whose influence is still present in the new work. Our continuing thanks to:

- **Joanne Dresner**, who initiated the project and helped conceptualize the general approach of *Focus on Grammar*
- Our editors for the first three editions: **Nancy Perry**, **Penny Laporte**, **Louisa Hellegers**, **Joan Saslow**, **Laura Le Dréan**, and **Françoise Leffler**, for helping to bring the books to fruition
- **Sharon Hilles**, our grammar consultant, for her insight and advice on the first edition

In the fourth edition, *Focus on Grammar* has continued to evolve as we update materials and respond to the valuable feedback from teachers and students who have been using the series. We are grateful to the following editors and colleagues:

- The Pearson *FOG* team, in particular **Debbie Sistino** for overseeing the project and for her down-to-earth approach based on years of experience and knowledge of the field; **Lise Minovitz** for her enthusiasm and alacrity in answering our queries; and **Rosa Chapinal** for her courteous and competent administrative support.
- **Françoise Leffler**, our multi-talented editor, for her continued dedication to the series and for helping improve *Focus on Grammar* with each new edition. With her ear for natural language, eye for detail, analytical mind, and sense of style, she is truly an editor *extraordinaire*.
- **Robert Ruvo** for piloting the book through its many stages of production
- **Irene Schoenberg** and **Jay Maurer** for their suggestions and support, and Irene for generously sharing her experience in teaching with the first three editions of this book
- **Irene Frankel** for reviewing Unit 29 and offering us some good tips of her own
- **Sharon Goldstein** for her intelligent, thoughtful, and practical suggestions

Finally, we are grateful, as always, to **Rick Smith** and **Luke Frances** for their helpful input and for standing by and supporting us as we navigated our way through our fourth *FOG*.

REVIEWERS

We are grateful to the following reviewers for their many helpful comments:

Aida Aganagic, Seneca College, Toronto, Canada; **Aftab Ahmed**, American University of Sharjah, Sharjah, United Arab Emirates; **Todd Allen**, English Language Institute, Gainesville, FL; **Anthony Anderson**, University of Texas, Austin, TX; **Anna K. Andrade**, ASA Institute, New York, NY; **Bayda Asbridge**, Worcester State College, Worcester, MA; **Raquel Ashkenasi**, American Language Institute, La Jolla, CA; **James Bakker**, Mt. San Antonio College, Walnut, CA; **Kate Baldrige-Hale**, Harper College, Palatine, IL; **Leticia S. Banks**, ALCI-SDUSM, San Marcos, CA; **Aegina Barnes**, York College CUNY, Forest Hills, NY; **Sarah Barnhardt**, Community College of Baltimore County, Reisterstown, MD; **Kimberly Becker**, Nashville State Community College, Nashville, TN; **Holly Bell**, California State University, San Marcos, CA; **Anne Bliss**, University of Colorado, Boulder, CO; **Diana Booth**, Elgin Community College, Elgin, IL; **Barbara Boyer**, South Plainfield High School, South Plainfield, NJ; **Janna Brink**, Mt. San Antonio College, Walnut, CA; **AJ Brown**, Portland State University, Portland, OR; **Amanda Burgoyne**, Worcester State College, Worcester, MA; **Brenda Burlingame**, Independence High School, Charlotte, NC; **Sandra Byrd**, Shelby County High School and Kentucky State University, Shelbyville, KY; **Edward Carlstedt**, American University of Sharjah, Sharjah, United Arab Emirates; **Sean Cochran**, American Language Institute, Fullerton, CA; **Yanely Cordero**, Miami Dade College, Miami, FL; **Lin Cui**, William Rainey Harper College, Palatine, IL; **Sheila Detweiler**, College Lake County, Libertyville, IL; **Ann Duncan**, University of Texas, Austin, TX; **Debra Edell**, Merrill Middle School, Denver, CO; **Virginia Edwards**, Chandler-Gilbert Community College, Chandler, AZ; **Kenneth Fackler**, University of Tennessee, Martin, TN; **Jennifer Farnell**, American Language Program, Stamford, CT; **Allen P. Feiste**, Suwon University, Hwaseong, South Korea; **Mina Fowler**, Mt. San Antonio Community College, Rancho Cucamonga, CA; **Rosemary Franklin**, University of Cincinnati, Cincinnati, OH; **Christiane Galvani**, Texas Southern University, Sugar Land, TX; **Chester Gates**, Community College of Baltimore County, Baltimore, MD; **Luka Gavrilovic**, Quest Language Studies, Toronto, Canada; **Sally Gearhart**, Santa Rosa Community College, Santa Rosa, CA; **Shannon Gerrity**, James Lick Middle School, San Francisco, CA; **Jeanette Gerrity Gomez**, Prince George's Community College, Largo, MD; **Carlos Gonzalez**, Miami Dade College, Miami, FL; **Therese Gormley Hirmer**, University of Guelph, Guelph, Canada; **Sudeepa Gulati**, Long Beach City College, Long Beach, CA; **Anthony Halderman**, Cuesta College, San Luis Obispo, CA; **Ann A. Hall**, University of Texas, Austin, TX; **Cora Higgins**, Boston Academy of English, Boston, MA; **Michelle Hilton**, South Lane School District, Cottage Grove, OR; **Nicole Hines**, Troy University, Atlanta, GA; **Rosemary Hiruma**, American Language Institute, Long Beach, CA; **Harriet Hoffman**, University of Texas, Austin, TX; **Leah Holck**, Michigan State University, East Lansing, MI; **Christy Hunt**, English for Internationals, Roswell, GA; **Osmany Hurtado**, Miami Dade College, Miami, FL; **Isabel Innocenti**, Miami Dade College, Miami, FL; **Donna Janian**, Oxford Intensive School of English, Medford, MA; **Scott Jenison**, Antelope Valley College, Lancaster, CA; **Grace Kim**, Mt. San Antonio College, Diamond Bar, CA; **Brian King**, ELS Language Center, Chicago, IL; **Pam Kopitzke**, Modesto Junior College, Modesto, CA; **Elena Lattarulo**, American Language Institute, San Diego, CA; **Karen Lavaty**, Mt. San Antonio College, Glendora, CA; **JJ Lee-Gilbert**, Menlo-Atherton High School, Foster City, CA; **Ruth Luman**, Modesto Junior College, Modesto, CA; **Yvette Lyons**, Tarrant County College, Fort Worth, TX; **Janet Magnoni**, Diablo Valley College, Pleasant Hill, CA; **Meg Maher**, YWCA Princeton, Princeton, NJ; **Carmen Marquez-Rivera**, Curie Metropolitan High School, Chicago, IL; **Meredith Massey**, Prince George's Community College, Hyattsville, MD; **Linda Maynard**, Coastline Community College, Westminster, CA; **Eve Mazereeuw**, University of Guelph, Guelph, Canada; **Susanne McLaughlin**, Roosevelt University, Chicago, IL; **Madeline Medeiros**, Cuesta College, San Luis Obispo, CA; **Gioconda Melendez**, Miami Dade College, Miami, FL; **Marcia Menaker**, Passaic County Community College, Morris Plains, NJ; **Seabrook Mendoza**, Cal State San Marcos University, Wildomar, CA; **Anadalia Mendoza**, Felix Varela Senior High School, Miami, FL; **Charmaine Mergulhao**, Quest Language Studies, Toronto, Canada; **Dana Miho**, Mt. San Antonio College, San Jacinto, CA; **Sonia Nelson**, Centennial Middle School, Portland, OR; **Manuel Niebla**, Miami Dade College, Miami, FL; **Alice Nitta**, Leeward Community College, Pearl City, HI; **Gabriela Oliva**, Quest Language Studies, Toronto, Canada; **Sara Packer**, Portland State University, Portland, OR; **Lesley Painter**, New School, New York, NY; **Carlos Paz-Perez**, Miami Dade College, Miami, FL; **Ileana Perez**, Miami Dade College, Miami, FL; **Barbara Pogue**, Essex County College, Newark, NJ; **Phillips Potash**, University of Texas, Austin, TX; **Jada Pothina**, University of Texas, Austin, TX; **Ewa Pratt**, Des Moines Area Community College, Des Moines, IA; **Pedro Prentt**, Hudson County Community College, Jersey City, NJ; **Maida Purdy**, Miami Dade College, Miami, FL; **Dolores Quiles**, SUNY Ulster, Stone Ridge, NY; **Mark Rau**, American River College, Sacramento, CA; **Lynne Raxlen**, Seneca College, Toronto, Canada; **Lauren Rein**, English for Internationals, Sandy Springs, GA; **Diana Rivers**, NOCCCD, Cypress, CA; **Silvia Rodriguez**, Santa Ana College, Mission Viejo, CA; **Rolando Romero**, Miami Dade College, Miami, FL; **Pedro Rosabal**, Miami Dade College, Miami, FL; **Natalie Rublik**, University of Quebec, Chicoutimi, Quebec, Canada; **Matilde Sanchez**, Oxnard College, Oxnard, CA; **Therese Sarkis-Kruse**, Wilson Commencement, Rochester, NY; **Mike Sfiropoulos**, Palm Beach Community College, Boynton Beach, FL; **Amy Shearon**, Rice University, Houston, TX; **Sara Shore**, Modesto Junior College, Modesto, CA; **Patricia Silva**, Richard Daley College, Chicago, IL; **Stephanie Solomon**, Seattle Central Community College, Vashon, WA; **Roberta Steinberg**, Mount Ida College, Newton, MA; **Teresa Szymula**, Curie Metropolitan High School, Chicago, IL; **Hui-Lien Tang**, Jasper High School, Plano, TX; **Christine Tierney**, Houston Community College, Sugar Land, TX; **Ileana Torres**, Miami Dade College, Miami, FL; **Michelle Van Slyke**, Western Washington University, Bellingham, WA; **Melissa Villamil**, Houston Community College, Sugar Land, TX; **Elizabeth Wagenheim**, Prince George's Community College, Lago, MD; **Mark Wagner**, Worcester State College, Worcester, MA; **Angela Waigand**, American University of Sharjah, Sharjah, United Arab Emirates; **Merari Weber**, Metropolitan Skills Center, Los Angeles, CA; **Sonia Wei**, Seneca College, Toronto, Canada; and **Vicki Woodward**, Indiana University, Bloomington, IN.

PRESENT AND PAST: REVIEW AND EXPANSION

UNIT	GRAMMAR FOCUS	THEME
1	Simple Present and Present Progressive	Names
2	Simple Past and Past Progressive	First Meetings
3	Simple Past, Present Perfect, and Present Perfect Progressive	Hobbies and Interests
4	Past Perfect and Past Perfect Progressive	Musicians

Simple Present and Present Progressive
NAMES

Continues.

STEP 1 GRAMMAR IN CONTEXT

Before You Read

Look at the title of the article and at the chart.
Discuss the questions.

1. What do you think the title means?
2. What are some common first and last names in your native language?
3. Do you have a nickname[1]? If yes, what is it? How did you get it?

Common Last Names around the World	
ARABIC	Ali, Ahmed, Haddad
CHINESE	Zhang, Wang, Chen
ENGLISH	Smith, Jones, Williams
JAPANESE	Sato, Suzuki, Takahashi
KOREAN	Kim, Lee, Park
RUSSIAN	Ivanov, Smirnov, Vasilev
SPANISH	García, Fernandez, Lopez
TURKISH	Özkan, Akcan, Gürbüz

Read

Read the school newsletter article about names.

What's in a Name?

Hi. My name **is** Yevdokiya Ivanova. I**'m** from Russia, but this year I**'m living** and **working** in Canada. Yevdokiya **is** an old-fashioned name, but it**'s coming back** into style. My classmates **find** it difficult to pronounce, so they **call** me by my nickname— Dusya. In my country, people always **call** their teachers by a first and a middle name, for example, Viktor Antonovich. The middle name **comes** from the father's first name and **means** "son of Anton." We **don't use** titles like "Mr." or "Professor." Here, some teachers actually **prefer** to be called by just their first name. At first, this was very hard for me to do. It still **seems** a little disrespectful,[2] but I**'m getting** used to it.

Hola![3] My name **is** Jorge Santiago García de Gonzalez, and I**'m** from Mexico City. I**'m studying** English here at the language institute. Jorge **is** my first, or given, name; Santiago, my middle name; García **comes** from my father (it**'s** his last name); and Gonzalez from my mother (it**'s** her last name). People often **think** my name **is** Mr. Gonzalez, but it**'s** actually Mr. García. Of course in class, everyone just **calls** me Jorge. People here **find** my name a "mouthful," but to me it **seems** perfectly normal. Some of my new friends **are trying** to convince me to call myself "George" while I**'m** here, but I **like** my name, and I **don't want** to lose my identity.

[1] *nickname:* a funny name or a shorter form of a person's first name, usually given by friends or family

[2] *disrespectful:* not polite
[3] *hola:* hello in Spanish

After You Read

A | Vocabulary: *Circle the letter of the word or phrase that best completes each sentence.*

1. If a name is in **style**, many people _____ it.
   a. have
   b. don't like
   c. have to spell

2. _____ is NOT an example of a **title**.
   a. *President*
   b. *Doctor*
   c. *John*

3. A _____ is an example of an **institute**.
   a. house
   b. school
   c. park

4. If you **convince** a person, you _____ that person's opinion.
   a. ask
   b. explain
   c. change

5. If you **actually** like your name, this means you _____.
   a. didn't like it before
   b. truly like it
   c. pretend to like it

B | Comprehension: *Check (✓)* **True** *or* **False**. *Correct the false statements.*

	True	False
1. Yevdokiya is now in Russia.	☐	☒
2. Her classmates call her by her nickname.	☒	☐
3. In Russia, she calls her teacher by his first name only.	☐	☒
4. Jorge is in Mexico City.	☐	☒
5. His classmates think his name is hard to say.	☒	☐
6. He's going to change his first name.	☐	☒

SIMPLE PRESENT

Affirmative Statements

They **live** in Mexico.
She always **works** here.

Negative Statements

They **don't live** in Mexico.
She **doesn't work** here.

Yes / No Questions

Do they **live** in Mexico?
Does she **work** here?

Short Answers

Yes, they **do**.
Yes, she **does**.

No, they **don't**.
No, she **doesn't**.

Wh- Questions

Where **do** they **live**?
Why **does** she **work** so hard?
Who **teaches** that class?

PRESENT PROGRESSIVE

Affirmative Statements

They**'re living** in Mexico now.
She**'s working** here today.

Negative Statements

They **aren't living** in Mexico now.
She **isn't working** here now.

Yes / No Questions

Are they **living** in Mexico now?
Is she **working** here now?

Short Answers

Yes, they **are**.
Yes, she **is**.

No, they **aren't**.
No, she **isn't**.

Wh- Questions

Where **are** they **living** these days?
Why **is** she **working** so hard?
Who**'s teaching** that class now?

GRAMMAR NOTES

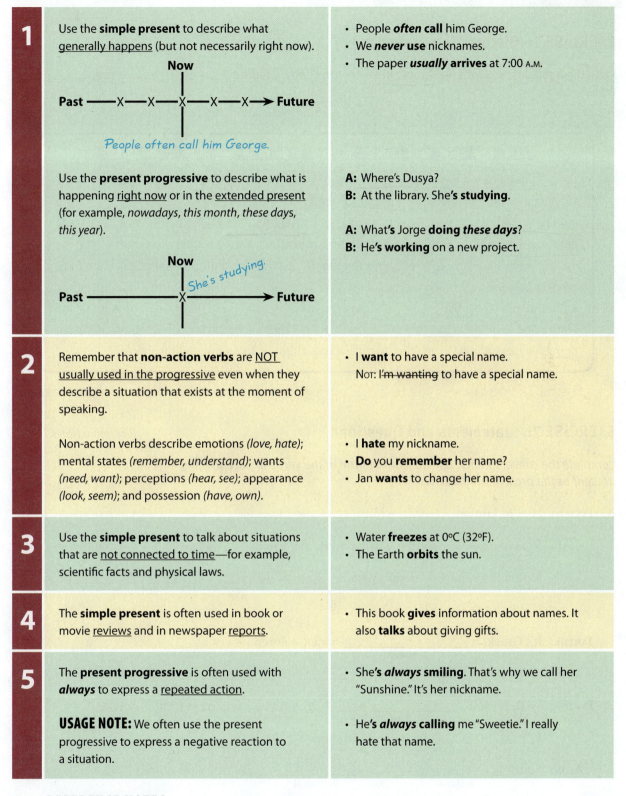

1 Use the **simple present** to describe what <u>generally happens</u> (but not necessarily right now).

Now

Past —X—X—X—X—X—→ Future

People often call him George.

- People ***often* call** him George.
- We ***never* use** nicknames.
- The paper ***usually* arrives** at 7:00 A.M.

Use the **present progressive** to describe what is happening <u>right now</u> or in the <u>extended present</u> (for example, *nowadays*, *this month*, *these days*, *this year*).

Now

She's studying.

Past ————X————→ Future

A: Where's Dusya?
B: At the library. She**'s studying**.

A: What**'s** Jorge **doing** *these days*?
B: He**'s working** on a new project.

2 Remember that **non-action verbs** are <u>NOT usually used in the progressive</u> even when they describe a situation that exists at the moment of speaking.

Non-action verbs describe emotions (*love*, *hate*); mental states (*remember*, *understand*); wants (*need*, *want*); perceptions (*hear*, *see*); appearance (*look*, *seem*); and possession (*have*, *own*).

- I **want** to have a special name.
  Not: I'm wanting to have a special name.

- I **hate** my nickname.
- **Do** you **remember** her name?
- Jan **wants** to change her name.

3 Use the **simple present** to talk about situations that are <u>not connected to time</u>—for example, scientific facts and physical laws.

- Water **freezes** at 0ºC (32ºF).
- The Earth **orbits** the sun.

4 The **simple present** is often used in book or movie <u>reviews</u> and in newspaper <u>reports</u>.

- This book **gives** information about names. It also **talks** about giving gifts.

5 The **present progressive** is often used with ***always*** to express a <u>repeated action</u>.

USAGE NOTE: We often use the present progressive to express a negative reaction to a situation.

- She**'s** *always* **smiling**. That's why we call her "Sunshine." It's her nickname.

- He**'s** *always* **calling** me "Sweetie." I really hate that name.

REFERENCE NOTES
For a list of **non-action verbs**, see Appendix 2 on page A-2.
For **spelling rules** on forming the **present progressive**, see Appendix 23 on page A-11.
For **spelling rules** on forming the third-person singular of the **simple present**, see Appendix 22 on page A-11.
For **pronunciation rules** for the **simple present**, see Appendix 29 on page A-14.

EXERCISE 1: Discover the Grammar

Read the book review. Circle the simple present verbs and underline the present progressive verbs.

> # ACROSS CULTURES
>
> Are you living or working in a foreign country? Do you worry about making a mistake with someone's name or title? You are right to be concerned. Naming systems vary a lot from culture to culture, and people tend to have very strong feelings about their names. Well, now help is available in the form of an interesting and practical book by Terri Morrison. *Kiss, Bow, or Shake Hands: How to Do Business in Sixty Countries* gives information on cross-cultural naming customs and much more. And it's not just for businesspeople. In today's shrinking world, people are traveling abroad in record numbers. They're flying to all corners of the world, and they're exchanging emails with people they've never actually met. So, if you're doing business abroad or making friends across cultures, I recommend this book.

EXERCISE 2: Statements and Questions

(Grammar Notes 1–3, 5)

Complete the conversations. Use the correct form of the verbs in parentheses—the simple present or the present progressive.

A. **IANTHA:** Hi, I'm Iantha.

ALAN: Nice to meet you, Iantha. I'm Alan, but my friends _____call_____ me Al.
1. (call)

Iantha is an unusual name. Where _____does_____ it _____come_____ from?
2. (come)

Is it Latin or Greek?

IANTHA: It's Greek. It _____means_____ "violet-colored flower."
3. (mean)

ALAN: That's pretty. What _____do_____ you _____doing_____, Iantha?
4. (do)

IANTHA: Well, I usually _____sell_____ computer equipment, but right now
5. (sell)

I _am working_ at a flower shop. My uncle _____owns_____ it.
6. (work) **7. (own)**

ALAN: You _are joking_ ! I _____guess_____ it's true that names
8. (joke) **9. (guess)**

influence our lives!
10. (influence)

B. **MARIO:** I _am trying_ to find Greg Costanza. _____Do_____ you
1. (try)

_____know_____ him?
2. (know)

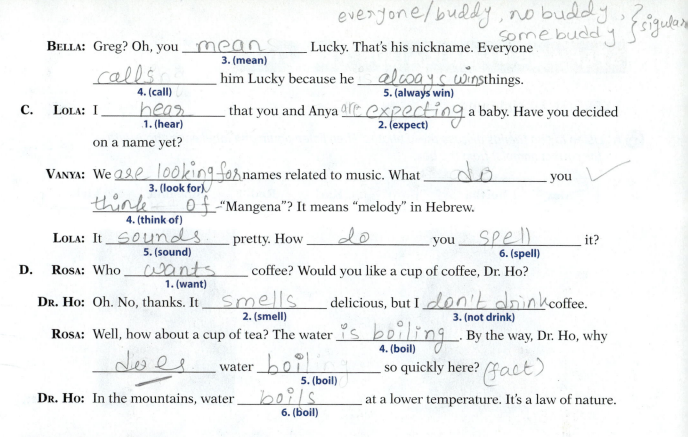

everyone/buddy, no buddy, somebuddy {sigular

BELLA: Greg? Oh, you _mean_ Lucky. That's his nickname. Everyone

3. (mean)

calls him Lucky because he _always wins_ things.

4. (call)   5. (always win)

C.   LOLA: I _hear_ that you and Anya _are expecting_ a baby. Have you decided

1. (hear)   2. (expect)

on a name yet?

VANYA: We _are looking for_ names related to music. What _do_ you ✓

3. (look for)

think of "Mangena"? It means "melody" in Hebrew.

4. (think of)

LOLA: It _sounds_ pretty. How _do_ you _spell_ it?

5. (sound)   6. (spell)

D.   ROSA: Who _wants_ coffee? Would you like a cup of coffee, Dr. Ho?

1. (want)

DR. HO: Oh. No, thanks. It _smells_ delicious, but I _don't drink_ coffee.

2. (smell)   3. (not drink)

ROSA: Well, how about a cup of tea? The water _is boiling_. By the way, Dr. Ho, why

4. (boil)

does water _boiling_ so quickly here? (fact)

5. (boil)

DR. HO: In the mountains, water _boils_ at a lower temperature. It's a law of nature.

6. (boil)

EXERCISE 3: Editing

Read this post to a class electronic bulletin board. There are eleven mistakes in the use of the simple present and the present progressive. The first mistake is already corrected. Find and correct ten more.

www.classbulletinboard.org

CLASS BULLETIN BOARD   [Follow Ups]   [Post a Reply]   [Message Board Index]

Posted February 16, 2012, at 15:30:03

I'm writing

Hi, everybody. ~~I write~~ this note to introduce myself to you, my classmates in English 047. Our teacher is

~~s~~
wanting a profile from each of us. At first I was confused by this assignment because my English dictionary

~~s~~
is defining *profile* as "a side view of someone's head." I thought, "Why does she wants that? She sees my

head every day!" Then I saw the next definition: "a short description of a person's life and character." OK,

then. Here is my profile:

call.

My name is Peter Holzer. Some of my friends ~~are calling~~ me Pay-Ha because that is how my initials

sound   *ing*
actually ~~sounding~~ in German. I am study English here in Miami because I want to attend the Aspen Institute

does
of International Leadership in Colorado. Maybe are you asking yourself, "Why he wants to leave Miami for

you are

come
Colorado?" The answer is snow! I am coming from Austria, so I love to ski. It's part of my identity. In fact, my

nickname in my family is Blitz (lightning) because always I'm trying to improve my speed.

Simple Present and Present Progressive   **7**

EXERCISE 4: Listening

A | *Listen to two friends discuss these photos. Then listen again and label each photo with the correct name(s) from the box.*

| Alex | Bertha | "Bozo" | Karl | Red | "Sunshine" | Vicki |

a. _____

b. _____ *Alex* _____

c. _____

d. _____

e. _____

f. _____ and _____

B | *Read the sentences. Listen again and circle the correct answers.*

1. Nowadays, more and more people are giving boys / (girls) names like *Alex*.

2. Red got his nickname because of his clothes / hair.

3. Bozo has / doesn't have a headache.

4. Janine agrees that her cousin's photo matches / doesn't match her nickname.

5. Janine's friend recognizes / doesn't recognize Karl.

6. Vicki and Bertha are mother and daughter / aunt and niece.

EXERCISE 5: Pronunciation

A | *Read and listen to the Pronunciation Note.*

> **Pronunciation Note**
>
> When we **compare two things**, we put **stress** on the **information that is different**. For example, when we compare what we **usually do** with what we are **doing now**, we put stress on:
>
> - the **things we are comparing**
> - **adverbs and time words** or expressions, such as *usually*, *now*, and *these days*
>
> EXAMPLES: I **usually** take the **train** home, but **these days** I'm taking the **bus**.
>
> Sara **normally washes** the dishes, but **now** she's **drying** them.

B | *Listen to the conversations. Put a dot (•) over the words in the answers that have the most stress.*

1. **A:** What does she drink?

   B: She often drinks coffee, but at the moment she's drinking tea.

2. **A:** Hi Tiffany. Are you making dinner now?

   B: I'm not making dinner. I'm eating dinner!

3. **A:** Where do you study?

   B: I often study at home, but these days I'm studying at the library.

4. **A:** What color jacket does she wear?

   B: She normally wears red, but right now she's wearing black.

5. **A:** What do they call him?

   B: They usually call him Bill, but today they're calling him William.

(continued on next page)

6. A: Does he speak Spanish?

    B: He doesn't speak Spanish, but he reads it very well.

7. A: How does he get to school?

    B: He generally takes the bus, but this week he's taking the train.

C | *Listen again to the conversations and repeat the answers. Then practice the conversations with a partner.*

EXERCISE 6: Find Someone Who . . .

A | *Write down your full name on a piece of paper. Your teacher will collect all the papers and redistribute them. Walk around the room. Introduce yourself to other students and try to find the person whose name you have on your piece of paper.*

> **EXAMPLE:**   **A:** Hi. I'm Jelena.
>   **B:** I'm Eddy.
>   **A:** I'm looking for Kadin Al-Tattany. Do you know him?
>   **B:** I think that's him over there. OR Sorry, I don't.

B | *When you find the person you are looking for, find out about his or her name. You can ask some of these questions:*

- What does your name mean?
- Which part of your name is your family name?
- Do you use a title? (for example, Ms., Miss, Mrs., Mr.)
- What do your friends call you?
- Do you have a nickname?
- What do you prefer to be called?
- How do you feel about your name?
- *Other:* _____

> **EXAMPLE:**   **A:** What does Kadin mean?
>   **B:** It means "friend" or "companion" in Arabic.
>   OR I don't actually know what it means.

You can also ask some general questions such as these:

- Where do you come from?
- Where are you living now?
- Why are you studying English?
- *Other:* _____

C | *Finally, introduce your classmate to the rest of the class.*

> **EXAMPLE:**   This is Henka Krol. Henka comes from Poland.
>   Her name means "ruler of the house or home."

EXERCISE 7: Writing

A | *Write a profile to introduce yourself to your class. Write about your name, your interests and hobbies, and your plans. Use the simple present and the present progressive. You can use the profile in Exercise 3 on page 7 as a model.*

EXAMPLE: My name is Thuy Nguyen, but my American friends call me Tina.

B | *Check your work. Use the Editing Checklist.*

Editing Checklist
Did you use . . . ? ☐ the simple present for things that generally happen ☐ the present progressive for things happening right now or in the extended present ☐ the simple present with non-action verbs ☐ the present progressive with **always** for repeated actions

Check your answers on page UR-1.

Do you need to review anything?

A | Circle the correct words to complete the sentences.

1. Ekaterina is helping / (helps) me with my Russian homework every weekend.

2. Felix is working / works on a new project these days.

3. Are / Do you ever talk on your cell phone while you're driving?

4. I don't understanding / understand what this word means. Can you explain it?

5. We usually go / go usually to the beach for vacation.

B | Complete the conversation with the simple present or present progressive form of the verbs in parentheses.

ANA: Hi, Kim! I _am looking for_ Jeff Goodale. Is he here?
     1. (look for)

KIM: I _think_ he's here somewhere.
     2. (think)

ANA: He _isn't carrying_ a cell phone today, so I _need_ to give him
     3. (not carry)   **4. (need)**
     a message from Lynn.

KIM: I _see_ him! He _is standing_ next to Kevin.
     5. (see)   **6. (stand)**

ANA: Jeff, hi. Call Lynn, OK? She _is waiting_ for your call right now.
     7. (wait)

JEFF: That _sounds_ serious! Can I use your phone?
      8. (sound)

ANA: Sure. I _don't believe_ it's anything serious. She just _wants_
     9. (not believe)   **10. (want)**
     you to buy a new cell phone.

C | Find and correct five mistakes.

Hi Leda,

                     are doing
How do you do these days? We're all fine. I'm writing to tell you that we, not living in
                                                                     do

                                              are expecting
California anymore. We just moved to Oregon. Also, we expect a baby! We're looking for an

interesting name for our new daughter. Do you have any ideas? Right now, we're thinking about

                          has
Gabriella because it's having good nicknames. For example, *Gabby*, *Bree*, and *Ella* all seem good

       do
to us. How are those nicknames sound to you? We hope you'll write soon and tell us your news.

Love,

Samantha

Simple Past and Past Progressive /continuous
FIRST MEETINGS

STEP 1 GRAMMAR IN CONTEXT

Before You Read

Look at the photos here and on the next page. Discuss the questions.

1. Which couples do you recognize?
2. What do you know about them?
3. Do you know how they met?

Read

Read the article about four famous couples.

SUPER COUPLES

Cover Story by Dennis Brooks

BEARING LOIS IN HIS ARMS SUPERMAN HEADS TOWARD THE CITY — —

It's a bird, . . . it's a plane, . . . it's Superman! Disguised as Clark Kent, this world-famous character **met** Lois Lane while the two **were working** as newspaper reporters for the *Daily Planet*. At first Lane **wasn't** interested in mild-mannered[1] Kent—she **wanted** to cover stories about "The Man of Steel." In time, she **changed** her mind. When Kent **proposed**, Lane **accepted**. (And she **didn't** even **know** he **was** Superman!)

Like Superman and Lois Lane, some names just seem to belong together: Marie and Pierre Curie, Diego Rivera and Frida Kahlo, or Steffi Graf and Andre Agassi. What **were** these other super couples **doing** when they **met**? What **did** they **accomplish** together? Let's find out.

(continued on next page)

Superman and Lois Lane

---

[1] *mild-mannered:* behaving in a quiet, gentle way

SUPER COUPLES

Marie and Pierre Curie

Frida Kahlo and Diego Rivera

Steffi Graf and Andre Agassi

When she **was** 24, Maria Sklodowska **left** Poland and **moved** to Paris. While she **was studying** at the Sorbonne,[2] she **met** physicist Pierre Curie. She **was planning** to return to Poland after her studies, but the two scientists **fell** in love and **got** married. While they **were raising** their daughters, they **were** also **doing** research on radioactivity. In 1903, the Curies **won** the Nobel Prize in physics. Then, in 1906, a horse-drawn carriage **hit** and **killed** Pierre while he **was** out **walking**. When Marie **recovered** from the shock, she **continued** their work. In 1911, she **received** her second Nobel Prize.

Born in Guanajuato, Mexico, in 1886, Diego Rivera **began** painting at a young age. He **became** famous for his large murals,[3] which he **painted** for universities and other public buildings. In 1922 he **met** Frida Kahlo for the first time while he **was working** on one of his murals. It **was** at the school that the 15-year-old Kahlo **was attending**. A few years later, Kahlo **was** in a serious bus accident. While she **was recovering**, she **started** painting from bed. One day she **went** to see Rivera to ask him for career advice. He **was** very impressed with her work. The two **fell** in love and **got** married. Today they are considered two of Mexico's greatest, most influential artists.

Steffi Graf first **picked up** a tennis racket when she **was** only three years old. She **went on** to become the best women's tennis player in the world—winning all four Grand Slam singles and the Olympic gold medal in a year. Her career **was going** great until she **suffered** a series of injuries while she **was playing**. She **was** also deeply shocked after a disturbed[4] fan **stabbed** her biggest opponent in an attempt to help Graf's career. But she **continued** to win many tournaments until she **retired**. She **got together** with future-husband Andre Agassi while they both **were competing** in Paris. He **was** the number 1 professional male American tennis player in the world; she **was** ranked the number 1 female German player. The superstars **started** dating and **married** a few years later.

---

[2] **Sorbonne:** the University of Paris, in Paris, France
[3] **mural:** a painting on a wall
[4] **disturbed:** having emotional problems

After You Read

A | Vocabulary: *Complete the sentences with the words from the box.*

couple	cover	influential	opponent	recover	research

1. I was doing _research_ at the university on the psychology of sports.

2. I met a very interesting _couple_ in my program. The three of us became good friends. We spent a lot of time together.

3. The woman taught me how to deal with losing to a(n) _opponent_ on the tennis court. It really helped my game.

4. The man was having some psychological problems. It took him many months to _recover_ from his illness.

5. After that, he became a very _influential_ writer. He changed people's opinions about mental illness.

6. All the newspapers wanted to _cover_ his story.

B | Comprehension: *Circle the word that best completes each sentence.*

1. Clark Kent met Lois Lane before / **during** / after his time at the *Daily Planet*.

2. Lane found out Kent was Superman before / during / **after** Kent's marriage proposal.

3. Maria Sklodowska met Pierre Curie before / **during** / after her move to Paris.

4. **Before** / During / After her marriage, Sklodowska wanted to return to Poland.

5. Diego Rivera began painting murals before / **during** / after his project at the school.

6. Frida Kahlo began painting before / **during** / after her recovery from the bus accident.

7. Steffi Graf was injured several times before / **during** / after games.

8. She married Andre Agassi before / **during** / after the competition in Paris.

SIMPLE PAST

withdid noted, ing

Affirmative Statements
Marie **studied** at the Sorbonne.

Negative Statements
Lois **didn't plan** to marry Clark at first.

Yes / No Questions	Short Answers
Did he **teach**?	**Yes**, he **did**. **No**, he **didn't**.

Wh- Questions
Where **did** they **play** tennis? Who **won**?

Simple Past and Simple Past
He **won** when he **played** there.

Simple Past and Past Progressive
She **met** him while she **was studying**.

PAST PROGRESSIVE

Affirmative Statements
She **was studying** at the Sorbonne in 1892.

Negative Statements
She **wasn't planning** to get married.

Yes / No Questions	Short Answers
Was he **doing** research?	**Yes**, he **was**. **No**, he **wasn't**.

Wh- Questions
Where **were** they **playing** tennis? Who **was winning**?

Past Progressive and Past Progressive
He **was winning** while he **was playing** there.

Past Progressive and Simple Past
She **was studying** when she **met** him.

GRAMMAR NOTES

1 Use the **simple past** to describe an action that was <u>completed</u> at a specific time in the past. The simple past focuses on the <u>completion</u> of the past action.

- Marie **moved** to Paris in 1891.
- The Curies **won** the Nobel Prize in 1903.
- She **researched** uranium.
  (*She completed her research.*)

2 Use the **past progressive** to describe an action that was <u>in progress</u> at a specific time in the past. The action began before the specific time and may or may not continue after the specific time. The past progressive focuses on the <u>duration</u> of the action, not its completion.

- The Curies **were living** in Paris in 1895.
- Marie **was studying** at the Sorbonne.
- During 1897, she **was researching** uranium.
  (*Her work was continuing.*)

REMEMBER: **Non-action verbs** are NOT usually used in the progressive.

- Marie **had** a degree in physics.
  NOT: Marie ~~was having~~ a degree in physics.

3 Use the **past progressive** with the **simple past** to talk about an action that was <u>interrupted by another action</u>. Use the simple past for the interrupting action.

- They **were driving** to work when they **saw** the accident.

- Use **while** to introduce the **past progressive** action.
- Use **when** to introduce the **simple past** action.

- **While** he **was walking**, the car **hit** him.

- **When** the car **hit** him, he **was walking**.

4 You can use the **past progressive** with **while** or **when** to talk about two actions <u>in progress at the same time</u> in the past. Use the past progressive in both clauses.

- **While** Clark **was leaving** the newsroom, Lois **was calling** the police.
- **When** Clark **was leaving** the newsroom, Lois **was calling** the police.

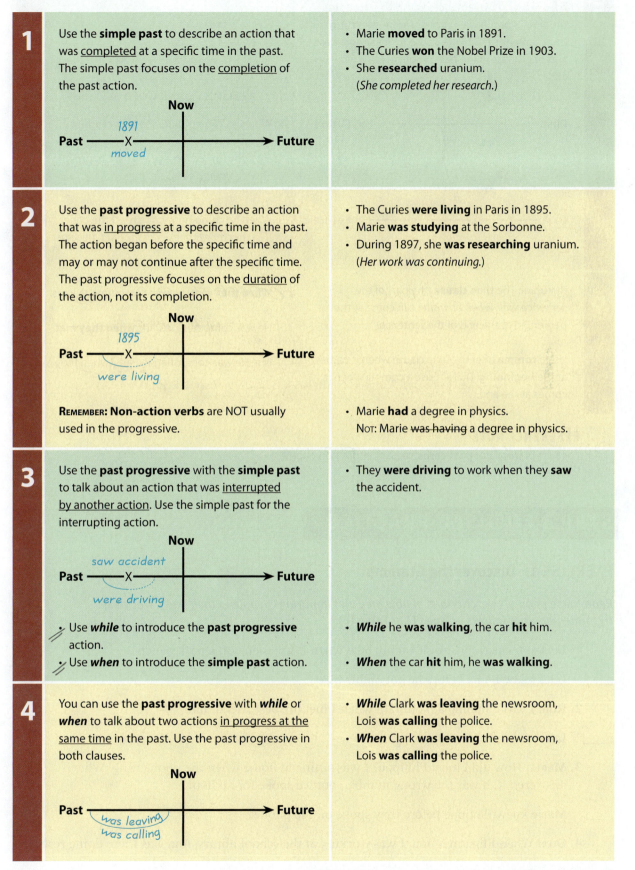

(continued on next page)

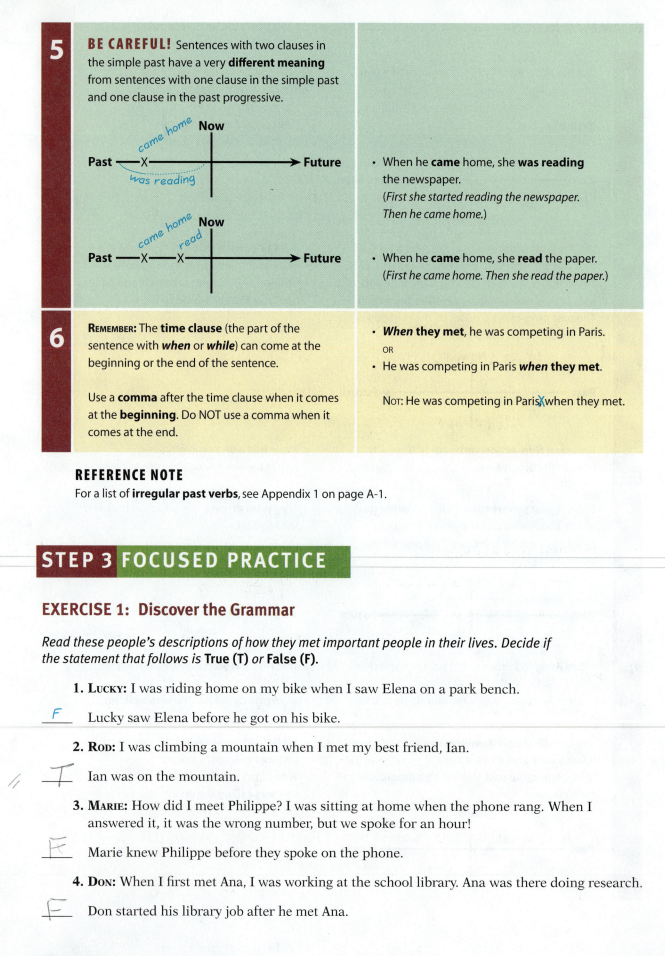

5 **BE CAREFUL!** Sentences with two clauses in the simple past have a very **different meaning** from sentences with one clause in the simple past and one clause in the past progressive.

- When he **came** home, she **was reading** the newspaper.
  (*First she started reading the newspaper. Then he came home.*)

- When he **came** home, she **read** the paper.
  (*First he came home. Then she read the paper.*)

6 REMEMBER: The **time clause** (the part of the sentence with **when** or **while**) can come at the beginning or the end of the sentence.

Use a **comma** after the time clause when it comes at the **beginning**. Do NOT use a comma when it comes at the end.

- **When** they met, he was competing in Paris.
  OR
- He was competing in Paris **when** they met.

  NOT: He was competing in Paris✗when they met.

REFERENCE NOTE
For a list of **irregular past verbs**, see Appendix 1 on page A-1.

STEP 3 FOCUSED PRACTICE

EXERCISE 1: Discover the Grammar

Read these people's descriptions of how they met important people in their lives. Decide if the statement that follows is True (T) or False (F).

1. LUCKY: I was riding home on my bike when I saw Elena on a park bench.

  _F_   Lucky saw Elena before he got on his bike.

2. ROD: I was climbing a mountain when I met my best friend, Ian.

  _T_   Ian was on the mountain.

3. MARIE: How did I meet Philippe? I was sitting at home when the phone rang. When I answered it, it was the wrong number, but we spoke for an hour!

  _F_   Marie knew Philippe before they spoke on the phone.

4. DON: When I first met Ana, I was working at the school library. Ana was there doing research.

  _F_   Don started his library job after he met Ana.

5. TONY: How did I meet my wife? Actually, it was kind of like a blind date. My cousins invited her to dinner while I was living at their place.

F   Tony moved in with his cousins after he met his wife.

6. MONICA: I was taking an English class while Dania was taking Spanish. We met in the hall during a break.

T   Monica and Dania were students at the same time.

EXERCISE 2: Simple Past or Past Progressive   *(Grammar Notes 1–6)*

Complete the conversations. Circle the correct verbs.

A.   **LILY:** Guess what! I was seeing / **saw** Andre Agassi and Steffi Graf at Club Rio last night.
1.

   TONY: Really? They're such a great couple! What **were** / did they **do** / doing there?
2.   3.

   LILY: They **were dancing** / danced near us on the dance floor.
4.

   TONY: Wow! Were / **Did** you getting / **get** their autographs?
5.   6.

   LILY: Yes. And then Graf was giving / **gave** me her pen!
7.

   TONY: Awesome! Were / **Did** you bringing / **bring** it with you? I want to see it!
8.   9.

   LILY: No. It was falling / **fell** out of my pocket when someone was bumping / **bumped** into
10.   11.

me. I never was finding / **found** it.
12.

B.   **TARO:** What **were** / did you **doing** / do when you **were spraining** / sprained your wrist?
1.   2.   3.

   KIWA: I was **playing** / played tennis with my boyfriend. We **were pretending** / pretended to be
4.   5.

Agassi and Graf. I was hurting / **hurt** myself while I **was hitting** / hit the ball!
6.   7.

   TARO: Sounds like he's a pretty tough opponent! I hope you recover soon.

C.   **JASON:** Are you OK, Erin? Were / **Did** you crying / **cry**?
1.   2.

   ERIN: Yes, but how were / **did** you knowing / **know**? I **wasn't crying** / didn't cry when you
3.   4.   5.

were coming / **came** in.
6.

   JASON: Your eyes are red.

   ERIN: The movie *Frida* was on TV. It's about the Mexican painter Frida Kahlo.

Were you ever seeing / **Did you ever see** it? It's so sad. While I was watching / **watched**
7.   8.

it, I **was thinking** / thought about her life. She had so many physical problems and she
9.

never really was recovering / **recovered** from them.
10.

EXERCISE 3: Simple Past or Past Progressive

(Grammar Notes 1–6)

Complete the conversations. Use the correct form of the verbs in parentheses—simple past or past progressive.

A. **PAZ:** What _____*were*_____ you _____*looking*_____ at just then? You *smiled*
  1. (look)   **2. (smile)**

  EVA: I __*watched*__ the video of Nicole's wedding. She *was looking* so happy.
  3. (watch)   **4. (look)**

  PAZ: How __*did*__ she and Matt __*met*__ ?
  5. (meet)

  EVA: At my graduation party. Matt almost *wasn't coming*. He *covered* a big
  6. (not come)   **7. (cover)**

  story for the newspaper. Luckily, his plans __*changed*__ . The rest is history.
  8. (change)

B. **DAN:** I __*found*__ your Superman web page while I *was surfing* the Internet.
  1. (find)   **2. (surf)**

  It's great.

  DEE: Thanks. When __*were*__ you __*becoming*__ a Superman fan?
  3. (become)

  DAN: Years ago. I *was reading* a comic book when I *decided* to marry Lois
  4. (read)   **5. (decide)**

  Lane! Just kidding. I __*wanted*__ to *draw* Lois Lane and Superman.
  6. (want)

  DEE: Me too. I *was studying* graphic arts when I __*started*__ my web page.
  7. (study)   **8. (start)**

  DAN: So, it seems like Superman was influential in *both* our lives!

C. **LARA:** __*Was*__ Jason *surprising* you when he __*came*__ over
  1. (surprise)   **2. (come)**

  last night?

  ERIN: Yes! I *was watching* a tennis match on TV when he *knocked* on the
  3. (watch)   **4. (knock)**

  door. When the game __*ended*__ , we *were having* a delicious dinner.
  5. (end)   **6. (have)**

  And while we *were eating*, Jason __*asked*__ me to marry him!
  7. (eat)   **8. (ask)**

  LARA: That's great. Congratulations!

EXERCISE 4: Connecting Clauses: *When* or *While*

(Grammar Notes 2–6)

*This timeline shows some important events in Monique's life. Use the timeline and the cues on the next page to write sentences about her. Use **when** or **while** and the simple past or past progressive. There is more than one way to write some of the sentences.*

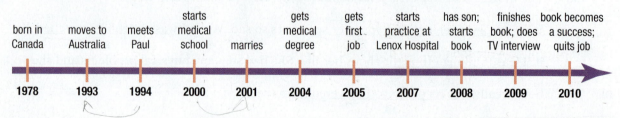

born in Canada	moves to Australia	meets Paul	starts medical school	marries	gets medical degree	gets first job	starts practice at Lenox Hospital	has son; starts book	finishes book; does TV interview	book becomes a success; quits job
1978	1993	1994	2000	2001	2004	2005	2007	2008	2009	2010

1. moves to Australia / meets Paul   *She met Paul when she moved to Australia.*

2. gets married / studies medicine   *She got married while she was studying medicine.*

3. lives in Australia / gets married   she got married while she was in Aus.

4. has medical degree / gets her first job   ~~when~~ she had the medical degree BY ~~her~~ she got the ~~her~~ 1st job.

   while she was

5. practices medicine at Lenox Hospital / has her son   she had ~~her~~ son while she practiced at M a L.H.

6. writes a book / works at Lenox Hospital   She wrote a book while she was working at L.H.

7. does a TV interview / finishes her book   she did TV interview when she finished her book.

8. leaves her job / her book becomes a success   Her book becomed success while she ~~teaved~~ her job.

   left

EXERCISE 5: Editing

*Read Monique's email to a friend. There are eleven mistakes in the use of the simple past
and the past progressive. The first mistake is already corrected. Find and correct ten more.*

Hi Crystal,

I was writing chapter two of my new book when I ~~was thinking~~ *thought* of you. The last time I saw you,

you walked down the aisle to marry Dave. That was more than two years ago. How are you? How

is married life?

A lot has happened in my life since that time. While I worked at Lenox Hospital, I began writing.

In 2004, I was publishing a book on women's health issues. It was quite successful here in Australia.

I even got interviewed on TV. When I was getting a contract to write a second book, I decided to

quit my hospital job to write full-time. That's what I'm doing now. Paul too has had a career

change. While I was writing, he was attending law school. He was getting his degree last summer.

Oh, the reason I thought of you while I wrote was because the chapter was about rashes. Remember

the time you were getting that terrible rash? We rode our bikes when you were falling into a patch

Plant/vine rasses/scatch.

of poison ivy. And that's how you met Dave! When you were falling off the bike, he offered to give

us a ride home. Life's funny, isn't it?

Well, please write soon, and send my love to Dave. I miss you!

Monique

EXERCISE 6: Listening

A | *Look at the pictures. Then listen to a woman explain how she met her husband. Listen again and circle the letter of the series of pictures that illustrates the story.*

A.

B.

C.

	True	False
1. The couple worked for a ~~movie company~~. *newspaper*	☐	☑
2. They didn't know each other well before they got an assignment together.	☐	☐
3. They were covering a story about neighborhood crime.	☐	☐
4. They had an appointment at a coffee shop.	☐	☐
5. They were at the coffee shop for several hours.	☐	☐
6. They got married a few years after.	☐	☐

EXERCISE 7: Pronunciation

A | *Read and listen to the Pronunciation Note.*

Pronunciation Note

When a **time clause begins a sentence**:

We usually **pause** briefly at the **end of the time clause** (at the **comma** in written sentences).

EXAMPLE: While we were talking, the rain started. ➜
"While we were talking [PAUSE] the rain started."

The voice **falls** and then **rises a little** at the **end of the time clause** to show that the sentence **isn't finished**.

The voice **falls lower** at the **end of the second clause** to show that the sentence **is finished**.

EXAMPLE: While we were talking, the rain started.

B | *Listen to the sentences. Add a comma where you hear the pause at the end of each time clause. Then practice the conversations with a partner.*

1. **A:** What did you do when the rain started?

   B: When it started to rain we went inside.

2. **A:** What did you do during the storm?

   B: While it was raining we were talking.

3. **A:** What did you do after the storm?

   B: When the storm was over we left.

4. **A:** What happened while you were leaving?

   B: While we were leaving the sun came out.

5. **A:** What did you do when you got home?

   B: When we got home we turned on the TV.

6. **A:** When did you get the phone call?

   B: While I was exercising the phone rang.

EXERCISE 8: What About You?

Work in small groups. Think about the first time you met someone who became influential in your life: a best friend, teacher, boyfriend or girlfriend, husband or wife. Tell your classmates about the meeting. What were you doing? What happened then? How did that person influence your life?

>   **EXAMPLE:**   I was walking to class when this guy came over and asked me for the time . . .

EXERCISE 9: Ask and Answer

Complete the timeline with some important events in your life. Include your first meeting with someone who is significant to you. Show your timeline to a classmate. Answer your classmate's questions.

Event

Year

>   **EXAMPLE:**   **A:** Where did you meet your wife?
>   **B:** I was studying medicine, and she was in my class.

EXERCISE 10: Writing

A | *Write two paragraphs about a relationship that is important to you. Use the simple past and past progressive. Follow these steps:*

1. In the first paragraph answer the questions:

      • How did you meet?

      • What were you doing when you met?

      • What were your first impressions of the person?

2. In the second paragraph, describe some events in the relationship.

>   **EXAMPLE:**   I met my friend Dania while I was living in Germany . . .

B | *Check your work. Use the Editing Checklist.*

Editing Checklist
Did you use . . . ?   ☐ the simple past   ☐ the past progressive   ☐ *when* or *while*   ☐ commas after time clauses at the beginning of a sentence

Check your answers on page UR-1.
Do you need to review anything?

A | Circle the correct words to complete the sentences.

1. I first (met) / was meeting my wife in 2002.

2. She worked / (was working) at the museum the day I went to see a Picasso exhibit.

3. (I saw) / was seeing her as soon as I walked into the room.

4. She (had) / was having long dark hair and a beautiful smile.

5. While / (When) I had a question about a painting, I went over to speak to her.

6. The whole time she was talking, I thought / (was thinking) about asking her on a date.

7. When I left the museum, she (gave) / was giving me her phone number.

B | Complete the conversation with the simple past or past progressive form of the verbs in parentheses.

A: What _____were_____ you _____doing_____ when you first _____met_____ Ed?
                                    1. (do)   **2. (meet)**

B: We _____were waiting_____ for a bus. We started to talk, and, as they say, "The rest is history."
       3. (wait)

What about you? How did you meet Karl?

A: Oh, Karl and I _____met_____ in school when we _____were studying_____ English. I
                        4. (meet)   **5. (study)**

_____noticed_____ him as soon as I _____entered_____ the room on the first day of class.
   6. (notice)   **7. (enter)**

B: It sounds like it was love at first sight!

C | Find and correct six mistakes.

    It was 2005. I ~~studied~~ *was ...ing* French in Paris ~~while~~ *when* I met Paul. Like me, Paul was from California.

We were both taking the same 9:00 A.M. conversation class. After class we always ~~were going~~ *went*

to a café with some of our classmates. One day, while we ~~was~~ *were* drinking café au lait, Paul ~~was~~

~~asking~~ *asked* me to go to a movie with him. After that, we started to spend most of our free time

together. We really got to know each other well, and we discovered that we had a lot of similar

interests. When the course was over, we left Paris and ~~were going~~ *went* back to California together.

The next year we got married!

Simple Past, Present Perfect, and Present Perfect Progressive

HOBBIES AND INTERESTS

STEP 1 GRAMMAR IN CONTEXT

Before You Read

Look at the photo. Discuss the questions.

1. What are the people doing?
2. Have you ever participated in an adventure sport?
3. What do you like to do in your free time?

Read

Read the personal website.

www.jumpforjoy.com

JUMPING FOR JOY

Hi, I'm Jason Barricelli. I**'ve been building** this website for a while, and now I'm almost finished. I**'ve written** this page to introduce myself.

I**'ve** always **been** a work-hard, play-hard kind of guy. I **grew up** in Perth, Australia, and my family **did** adventure sports like rock climbing. Lately, some people **have called** these activities "extreme sports," but to me they**'ve** always **seemed** like normal fun.

We've been falling for an awfully long time!

I**'ve been working** on a master's degree for a couple of years, but I still take time out to play. Since I **moved** to Sydney, I**'ve learned** how to skydive. This month, I**'ve** already **made** five jumps.

Yes, I have a social life too. In fact, last month I **got** engaged to a fantastic woman. Here's a picture of the two of us jumping together.

Joy **hasn't been skydiving** that long, but she **wanted** to celebrate our engagement with a jump.

I**'ve included** more pictures of this historic jump. Just click on the plane to continue.

Next   My Family   Other Interests   Home

After You Read

A | Vocabulary: *Circle the letter of the word or phrase that best completes each sentence.*

1. Someone who is **engaged** is planning to _____.
   a. get married
   b. find a marriage partner
   c. get a master's degree

2. An example of an **extreme** sport is _____.
   a. tennis
   b. mountain biking
   c. swimming in a pool

3. One reason people **celebrate** an event is to _____.
   a. show that the event is important
   b. criticize the event
   c. help them forget the event

4. To **introduce** yourself, you can _____.
   a. leave the room
   b. explain something
   c. say your name

5. A **fantastic** person is usually _____.
   a. imaginary
   b. very special
   c. very strange

6. An **historic** event in your life is one that is very _____.
   a. important
   b. interesting
   c. dangerous

B | Comprehension: *Check (✓) the correct box for each event in Jason's life.*

	Finished	Unfinished
1. build a website	☐	☐
2. live in Perth, Australia	☐	☐
3. get a master's degree	☐	☐
4. live in Sydney, Australia	☐	☐
5. learn to skydive	☐	☐
6. get engaged	☐	☐

SIMPLE PAST

PRESENT PERFECT
PRESENT PERFECT PROGRESSIVE

Affirmative Statements
I **built** a website last month.

Affirmative Statements
I**'ve built** a website. I**'ve been building** a website this month.

Negative Statements
She **didn't write** last week.

Negative Statements
She **hasn't written** many letters. She **hasn't been writing** lately.

Yes / No Questions	Short Answers
Did he **move**?	**Yes**, he **did**. **No**, he **didn't**.

Yes / No Questions	Short Answers
Has he **moved**? **Has** he **been living** in Perth?	**Yes**, he **has**. **No**, he **hasn't**.

Wh- Questions
Where **did** he **work**?
Who **lived** in Perth?

Wh- Questions
Where **has** he **worked**? Where **has** he **been working**?
Who**'s lived** in Perth? Who**'s been living** in Perth?

GRAMMAR NOTES

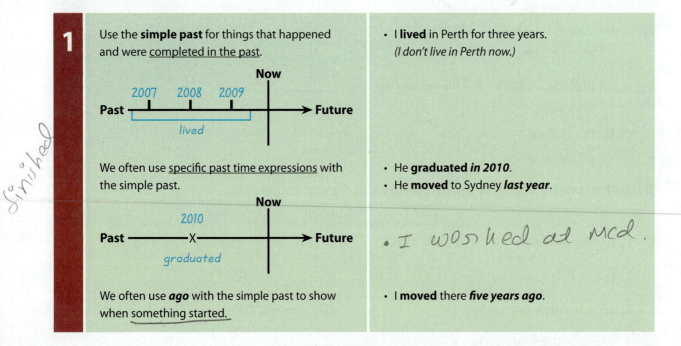

1 Use the **simple past** for things that happened and were <u>completed in the past</u>.

2007 2008 2009 Now
Past ——————————→ Future
lived

We often use <u>specific past time expressions</u> with the simple past.

2010 Now
Past ———X———→ Future
graduated

We often use *ago* with the simple past to show when <u>something started.</u>

- I **lived** in Perth for three years.
  (I don't live in Perth now.)

- He **graduated** *in 2010*.
- He **moved** to Sydney *last year*.

- I worked at Mcd.

- I **moved** there *five years ago*.

finished

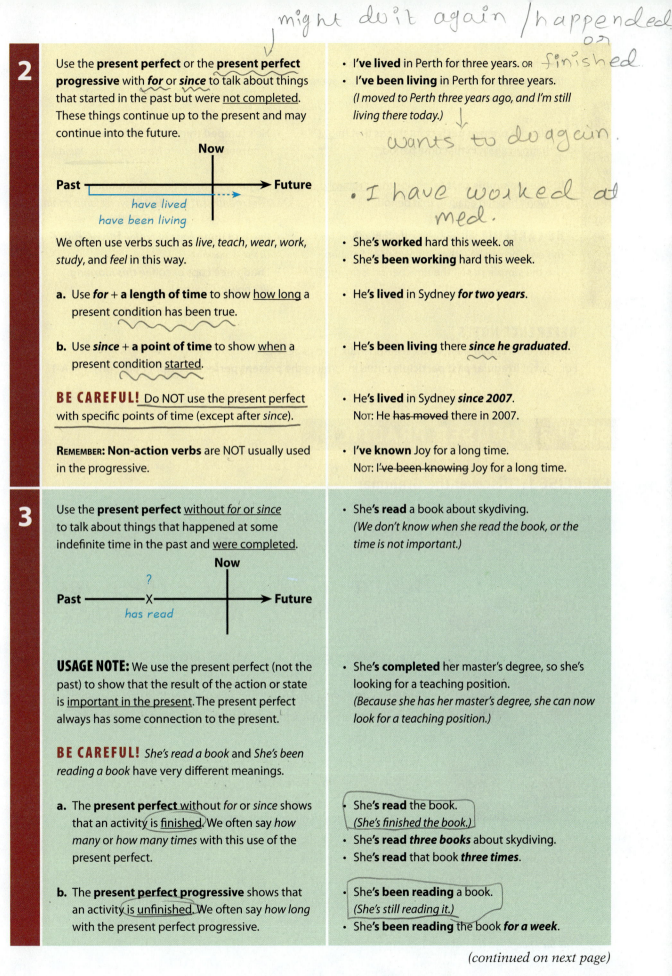

2 Use the **present perfect** or the **present perfect progressive** with *for* or *since* to talk about things that started in the past but were <u>not completed</u>. These things continue up to the present and may continue into the future.

[handwritten: might do it again / happened or finished]

Now

Past ──────────────────► Future

have lived
have been living

We often use verbs such as *live*, *teach*, *wear*, *work*, *study*, and *feel* in this way.

a. Use *for* + **a length of time** to show <u>how long</u> a present condition has been true.

b. Use *since* + **a point of time** to show <u>when</u> a present condition <u>started</u>.

BE CAREFUL! Do NOT use the present perfect with specific points of time (except after *since*).

REMEMBER: Non-action verbs are NOT usually used in the progressive.

- I**'ve lived** in Perth for three years. OR
- I**'ve been living** in Perth for three years.
  (*I moved to Perth three years ago, and I'm still living there today.*)

[handwritten: wants to do again]

[handwritten: • I have worked at med.]

- She**'s worked** hard this week. OR
- She**'s been working** hard this week.

- He**'s lived** in Sydney **for two years**.

- He**'s been living** there **since he graduated**.

- He**'s lived** in Sydney **since 2007**.
  NOT: He ~~has moved~~ there in 2007.

- I**'ve known** Joy for a long time.
  NOT: I~~'ve been knowing~~ Joy for a long time.

3 Use the **present perfect** <u>without</u> *for* or *since* to talk about things that happened at some indefinite time in the past and <u>were completed</u>.

Now

?
Past ──────X────────────► Future
        has read

USAGE NOTE: We use the present perfect (not the past) to show that the result of the action or state is <u>important in the present</u>. The present perfect always has some connection to the present.

BE CAREFUL! *She's read a book* and *She's been reading a book* have very different meanings.

a. The **present perfect** without *for* or *since* shows that an activity is (finished). We often say *how many* or *how many times* with this use of the present perfect.

b. The **present perfect progressive** shows that an activity is unfinished. We often say *how long* with the present perfect progressive.

- She**'s read** a book about skydiving.
  (*We don't know when she read the book, or the time is not important.*)

- She**'s completed** her master's degree, so she's looking for a teaching position.
  (*Because she has her master's degree, she can now look for a teaching position.*)

- She**'s read** the book.
  (*She's finished the book.*)
- She**'s read** *three books* about skydiving.
- She**'s read** that book *three times*.

- She**'s been reading** a book.
  (*She's still reading it.*)
- She**'s been reading** the book *for a week*.

(continued on next page)

4 Use the **present perfect** or the **simple past** with time expressions for <u>unfinished time periods</u> such as *today*, *this week*, *this month*, and *this year*.

a. Use the **present perfect** for things that <u>might happen again</u> in that time period.

b. Use the **simple past** for things that <u>probably won't happen again</u> in that period.

BE CAREFUL! This morning, this afternoon, and this evening can be either unfinished or finished. Use the **simple past** if the time period is <u>finished</u>.

- He**'s jumped** three times **this month**. *(The month isn't over. He might jump again.)*

- He **jumped** three times **this month**. *(The month isn't over, but he won't jump again.)*

- I**'ve had** three cups of coffee **this morning**. *(It's still morning.)*
- I **had** three cups of coffee **this morning**. *(It's now afternoon.)*

REFERENCE NOTES

For a list of **irregular past verbs**, see Appendix 1 on page A-1.
For a list of **irregular past participles** used in forming the **present perfect**, see Appendix 1 on page A-1.

STEP 3 FOCUSED PRACTICE

EXERCISE 1: Discover the Grammar

A | *Read this newspaper article about a wedding. Circle the simple past verbs and underline the present perfect verbs.*

Board and Eruc Tie the Knot[1]

get married

Nancy Board and Erden Eruc of Seattle, Washington, have always loved the outdoors, so Alaska was a natural choice to celebrate their wedding. Nancy flew there for the June 7 ceremony, but Erden started in February and rode his bike. Then he climbed Mount Denali. Unfortunately, he ran into some bad weather, so the historic event was a week late. Nancy understood. She herself has been doing extreme sports for years.

Erden, an engineer, has earned degrees from universities in Turkey and the United States. He has been climbing since he was 11. In 2003, he left his job to begin an around-the-world trip powered only by human effort. Since then, he has been climbing, hiking, biking, and rowing his way across several continents. So far, he has climbed Mount Denali in Alaska, and he has rowed across two oceans (the Atlantic and the Pacific).

Nancy, a psychotherapist, recently founded a new business in Seattle. She and her co-founder *started* have been using their outdoor experience to teach leadership skills to women in Australia, Canada, South Africa, and the United States. ↳*Infinitive*

---
[1] *tie the knot:* to get married

I founded a scl.
I found it. It's Here.

B | *Now read the statements and check (✓)* **True, False,** *or* **?** *(the information isn't in the article).*

	True	False	?
1. The couple's love of the outdoors began ~~after~~ *before* their wedding.	☐	☑	☐
2. They got married on June 7.	☐	☑	☐
3. Erden left for Alaska before Nancy.	☑	☐	☐
4. Nancy started adventure sports ~~a year ago~~ *ten years*.	☐	☑	☐
5. Erden got his degree in Turkey in 1989.	☐	☐	☑
6. He started climbing at the age of 11.	☑	☐	☐
7. He started his around-the-world trip in 2003.	☑	☐	☐
8. He crossed the Pacific in a boat in 2009.	☐	☐	☑
9. Nancy started her business in 2010.	☐	☐	☑
10. She teaches leadership skills.	☑	☐	☐

EXERCISE 2: Simple Past, Present Perfect, or Present Perfect Progressive

(Grammar Notes 1–3)

Complete the article about another hobby—collecting toys. Circle the correct verbs.

MOVE OVER, BARBIE!

Ty Warner (has been making) / made toys since 1986.
1.

In 1992, he has gotten / (got) the idea to make stuffed
2.

animals that children could afford. The first nine Beanie

Babies have appeared / (appeared) in stores just one year
3.

later. Pattie the Platypus and her eight companions

have sold out / (sold out) immediately. In the 1990s, the
4.

fad (has become) / (became) an international craze, and
5.

the Beanies are still popular. More than 2 billion fans (have visited) / have been visiting Ty's
6.

website. The growth of eBay,[1] which has started / (started) around the same time as the Beanies,
7.

(has been keeping) / kept the collecting craze going to this day. In fact, a few years ago, one
8.

collector has been buying / (bought) a Beanie Bear on eBay for an amazing $24,000. Which
9.

reminds me—I'd like to discuss some trades. (Have you found) / Have you been finding Nana
10.

the Monkey yet?

---

[1] *eBay:* a website where people and companies can buy and sell a lot of different things

EXERCISE 3: Simple Past, Present Perfect, or Present Perfect Progressive

(Grammar Notes 1–4)

Complete the paragraphs about other people's interests. Use the correct form of the verbs in parentheses—simple past, present perfect, or present perfect progressive. Sometimes more than one answer is correct.

A. May ___*has been taking*___ photos ever since her parents ___bought___ her a camera when
　　　　　1. (take)　　　　　　　　　　　　　　　　　**2. (buy)**

she ___was___ only 10. At first she only ___took___ color snapshots of friends
　　　3. (be)　　　　　　　　　　　　　**4. (take)**

and family, but then she ___changed___ to black and white. Lately she ___has been shooting___
　　　　　　　　　　　5. (change)　　　　　　　　　　　　　　　**6. (shoot)**

a lot of nature photographs. This year she ___has completed___ in three amateur photography
　　　　　　　　　　　　　　　　　7. (compete)

contests—and it's only April! In fact, last month she ___won___ second prize for her
　　　　　　　　　　　　　　　　　　　　　　8. (win)

nighttime photo of a lightning storm.

B. Carlos ___has begun___ playing music when he ___got___ an electric guitar for
　　　　　1. (begin)　　　　　　　　　　　　　**2. (get)**

his 12th birthday. He ___has not stopped___ playing since. In fact, the guitar ___has become___
　　　　　　　　3. (not stop)　　　　　　　　　　　　　　　**4. (become)**

more than just a way of having some fun with his friends. Last year he ___joined___
　　　　　　　　　　　　　　　　　　　　　　　　　5. (join)

a local band. Since then, they ___have been ing___ all over town. So far this year, the band
　　　　　　　　　　　6. (perform)

___has given___ six concerts, and they have plans for many more.
　　7. (give)

C. Kate ___found___ a beautiful old stamp last month. It is now part of the fantastic
　　　　1. (find)

collection she ___has been ing___ on for the past two years. At first she just ___saved___
　　　　　　　2. (work)　　　　　　　　　　　　　　　　　　　　**3. (save)**

stamps from letters that she ___got___ from friends. After some time, however,
　　　　　　　　　　　　4. (get)

she ___begun___ to look more actively for stamps. Lately, she ___has been buying___
　　　5. (begin)　　　　　　　　　　　　　　　　　　　　**6. (buy)**

them from special stores and ___traded___ stamps with other collectors. So far she
　　　　　　　　　　　　　7. (trade)

has ___found___ over 200 stamps from all over the world.
　　8. (find)

EXERCISE 4: Editing

Read the email message. There are nine mistakes in the use of the simple past, the present perfect, and the present perfect progressive. The first mistake is already corrected. Find and correct eight more.

Dear Erden,

've been doing
I'm doing adventure sports since I got engaged, and this year I've been joining a climbing *ed*

have beening
club. All the members followed your fantastic trip on the Around-n-Over website since

last January, but I haven't been written to you before. I have a few questions. I know

ed
you've been climbing Mount Erciyes in Turkey many years ago. Will you climb it again on

ed
this project? Also, you've traveling to different continents. How have you communicated

saw
with people? Did you study other languages before your trip? Last month, I've seen an

been
article about your project in *Hooked on the Outdoors Magazine*. You've became famous!

ed
Have you received many emails since you start your project?

Thanks for answering my questions, and good luck!

Lise Bettmann

STEP 4 COMMUNICATION PRACTICE

EXERCISE 5: Listening

A | *Jason and Joy have been planning their honeymoon trip. Read the sentences from their conversation. Then listen to their conversation. Listen again and circle the correct verbs to complete the sentences.*

1. You wouldn't believe the lines down here. I waited / 've been waiting for 40 minutes.

2. I've been getting / got them on the way over here.

3. I've read / been reading it. I found some fantastic locations.

4. I called / 've been calling all morning, but I didn't get / haven't gotten through.

5. I had to / 've had to wait more than half an hour.

6. Have you looked / Did you look for a bathing suit?

B | *Now read Jason and Joy's* **To Do** *list. Which things have they already done? Check (✓) the ones you remember. Then listen again and check your answers.*

To Do

☐ renew passport (Jason) _____

✓ pick up plane tickets _____

☐ read skydiving guide _____

☐ make reservations at Hotel Splendor _____

☐ stop mail for two weeks _____

☐ buy bathing suit (Joy) _____

EXERCISE 6: Pronunciation

A | *Read and listen to the Pronunciation Note.*

Pronunciation Note

In **conversation**, we often pronounce *has he* "hazee" and *did he* "didee."

We don't pronounce the *h* in *he*.

EXAMPLES: **Has he** called you yet? → "**Hazee** called you yet?"
Did he tell you the news? → "**Didee** tell you the news?"

We often pronounce *have you* "havya" and *did you* "didja."

EXAMPLES: **Have you** heard about Jason? → "**Havya** heard about Jason?"
Did you meet Joy last night? → "**Didja** meet Joy last night?"

B | *Listen to the short conversations. Then listen again and complete the conversations with the words that you hear.*

1. **A:** _____ about Jason and Joy?
   (hear)

   B: Yeah, they just got engaged. It's great.

2. **A:** _____ Joy to skydive yet?
   (teach)

   B: Yes. She's already made three jumps.

3. **A:** How _____ them?
   (meet)

   B: A friend introduced us.

4. **A:** _____ skydiving?
   (try)

   B: No, extreme sports are too dangerous.

5. **A:** _____?
                       (graduate)

    B: No. One more year to go!

6. **A:** _____ here from Perth?
                       (move)

    B: Yes. Three years ago.

7. **A:** _____ them a long time?
                       (know)

    B: No, just a couple of years.

C | *Listen again to the conversations and repeat the questions. Then practice the conversations with a partner.*

EXERCISE 7: What About You?

Work in small groups. Talk about your hobbies and interests. What have you done in the past with your hobby? What have you been doing lately? Find out about other people's hobbies.

> **EXAMPLE:** **A:** Do you have any hobbies, Ben?
> **B:** Yes. My hobby has been photography since I was a kid. Recently I've been taking pictures of nature. I even won first prize in a contest last month. What about you? Do you have a hobby?
> **C:** I collect sneakers. I got my first pair of Nikes when I was 10, and I've been collecting different kinds of sneakers ever since. Recently I've been selling some of the older pairs on eBay. Last week I sold a really old pair of Air Jordans for $250.

EXERCISE 8: Ask and Answer

A | *What did you plan to accomplish last week? Make a list. Include things you did and things that you still haven't done. Do not check (✓) any of the items. Exchange lists with a partner.*

> **EXAMPLE:** ☐ Organize the photos on my computer
> ☐ Research photography contests on the Internet

B | *Now ask questions about your partner's list. Check (✓) the things that your partner has already done. Answer your partner's questions about your list. When you are done, compare your answers.*

> **EXAMPLE:** **A:** Have you organized your photos yet?
> **B:** Yes, I have. I organized them last week.

EXERCISE 9: Writing

A | *Write a few paragraphs about yourself for a personal website like the one on page 26. Tell about your interests and hobbies. Use the simple past, present perfect, and present perfect progressive.*

> **EXAMPLE:** Welcome! I'm Steffie Hart. I've been living in Tokyo since 2004. I built this website to record my experience here. I've posted a lot of photos. I hope you enjoy them.

B | *Check your work. Use the Editing Checklist.*

Editing Checklist

Did you use . . . ?

☐ the simple past for things that happened and were completed in the past

☐ the present perfect and present perfect progressive with **for** and **since** for things that started in the past but were not completed

☐ the present perfect without time words for things that were completed at an indefinite past time

☐ the present perfect progressive without time words for things that continue into the present

---

A | *Circle the correct words to complete the sentences.*

1. Tina and Raoul have gotten / (got) married in 2009.

2. Raoul lived / (has been living) in Chile his whole life. He never wants to move.

3. Tina has lived there (since) / for 2005.

4. Last week, I (read) / 've been reading two books about South America. They were both excellent.

5. Jason has (been playing) / played basketball for an hour. He should stop and start his

   homework. Could you tell him to come in soon?

6. Where (has) / was Jena been living?

7. This year, I studied / (ve been studying) photography. I'm really enjoying my class.

B | *Complete the sentences with the simple past, present perfect, or present perfect progressive form of the verbs in parentheses.*

Lisa _has been working_ on her stamp collection for five years, and she still enjoys it.
      1. (work)

Last year, she _discovered_ a very valuable stamp on an old letter in her attic.
               2. (discover)

At first, she _didn't know_ it was valuable.
              3. (not know)

She _found out_ after she _did_ some research on the Internet.
     4. (find out)   **5. (do)**

                    has
Since then, she ^ _been going_ to garage sales and flea markets every weekend.
                  6. (go)

                                                                    has
She _hasn't found_ another valuable stamp, but she ^ _been having_ a great
    7. (not find)   **8. (have)**

time searching.
                                              or
                                      has had

C | *Find and correct five mistakes.*

                have
A: How long ~~did~~ you been doing adventure sports?

     got
B: I've ~~gotten~~ interested five years ago, and I haven't stopped since then.

A: You're lucky to live here in Colorado. It's a great place for adventure sports.
   Have you d   or have been living
   ~~Did you live~~ here long?

                                                      lived
B: No, not long. I moved here last year. Before that, ~~I've been living~~ in Alaska.

               en
A: I haven't go ^ there yet, but I've heard it's great.

B: It *is* great. When you go, be sure to visit Denali National Park.

Past Perfect and Past Perfect Progressive
MUSICIANS

STEP 1 GRAMMAR IN CONTEXT

Before You Read

Look at the photo, the title, and the first paragraph of the article. Discuss the questions.

1. What is the man doing? Describe him.
2. What type of music do you like? Do you enjoy classical music? Which composers?
3. Why do you think the article is called "The People's Conductor"?

Read

Read the article about Gustavo Dudamel.

The People's Conductor

He's young. He's exciting. He's great-looking. He's "The Dude,[1]" and he's changing the way people around the world feel about classical music.[2]

Gustavo Dudamel grew up in Barquisimeto, Venezuela. A child prodigy,[3] he **had already started** taking music lessons by the early age of four. His father played the trombone in a salsa band, and young Dudamel **had been hoping** to take up the same instrument. But his arms were too short, and so he studied the violin instead.

Dudamel soon became part of El Sistema—a free national program that

teaches young Venezuelans, mostly from poor families, how to play instruments. Many of these kids **had been getting** into pretty serious trouble before participating in the program. El Sistema **has transformed** the lives of hundreds of thousands of them by taking them off the streets and introducing them to the power of music. "The music saved me. I'm sure of this," said Dudamel in a TV interview.

In El Sistema, Dudamel's amazing talent was obvious, and by the time he was 15, he **had become** the conductor of the Simón Bolívar National Youth Orchestra. But that wasn't the first time

---

[1]*dude:* a man (an informal word, used to express positive feelings about the person)
[2]*classical music:* a type of music that is considered to be important and serious and that has continuing artistic value, for example operas and symphonies
[3]*prodigy:* a very young person who has a great natural ability in a subject or skill

The People's Conductor

he **had led** an orchestra. According to Dudamel, he **had been conducting** in his imagination since he was six.

On October 3, 2009, Dudamel lifted his baton for the first time as music director of the famed Los Angeles Philharmonic. He was only 28, and he **had** just **signed** a five-year contract as conductor. Tickets for this free concert at the 18,000-seat Hollywood Bowl **had become** available two months earlier. By the time the Bowl's ticket office opened on August 1, hundreds of people **had** already **arrived**. They **had been lining up** for hours in the hot Californian sun. The tickets were gone in minutes. On October 3, that lucky audience, a mix of all ages and ethnic backgrounds, **had come** for one thing—to see "Gustavo the Great" conduct. They were not disappointed. By the end of the concert they **had** all **risen** to their feet and **had been applauding** enthusiastically for ten minutes.

Since then Dudamel's career has continued to skyrocket[4] as he conducts orchestras all over the world. Although he has become famous, he has never forgotten his roots[5] or how his life **had been** before he learned to make music. To help other young people, he set up a program in Los Angeles modeled on El Sistema—the program that **had changed** his life. He said, "You cannot imagine how it changes the life of a kid if you put a violin or a cello or a flute in his hand. You feel you have your world . . . and it changes your life. This happened to me." Dudamel's goal is to make sure this happens to many others and to spread his love of classical music around the world.

---

[4]***skyrocket:*** to improve a lot and very quickly
[5]***roots:*** the connection a person feels with a place because he or she was born there or his or her family lived there

After You Read

A | Vocabulary: *Complete the sentences with the words from the box.*

conducted	contract	enthusiastic	ethnic	participated	transformed

1. The experience _transformed_ her life. It really changed everything for her.

2. The reviewer loved the concert. He wrote a(n) _enthusiastic_ review about it.

3. How many times has Dudamel _conducted_ the orchestra this season?

4. The audience was a real ___ethnic___ mix. There were African Americans, Asians, Hispanics, and whites.

5. Many musicians and singers _participated_ in the event.

6. One violinist signed a(n) _contract_ with the orchestra for two years.

B | Comprehension: *Put these events in Dudamel's life in the correct chronological order (1 = first, 6 = last).*

_5_ He became conductor of the Simón Bolívar National Youth Orchestra.

_2_ He turned four.

_4_ Music saved him.

_3_ He became music director of the Los Angeles Philharmonic.

_1_ He started taking music lessons.

_6_ He became part of El Sistema.

STEP 2 GRAMMAR PRESENTATION

PAST PERFECT

Statements				
Subject	***Had (not)***	**Past Participle**		
I You He She It We You They	**had (not)**	**arrived**	in the U.S.	by then.
		become	famous	

Contractions	
I had	= **I'd**
you had	= **you'd**
he had	= **he'd**
she had	= **she'd**
we had	= **we'd**
they had	= **they'd**
had not	= **hadn't**

Yes / No Questions				
Had	**Subject**	**Past Participle**		
Had	you he they	**arrived**	in the U.S.	by then?
		become	famous	

Short Answers						
Affirmative			**Negative**		
Yes,	I he they	**had.**	**No,**	I he they	**hadn't.**

Wh- Questions					
***Wh-* Word**		***Had***	**Subject**	**Past Participle**	
How many	concerts	**had**	he	**given**	by then?

PAST PERFECT PROGRESSIVE

Statements			
Subject	***Had (not) been***	**Base Form + *-ing***	
I You He She It We You They	**had (not) been**	**playing**	all over the world by then.

40 UNIT 4

Yes / No Questions			
Had	**Subject**	*Been* + **Base Form** + *-ing*	
Had	you he they	**been playing**	all over the world by then?

Short Answers					
Affirmative			**Negative**		
Yes,	I he they	**had**.	**No**,	I he they	**hadn't**.

Wh- Questions				
Wh- **Word**	*Had*	**Subject**	*Been* + **Base Form** + *-ing*	
How long	**had**	he	**been playing**	classical music by then?

GRAMMAR NOTES

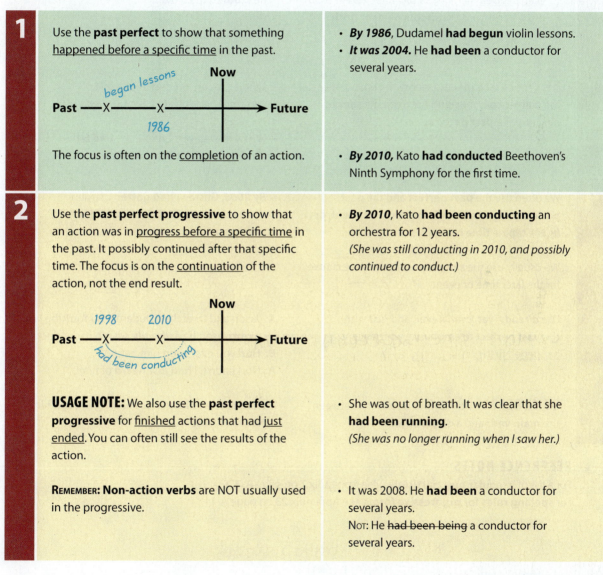

1 Use the **past perfect** to show that something happened before a specific time in the past.

The focus is often on the completion of an action.

- *By 1986*, Dudamel **had begun** violin lessons.
- *It was 2004.* He **had been** a conductor for several years.

- *By 2010,* Kato **had conducted** Beethoven's Ninth Symphony for the first time.

2 Use the **past perfect progressive** to show that an action was in progress before a specific time in the past. It possibly continued after that specific time. The focus is on the continuation of the action, not the end result.

- *By 2010*, Kato **had been conducting** an orchestra for 12 years.
  (She was still conducting in 2010, and possibly continued to conduct.)

USAGE NOTE: We also use the **past perfect progressive** for finished actions that had just ended. You can often still see the results of the action.

- She was out of breath. It was clear that she **had been running**.
  (She was no longer running when I saw her.)

REMEMBER: Non-action verbs are NOT usually used in the progressive.

- It was 2008. He **had been** a conductor for several years.
  Not: He ~~had been being~~ a conductor for several years.

(continued on next page)

3 Use the **past perfect** and the **past perfect progressive** with the **simple past** to show a relationship between two past events.

   a. Use the **past perfect** or the **past perfect progressive** for the <u>earlier event</u>. Use the **simple past** for the <u>later time or event</u>.

   b. When the <u>time relationship between two past events is clear</u> (as with *before*, *after*, and *as soon as*), we often use the **simple past for both events**.

BE CAREFUL! In sentences with *when*, notice the difference in meaning between the **simple past** and the **past perfect**.

- He **had been living** in Venezuela when he **won** a competition in Germany.
  (He was living in Venezuela. During that time, he won a competition in Germany.)

- *After* Dudamel **had joined** El Sistema, he **studied** the violin.
  OR
- *After* Dudamel **joined** El Sistema, he **studied** the violin.

- *When* the concert ended, she **left**.
  (First the concert ended. Then she left.)

- *When* the concert ended, she **had left**.
  (First she left. Then the concert ended.)

4 We often use the **past perfect** and the **past perfect progressive** with *by* + **time or event**, or *by the time* + **time clause**.

We usually use the **simple past** in the **time clause** for the later time or event.

Use *already*, *yet*, *ever*, *never*, and *just* with the **past perfect** to emphasize which event <u>happened first</u>.

BE CAREFUL! Do NOT put an adverb between the **main verb** and a **direct object**.

- *By 2006*, Gustavo **had gotten** married.
- *By the time we got tickets*, we **had been waiting** in line for an hour.

A: Jason and I watched Dudamel on YouTube last night. Jason **had** *already* **seen** him conduct.
B: **Had** you *ever* **seen** him before?
A: No, I hadn't. I **had** *just* **heard** of him!

- I hadn't **seen him yet**. OR I hadn't *yet* **seen him**.
  NOT: I hadn't ~~seen *yet* him~~.

REFERENCE NOTES
For a list of **irregular past participles**, see Appendix 1 on page A-1.
For **spelling rules for progressive forms**, see Appendix 23 on page A-11.

EXERCISE 1: Discover the Grammar

*Read each numbered situation. Decide if the description that follows is **True (T)** or **False (F)**.*
*If there is not enough information to know, write a question mark **(?)**.*

1. The talk show host invited the musician on her show because he had won a competition.

   ___F___ The musician won the competition after his appearance on the show.

2. Before the break, the musician had been explaining why he had chosen to play the violin.

   ___T___ The musician's explanation was finished.

3. It was 4:00 P.M. They had been selling tickets for an hour.

   ___T___ They were still selling tickets at 4:05.

4. When I found my seat, the concert started.

   ___F___ First the concert started. Then I found my seat.

5. When I found my seat, the concert had started.

   ___T___ First the concert started. Then I found my seat.

6. When I saw Mei Ling, she was very enthusiastic. She had been rehearsing with Dudamel.

   ___T___ She wasn't rehearsing when I saw her.

7. By the end of the concert, the audience had fallen in love with Dudamel.

   ___F___ The audience fell in love with Dudamel after the concert.

EXERCISE 2: Past Perfect: Statements with *Already* and *Yet*   *(Grammar Notes 1, 4)*

Look at some important events in Gustavo Dudamel's career. Then complete the sentences.
*Use the past perfect with **already** or **not yet**.*

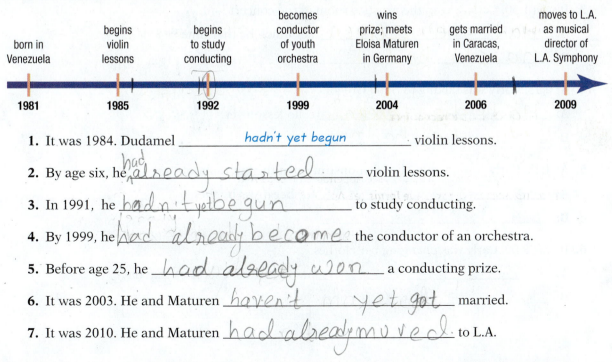

born in Venezuela	begins violin lessons	begins to study conducting	becomes conductor of youth orchestra	wins prize; meets Eloisa Maturen in Germany	gets married in Caracas, Venezuela	moves to L.A. as musical director of L.A. Symphony
1981	1985	1992	1999	2004	2006	2009

1. It was 1984. Dudamel _____ *hadn't yet begun* _____ violin lessons.

2. By age six, he ___had already started___ violin lessons.

3. In 1991, he ___hadn't yet begun___ to study conducting.

4. By 1999, he ___had already become___ the conductor of an orchestra.

5. Before age 25, he ___had already won___ a conducting prize.

6. It was 2003. He and Maturen ___haven't yet got___ married.

7. It was 2010. He and Maturen ___had already moved___ to L.A.

Past Perfect and Past Perfect Progressive   **43**

EXERCISE 3: Past Perfect: Questions and Short Answers

(Grammar Note 1)

Carly plays cello in an orchestra. Read her diary notes. Then complete the questions about her day and give short answers. Use the past perfect.

DATE: Thursday, May 18, 2012

8:30 took yoga class at the gym

10:00 started rehearsing at the concert hall for Saturday's concert

12:30 ate lunch

2:30 had cello lesson with Sofia Gregor

4:00 gave cello demonstration at Performing Arts High School

6:00 shopped for dress for Saturday night's concert

7:30 did relaxation exercises

8:30 ordered takeout

11:00 fell asleep—forgot to eat!

1. It was 9:30 A.M. Carly was at the gym.

   A: _____Had she taken_____ her yoga class yet?

   B: _____Yes, she had._____

2. At 10:00, Carly was at the concert hall.

   A: __Had she started__ for Saturday's concert yet?

   B: __yes, she had__

3. It was 1:30. Carly was in the practice room of the concert hall.

   A: __Had she eatten__ her lunch by that time?

   B: __no, she hadn't__

4. At 2:15, Carly was talking to Sofia Gregor.

   A: __Had she taken__ cello lesson yet?

   B: __No, she hadn't__

5. At 4:45, Carly was finishing her demonstration at the high school.

   A: __Had she bought__ for her dress by then?

   B: __No, she hadn't__

6. It was 8:00. Carly was changing her clothes.

   A: __Had she finished__ her relaxation exercises that day?

   B: __Yes, she hadn't__

7. At 10:00 Carly was listening to a CD of her last performance.

A: _had she ordered_ takeout yet?

B: _Yes, she had_

8. It was 11:00. Carly was sleeping.

A: _Had she eaten_ her dinner yet?

B: _No, she hadn't_

EXERCISE 4: Past Perfect Progressive: Statements

(Grammar Note 2)

Gustavo Dudamel was a musical child prodigy. Complete the information about two other prodigies. Use the past perfect progressive form of the verbs in parentheses.

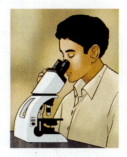

AKRIT JASWAL has been called "the world's smartest boy" and "the Mozart of modern medicine." By the age of six, he ___ *had* ___ already ___ *been reading* ___ Shakespeare in his native village in northern India. Even
1. (read)
more amazing, he _had been studing_ medical textbooks on his own. He
2. (study)
had been even observeing surgeries at local hospitals.
3. (observe)

Then at age seven, he operated on a young girl whose hand had been severely injured in a fire. The operation, which he performed for free in his home, was a success, and Jaswal became famous. His family _had been hopeing_ that their son could start medical school when he was eight, but he had
4. (hope)
to wait three years before he enrolled at Punjab University—the youngest student ever admitted.

Jaswal's dream is to someday find a cure for cancer.

JUDIT POLGAR is known as the strongest female chess player who has ever lived. In 1991, she became the youngest Grandmaster ever at age 15, not surprising since she _had been playing_ the game since she was five years old.
5. (play)
For five years, she _had been winning_ games against older chess masters. By
6. (win)
age 20, Polgar was ranked the 10th best player in the world—the first woman to achieve a rating in the top 10. In 2002, she defeated Garry Kasparov, the highest rated player in the world. It was a great personal victory. She had lost to Kasparov in 1994, and she _had been waiting_
7. (wait)
to try again. In 2000, Polgar married Gusztav Font. Font, a veterinarian, _had been treating_
8. (treat)
Polgar's dog when the two met. Between 2004 and 2007, the couple had two children, and Polgar competed less often. Because she _hadn't been completing_ as much, her rank dropped to 20th, but by
9. (not compete)
2008, Polgar was playing for Hungary in the Olympics, her career back on track.

EXERCISE 5: Past Perfect Progressive: Questions

(Grammar Note 4)

*A talk-show host is trying to get some background information on violinist Mei Ling before her interview. Use **before** or **when** and the words in parentheses to write questions with the past perfect progressive.*

1. Mei Ling quit her old job to play full-time.

What kind of work had she been doing when she quit her job to play full-time?
(what kind of work / she / do)

2. She signed a contract with the L.A. Philharmonic.

Had she ~~was~~ been living in LA, when she signed a
(she / live in Los Angeles) contract.

3. She gave her first solo performance.

Had she been practing long, before she gave
(she / practice long) her first solo
performance?

4. She won first prize in the Paganini Violin Competition.

Had she been competing a long time when she won
(she / compete a long time) competition?

5. Her bow[1] broke during the concert.

when
How long had she been playing, her bow broke?
(how long / she / play)

6. They took pictures of her in front of her home.

Had the newspaper reporter been following
her in front **(the newspaper reporters / follow her)** of her home.

7. She married the conductor Lorenzo Russo.

How long had they been dating before
(how long / they / date) she married the
conductor.

8. Mei Ling and her husband moved to Rome.

been
Where had they, living before they moved
(where / they / live) to Rome.

[1] **bow:** a long thin piece of wood with strings stretched tightly from one end to the other used for playing string instruments, such as the violin

EXERCISE 6: Past Perfect and Past Perfect Progressive

(Grammar Notes 1–4)

Complete this report on El Sistema. Use the past perfect or past perfect progressive form of the verbs in the boxes. Use the progressive form when possible. Some verbs can be used more than once.

situation		*notice*		*be visible*	
come up	help	observe	receive	show up	teach

It was 1975. José Antonio Abreu ___had received___ his degree in economics and
1.

had been teaching economics at Simón Bolívar University for years. As an economist, he
2.

had been observing the poverty he saw around him. As a trained musician, he _had come up_
3. _(need)_   **4.**

with a creative solution—a music program for children. El Sistema began in a parking garage in

1975. Abreu remembers the first night of the program. Only 11 children _had showed up_
5.

but, Abreu says, he still felt it was the start of something very big. It was. By 2009, Abreu

had received many prizes for his work, and he _had helped_ hundreds of thousands
6.   **7.**

of Venezuela's kids turn their lives around with music.

arrest	be	hope	live	work

Gustavo Dudamel, now a world-famous conductor, _had been_ one of those kids. He, in
8.

turn, has established similar organizations, such as The Youth Orchestra of Los Angeles. Canadian

singer Measha Brueggersgosman participated in the project, and in October 2009 the kids attended

Dudamel's concert at the Hollywood Bowl. They were wildly enthusiastic. "A lot of the people . . .

had never _being_ to a classical music concert before. . . .They were
9.

crying and screaming," she recalls. But Dudamel is only one of El Sistema's success stories. Here

are just two more out of thousands: At age nine, Edicson Ruiz _had been working_ at a Caracas
10.

supermarket to help support his family. El Sistema helped him put down the supermarket packages

and pick up the bow. He is now a successful double bass player with the Berlin Philarmonie. And

then there's Lennar Acosta. Before he got his clarinet, Acosta _had been living_ a life of crime.
11.

Police _had_ already _arrested_ the troubled youth nine times for robbery
12.

and drug use. But thanks to El Sistema, he traded in his gun for a musical instrument, and today he

is a clarinetist at the Caracas Youth Orchestra.

    This is what José Antonio Abreu _had hoped_ to accomplish when he began El Sistema
13.

more than three decades ago. For Abreu, music has always been more than just an art form. He calls

it a "weapon against poverty" and a way to change lives.

Dudamel and the Simón Bolívar Youth Orchestra

EXERCISE 7: Time Clauses

(Grammar Note 4)

A talk-show host is interviewing violinist Mei Ling about her career. Complete the interview. Determine the correct order of the sentences in parentheses and use the past perfect or past perfect progressive to express the event that occurred first. Use the progressive form when possible.

HOST: When did you decide to play the violin professionally?

LING: (I made up my mind to play professionally. / I was 10.)

By the time _____*I was 10, I had made up my mind to play professionally*_____.
1.

HOST: How did you get your first paying job?

LING: (I was performing with a group at college. / My professor recommended me.)

I had been performing the clg when my professor recommended me. clg.
2.
The job was with an opera company.

HOST: That was lucky! Did you work there for a long time?

LING: No. (The company closed. / I was working there for only a month.)

After the company closed I had working
3.
there for only a month.

HOST: Did you find another job performing?

LING: Yes, but not for a while. (I was teaching in a community music program. / City Orchestra called me.)

Before city orchestra called, I had been teaching in
4.   me   a community music
(I almost decided to stop performing. / I loved working with those kids.)   pro.
had
I almost decided to stop performing because
5.
I loved working with those kids.

HOST: Do you still keep in touch with the community program?

LING: Oh, sure. (We were planning an orchestra for the kids. / I left.)

we had been planning when
6.
I left. I still want to do that.

EXERCISE 8: Editing

Read this article about a singer. There are eight mistakes in the use of the past perfect and the past perfect progressive. The first mistake is already corrected. Find and correct seven more.

A Diva¹ with a Difference

Measha Brueggergosman was born in 1977 in New Brunswick, Canada. Her first-grade teacher urged Brueggergosman's parents to give her music lessons. They did, and by age 15, she ~~had been deciding~~ *had decided* on a singing career. Not growing up in a large cultural center, she didn't have the chance to attend concerts or the opera. However, by the time she enrolled at the University of Toronto, she listening to classical music on the radio for years, and she participated in her church's music program since she was a child.

After receiving her degree in Toronto, Brueggergosman moved to Düsseldorf, Germany, to study. By age 25, she had been performing internationally for several years and had won a number of important prizes. One enthusiastic judge said she'd never been meeting so young a singer with such perfect vocal control.

By her 30th birthday, Brueggergosman has become both a classical music sensation² and a popular celebrity. A diva with a Facebook fan club, she had been developed her own unique fashion style. She had also appearing on popular TV shows. Things had been going along fine when, in June 2009, she experienced a health crisis that led to emergency surgery. She had to cancel many performances, but she recovered in time to sing at the *Bienvenido Dudamel!* concert in L.A. four months later. When she took the stage at the Hollywood Bowl, it was clear why the soprano had been made such an impression on critics and audiences for the last 10 years. They had all fallen in love with her style as well as her beautiful voice. Brava Brueggergosman!

---

¹*diva:* a very successful female opera singer
²*sensation:* something or someone that causes a lot of excitement or interest

EXERCISE 9: Listening

A | *A radio host is interviewing several young musicians. Read the sentences. Then listen to the interview. Listen again and circle the words you hear.*

1. **JULIO:** I'd / (I hadn't) really been planning to study the trombone.

2. **MARTA:** (We'd) / We hadn't been playing in the same orchestra.

3. **KLAUS:** He'd / (He hadn't) gotten us tickets for a concert.

4. **LING:** (I'd / I hadn't) been dreaming of getting a violin of my own.

5. **ANTONIO:** I'd / (I hadn't) been doing my schoolwork.

B | *Read the statements. Then listen again to the interview and check (✓)* **True** *or* **False**. *Correct the false statements.*

	True	False
1. Before Julio started lessons, he'd wanted to play the ~~trombone~~. *flute*	☐	☑
2. Maria and Julio were good friends before the concert in Berlin.	☐	☐
3. Klaus had seen Dudamel conduct many times before the concert in Caracas.	☐	☐
4. Ling decided she wanted a violin before she turned 10.	☐	☐
5. After Antonio started making music, he spent less time hanging out with his friends.	☐	☐

EXERCISE 10: Pronunciation

A | *Read and listen to the Pronunciation Note.*

> **Pronunciation Note**
>
> In conversation, we often use the contraction **'d** for *had* in the **past perfect** or **past perfect progressive**.
>
> After **pronouns** (except *it*), we pronounce **'d** as /**d**/.
>
> **EXAMPLE:**   **We had** been there before.   →   "**We'd** been there before."
>
> After *it* and **nouns** we pronounce **'d** as a short extra syllable /ə**d**/.
>
> **EXAMPLES:**   **It had** been a great concert.   →   "**It'd** been a great concert."
> **My friends had** enjoyed it a lot.   →   "My **friends'd** enjoyed it a lot."
> **Rosa had** been rehearsing for weeks.   →   "**Rosa'd** been rehearsing for weeks."
>
> We do NOT usually write the contraction **'d** after a noun or *it*. We write *friends had* and *it had* (NOT: ~~friends'd~~ or ~~it'd~~).

B | *Listen to the conversations and repeat each statement.*

1. **A:** We'd been standing in line for hours.
   B: Yes. But it had been worth it.

2. **A:** Maria had come late.
   B: I know. Her seat had been taken.

3. **A:** I'd seen him conduct twice before.
   B: It was the first time my son had seen him.

4. **A:** The concert had been sold out.
   B: People had come from all over.

5. **A:** The day had been perfect.
   B: The audience had loved the performance.

C | *Practice the conversations with a partner.*

EXERCISE 11: What About You?

for By the time use. Past perfect (Had)

Think about what you did yesterday. Indicate whether it was or wasn't a busy day. Complete the sentences. Then compare your day with a classmate's.

EXAMPLE: **A:** By 9:00 A.M., I'd already been practicing the piano for two hours. What about you?
B: By 9:00 A.M., I hadn't even gotten up!

Yesterday was / wasn't a busy day for me.

1. By 9:00 A.M., _I'd already been finishing my breakfast._

2. By the time I got to work / school, _had already started at work._

3. By the time I had lunch, _I had already had my 1st class._

4. By the time I left work / school, _I had been waited in traffic._

5. By the time I had dinner, _my father had come from work._

6. By 9:00 P.M., I _had already brushed my teeth._

7. By the time I went to bed, I had done so much / little that I felt _tired._

EXERCISE 12: Conversation

Work in small groups. Talk about things you had never done before you began living here (or before a certain year). Possible topics: music, food, sports, clothing, entertainment, transportation.

EXAMPLE: **A:** Before I went to the Dudamel concert in Los Angeles, I wasn't really enthusiastic about classical music.
B: Me neither. I'd only listened to popular music.
C: I'd never been to a classical concert before.

EXERCISE 13: Game: Find the Differences

*Work with a partner. Look at the two pictures. There are eleven differences in the pictures. Find and discuss them. Use **by** + past perfect in your discussion.*

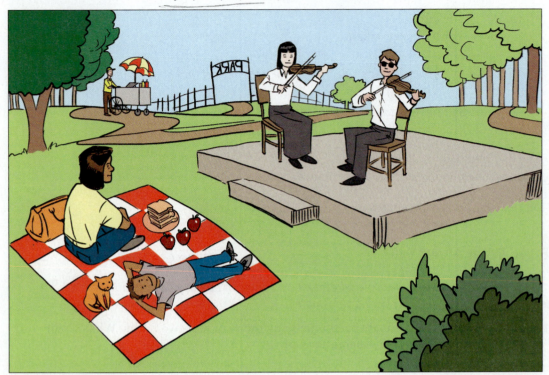

4:00 P.M.

6:00 P.M.

> **EXAMPLE:** **A:** At 4:00 the woman wasn't wearing a sweater. By 6:00 she had put her sweater on.
> **B:** And the boy had fallen asleep.

EXERCISE 14: Writing

A | *Find information in the library or on the Internet about the life and career of a musician or singer that you like. Make a timeline using seven or eight events in the artist's life and career.*

B | *Write two paragraphs about the artist you researched. For example, the first paragraph could be about the person's career. The second could be about the artist's personal life. Use the timeline to help you write sentences in the past perfect and past perfect progressive. If you can, download a photo of the artist for your essay.*

> **EXAMPLE:** Vanessa-Mae only uses her first name professionally. She was born in Singapore on October 27. By age five, she had been playing the piano for two years. By the time she was a teenager, she had already made three classical recordings . . .

C | *Check your work. Use the Editing Checklist.*

Editing Checklist

Did you use . . . ?
- ☐ the past perfect and the past perfect progressive
- ☐ the past perfect for things that began before a specific past time
- ☐ the past perfect progressive for things that were in progress before a specific past time
- ☐ time clauses to show the relationship between past events
- ☐ adverbs to emphasize the first event

A | Circle the correct words to complete the sentences.

1. By the time I was 10, I got / had gotten my first violin.

2. It was 2007. I have been studying / had been studying the violin for two years by then.

3. By 2010, I had graduated / had been graduating from Juilliard School of Music.

4. After I finished school, I moved / had been moving to Los Angeles.

5. I had given / hadn't given a concert yet.

B | Complete the interview with the simple past, past perfect, or past perfect progressive form of the verbs in parentheses. Use the past perfect progressive when possible.

A: You're only 25. How long _____ you _____ the violin when you
   1. (play)
_____ the Philharmonic Orchestra?
   2. (join)

B: Ten years. By the time I was 13, I _____ to become a professional,
   3. (decide)
and I _____ for three hours a day. My father was a musician, and he
   4. (practice)
_____ me to play the piano too.
   5. (teach)

A: _____ you _____ to this country yet?
   6. (come)

B: Yes. We _____ already _____ here. We _____ here for a year.
   7. (move)   **8. (live)**

A: Well, congratulations on winning the grand prize. Were you surprised?

B: Very! I _____ it, and I was very excited.
   9. (not expect)

C | Find and correct six mistakes.

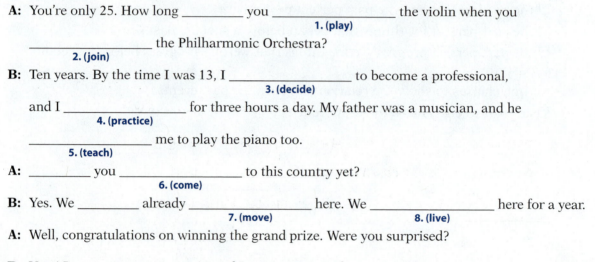

When five-year-old Sarah Chang enrolled in the Juilliard School of Music, she has already been playing the violin for more than a year. Her parents, both musicians, had been moving from Korea to further their careers. They had gave their daughter a violin as a fourth birthday present, and Sarah had been practiced hard since then. By seven, she already performed with several local orchestras. A child prodigy, Sarah became the youngest person to receive the Hollywood Bowl's Hall of Fame Award. She had already been receiving several awards including the Nan Pa Award—South Korea's highest prize for musical talent.

From Grammar to Writing
EDITING FOR VERB FORMS

When a paragraph includes more than one time frame (both present and past, for example), use correct verb forms to keep your meaning clear. You should also use **transitional words and phrases** such as *one day*, *now*, *at that time*, and *since then* to **signal a change in time**.

> SIMPLE PAST   PRESENT PERFECT
>
> **EXAMPLE:**   I **decided** to change my behavior. I **have been** much happier. ➔
> *One day* I **decided** to change my behavior. *Since then* I **have been** much happier.

1 | *Complete the student's paragraph about a phase in her life (a temporary period when she had particular kinds of behavior and feelings). Use the correct form of the verbs in parentheses.*

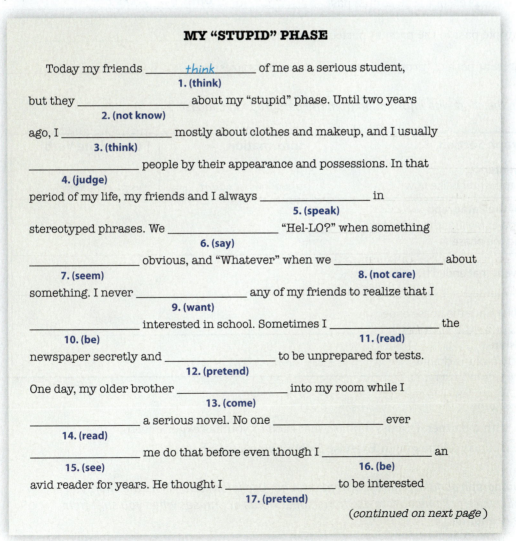

MY "STUPID" PHASE

Today my friends _____ *think* _____ of me as a serious student,
           1. (think)

but they _____ about my "stupid" phase. Until two years
    2. (not know)

ago, I _____ mostly about clothes and makeup, and I usually
    3. (think)

_____ people by their appearance and possessions. In that
4. (judge)

period of my life, my friends and I always _____ in
                        5. (speak)

stereotyped phrases. We _____ "Hel-LO?" when something
          6. (say)

_____ obvious, and "Whatever" when we _____ about
7. (seem)   **8. (not care)**

something. I never _____ any of my friends to realize that I
          9. (want)

_____ interested in school. Sometimes I _____ the
10. (be)   **11. (read)**

newspaper secretly and _____ to be unprepared for tests.
          12. (pretend)

One day, my older brother _____ into my room while I
          13. (come)

_____ a serious novel. No one _____ ever
14. (read)

_____ me do that before even though I _____ an
15. (see)   **16. (be)**

avid reader for years. He thought I _____ to be interested
          17. (pretend)

(continued on next page)

in the book in order to impress a new boyfriend. I _____
18. (get)

angry when he _____ at me, so I _____ a
19. (laugh)   20. (make)

decision. I _____ hiding my real interests. Since that day, I
21. (stop)

_____ my news magazines proudly and _____
22. (carry)   23. (express)

opinions in class. For the last two years I _____ for tests
24. (prepare)

openly. Now I _____ for college, and I _____
25. (apply)   26. (feel)

proud of being a good student.

2 | Look at the paragraph in Exercise 1. Find the transitional words and phrases that signal a change in time.

1. the simple present to the simple past _____ *Until two years ago* _____

2. the simple past to the present perfect (progressive) _____

3. the present perfect (progressive) to the present progressive _____

3 | Complete the chart with information from the paragraph in Exercise 1.

Paragraph Section	Information	Form of the Verb
Topic Sentence • what the writer is like now	*a serious student*	*simple present*
Body of the Paragraph • habits and feelings the writer had during the phase		
• the event that ended the phase		
• behavior since the phase ended		
Conclusion • the results of the change		

4 | Before you write . . .
1. Work with a partner. Discuss a phase that each of you has experienced.
2. Make a chart like the one in Exercise 3 about your own phase.

5 | Write a paragraph about a phase you went through. Use information from the chart you made in Exercise 4. Remember to use transitional words or phrases when you shift from one time to another.

6 | *Exchange paragraphs with a different partner. Underline the verbs in your partner's paragraph. Circle the transitional words and phrases. Write a question mark (?) where something seems wrong or missing. Then answer the following questions.*

	Yes	No
1. Does each verb correctly express the time the author is writing about?	☐	☐
2. Is each verb formed correctly?	☐	☐
3. Are the shifts from one time to another time clearly marked with transitional words or phrases?	☐	☐

7 | *Work with your partner. Discuss each other's editing questions from Exercise 6. Then rewrite your own paragraph and make any necessary corrections.*

FUTURE: REVIEW AND EXPANSION

Before You Read

Look at the pictures. Discuss the questions.

1. What topics do you think the article will discuss?
2. What kinds of problems do you think people will face in the future?
3. How do you think they can solve them?

Read

Read the article about the future.

Cities of the Future
By Will Hapin, PhD

The world's population is exploding. By 2050, futurists[1] predict that 10 billion people **will be living** on the planet, up to 80 percent of them in cities. At the same time, the oceans are rising as global warming melts the ice at the North and South Poles. This means that while the population **is growing**, land **will be shrinking**. In addition, there **is not going to be** enough fresh water or oil and other types of fuel. Where **will** people **live** when room on dry land **gets** too crowded? How **will** 10 billion people **feed** themselves and **travel** from place to place? We**'re going to need** a lot of innovative solutions. Fortunately, some very creative people are already thinking about them. Here's what they are predicting:

Homes: Water World

Some futurists believe that as rising oceans **cover** the land, the oceans themselves **are going to become** valuable real estate.[2] People **will be building** floating cities, like the one in the picture, that **will use** solar, wind, and wave power.[3] Some cities **will** even **be traveling** long distances and **using** their large gardens to supply food. Science fiction? Maybe not. Some of the technology is already being used in underwater hotels and laboratories.

[1]*futurist:* someone who predicts future events and developments
[2]*real estate:* land and houses that people buy and sell
[3]*solar, wind, and wave power:* energy from the sun, wind, and ocean waves

Cities of the Future

Food: The Sky's the Limit

According to the United Nations Food and Agriculture Organization, the world **is going to need** 70 percent more food by 2050. This **will require** additional farmland equal to the size of Brazil. Where **will** we **find** it? Dr. Dickson Despommier, a professor at Columbia University, says urban farmers **will be growing** food on vertical farms, and that "sky farms" in New York **will produce** enough chicken, vegetables, and fruit to feed Manhattan. Instead of fuel-guzzling[4] farm machines, farmers **will be using** robots for difficult and dangerous work. The farms **will** also **save** energy because food **won't be traveling** into the city by truck from distant farms.

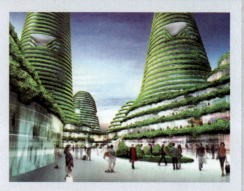

Travel: Back to the Future?

More than 50 years ago, luxurious airships—large "balloons" filled with helium[5]—carried passengers around Europe and across the Atlantic. However, after one terrible accident, people stopped traveling in them. Now, with fuel becoming more expensive, airships are coming back. A Spanish company is developing a solar-powered airship that **will fly** on sunshine during the day and **use** fuel only at night. Commuters **will be taking** airships to work, and the company predicts many other uses for the vehicles. For example, disaster relief organizations, such as the Red Cross and Red Crescent Societies, **will be using** them as flying hospitals to help earthquake and storm victims.

Earth and Beyond: The Space Elevator

What **will** vacationers of the future **do** when they **need** a break from their crowded cities? They**'ll** just **hop** on the space elevator—a "ribbon" from the Earth that **will carry** people into space. This amazing idea was first proposed in 1895 by Russian scientist Konstantin Tsiolkovsky. Now, new technology and materials are turning the elevator into a reality. Supporters of the idea claim the elevators **are going to make** space travel cheap and safe. By the end of the century, they say, tourists **will be visiting** sky hotels and even **traveling** to the Moon, Mars, and beyond. Next stop, the 10,000th floor!

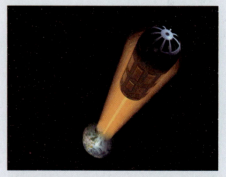

The future **is coming**, with all its opportunities and challenges. **Will** we **be** ready? With enough imagination and hard work, we **will be**!

---

[4]**fuel-guzzling:** using too much fuel. *Guzzle* means "to drink large amounts of something."
[5]**helium:** a gas that is lighter than air, often used to make balloons and airships float in the air

A I **Vocabulary:** *Circle the letter of the word or phrase that best completes each sentence.*

1. A **creative** or **innovative** plan is _____.
   a. new
   b. old
   c. easy

2. **Technology** is the _____ we use to do things.
   a. money and skills
   b. machines and knowledge
   c. people and animals

3. A _____ is NOT usually **vertical**.
   a. tall building
   b. tree
   c. desktop

4. A(n) _____ is an example of a **vehicle**.
   a. accident
   b. automobile
   c. hospital

5. A **challenge** is a task that is _____.
   a. new and difficult
   b. easy and safe
   c. in the far future

B I **Comprehension:** *Which of these statements are true* **Now**? *Which will be true only in the* **Future**? *Check (✓) the correct boxes.*

	Now	Future
1. The world's population is growing fast.	☑	☐
2. People are living on floating cities.	☐	☑
3. Tourists are staying in underwater hotels.	☐	☑
4. Sky farms are using robots as workers.	☐	☑
5. A company is building a solar-powered airship.	☑	☐
6. People are riding an elevator into space.	☐	☑

*Jane is having a meeting on mon.
  —Is Jane Having?
  —was jane having a ..?

STEP 2 GRAMMAR PRESENTATION

FUTURE

Affirmative Statements	
We **are going to take**	
We **will take**	
We **are taking**	the airship at 9:00.
We **take**	

Negative Statements	
We **are not going to take**	
We **will not take**	
We **are not taking**	the airship at 10:00.
We **don't take**	

Yes / No Questions	
Is she **going to take**	
Will she **take**	
Is she **taking**	the airship at 9:00?
Does she **take**	

Short Answers					
Affirmative			**Negative**		
Yes,	she **is.**		**No,**	she **isn't.**	
	she **will.**			she **won't.**	
	she **is.**			she **isn't.**	
	she **does.**			she **doesn't.**	

Wh- Questions	
When **is** she **going to take**	
When **will** she **take**	
When **is** she **taking**	the airship?
When **does** she **take**	

Fut. {
I will go.
I am going to
I see him on mon.
}

FUTURE PROGRESSIVE

Statements			
Subject	**Be (not) going to / Will (not)**	**Be + Base Form + -ing**	
People	**are (not) going to** **will (not)**	**be traveling**	to Mars by 2050.

Yes / No Questions				
Be / Will	**Subject**	**Going to**	**Be + Base Form + -ing**	
Are	they	**going to**	**be traveling**	to Mars?
Will				

Short Answers				
Affirmative		**Negative**		
Yes,	they **are.**	**No,**	they**'re not.**	
	they **will.**		they **won't.**	

Wh- Questions					
Wh- Word	**Be / Will**	**Subject**	**Going to**	**Be + Base Form + -ing**	
When	are	they	**going to**	**be traveling**	to Mars?
	will				

GRAMMAR NOTES

1 There are several ways to talk about the **future**. You can use:

- *be going to*
- *will*
- **present progressive**
- **simple present**

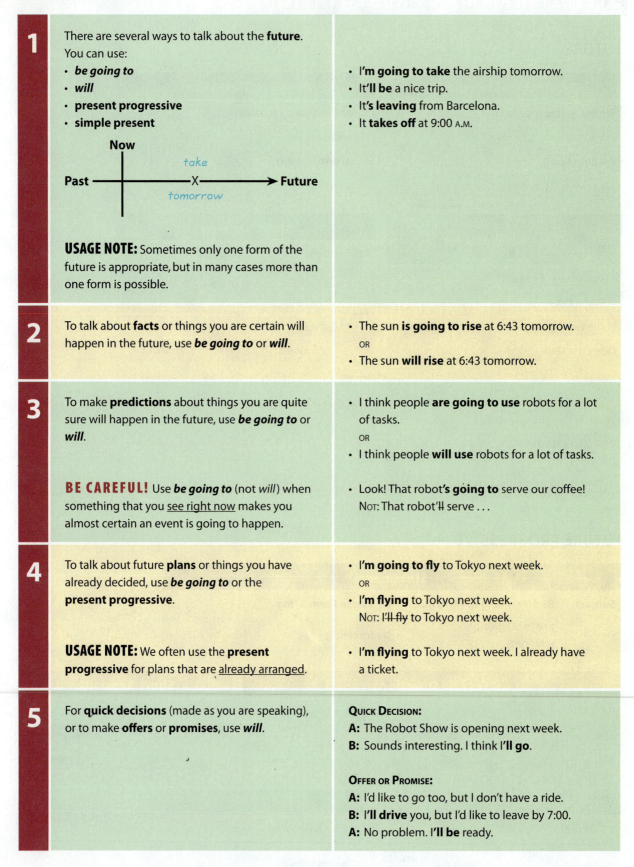

USAGE NOTE: Sometimes only one form of the future is appropriate, but in many cases more than one form is possible.

- I**'m going to take** the airship tomorrow.
- It**'ll be** a nice trip.
- It**'s leaving** from Barcelona.
- It **takes off** at 9:00 A.M.

2 To talk about **facts** or things you are certain will happen in the future, use *be going to* or *will*.

- The sun **is going to rise** at 6:43 tomorrow.
  OR
- The sun **will rise** at 6:43 tomorrow.

3 To make **predictions** about things you are quite sure will happen in the future, use *be going to* or *will*.

- I think people **are going to use** robots for a lot of tasks.
  OR
- I think people **will use** robots for a lot of tasks.

BE CAREFUL! Use *be going to* (not *will*) when something that you see right now makes you almost certain an event is going to happen.

- Look! That robot**'s going to** serve our coffee!
  NOT: That robot**'ll** serve . . .

4 To talk about future **plans** or things you have already decided, use *be going to* or the **present progressive**.

- I**'m going to fly** to Tokyo next week.
  OR
- I**'m flying** to Tokyo next week.
  NOT: I**'ll fly** to Tokyo next week.

USAGE NOTE: We often use the **present progressive** for plans that are already arranged.

- I**'m flying** to Tokyo next week. I already have a ticket.

5 For **quick decisions** (made as you are speaking), or to make **offers** or **promises**, use *will*.

QUICK DECISION:
A: The Robot Show is opening next week.
B: Sounds interesting. I think I**'ll go**.

OFFER OR PROMISE:
A: I'd like to go too, but I don't have a ride.
B: I**'ll drive** you, but I'd like to leave by 7:00.
A: No problem. I**'ll be** ready.

6	To talk about **scheduled future events** (timetables, programs, schedules), use the **simple present**. We often use verbs such as *leave*, *start*, *end*, and *begin* this way.	• The airship **leaves** at 9:00 A.M. • The conference **starts** tomorrow morning.
7	Use the **future progressive** with **be going to** or **will** to talk about actions that will be in progress at a specific time in the future. **Now** tomorrow **Past** ——————X————→ **Future** fly to Tokyo **USAGE NOTES:** **a.** We often use the **future progressive** instead of the future to make a question about someone's plans <u>more polite</u>. **b.** People often use the **future progressive** to ask indirectly for a favor. This makes the request <u>more polite</u>.	• At this time tomorrow, I**'m going to be flying** to Tokyo. OR • At this time tomorrow, I**'ll be flying** to Tokyo. • When **are** you **going to hand in** your paper? *(teacher to student)* • When **will** you **be grading** our tests? *(student to teacher)* • **Will** you **be going** by the post office tomorrow? I need some stamps.
8	In sentences with a **future time clause**: **a.** Use the future or the future progressive in the main clause. **b.** Use the **simple present** or the **present progressive** in the **time clause**. **BE CAREFUL!** Do NOT use the future or the future progressive in the time clause.	MAIN CLAUSE TIME CLAUSE • I**'ll call** when the robot **finishes** the laundry. • I**'ll be eating** while he **is dusting**. • I'll be making lunch while the robot **is cleaning**. Not: I'll be making lunch while the robot ~~will be cleaning~~.

(Before)
Tim clauses: By the time
        while
        After /Before

By the time you come, I will have read 20 pages.

"   the sem. ends, you will have learn Grammer.

Future and Future Progressive **65**

EXERCISE 1: Discover the Grammar

A | *Dr. Will Hapin just met his friend Dr. Nouvella Eon at a conference. Read the conversation and underline all the verbs that refer to the future.*

HAPIN: Nouvella! It's nice to see you. <u>Are you presenting</u> a paper today?

EON: Hi, Will! Yes. In fact my talk <u>starts</u> at two o'clock.

HAPIN: Oh, I think <u>I'll go</u>. What do you plan to talk about? <u>Will you be discussing</u> robots?

EON: Yes. <u>I'm focusing</u> on personal robots for household work. My talk is called "Creative Uses of Home Robots."

HAPIN: *I* want one of those! But seriously, you promised me an interview on personal robots. <u>Will you be getting</u> some free time in the next few weeks?

EON: I'm not sure. <u>I'll get</u> back to you, OK?

HAPIN: Great! Where's your son, by the way? Is he with you?

EON: No. Rocky stays in Denver with his grandparents in the summer. <u>I'm going to visit</u> him right after the conference. <u>He'll be</u> 10 years old in a few days. I can't believe it!

HAPIN: It's his birthday, huh? Here, take this little model of the flying car for him.

EON: Oh, <u>he's going to love</u> this! Thanks, Will. So, what are you working on these days?

HAPIN: Well, *Futurist Magazine* just published my story on cities of the future. And I'm still with the World Future Association. In fact, <u>I'm speaking</u> at a news conference next month about the space elevator.

EON: <u>That'll be</u> exciting! Good luck with it!

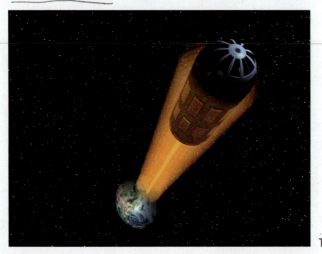

The space elevator

B | Complete the chart. List the 12 future verb forms in Part A. Then check (✓) the correct column for each form.

	Facts	Predictions	Plans	Quick Decisions	Offers and Promises	Schedules
1. *Are you presenting*			✓			
2.						
3.						
4.						
5.						
6.						
7.						
8.						
9.						
10.						
11.						
12.						

EXERCISE 2: Forms of the Future

(Grammar Notes 1–6)

Complete these conversations. Circle the correct words.

1. **Eon:** Which projects <u>do you report</u> / (are you going to report) on?

   Hapin: I haven't decided for sure. Probably flying cars.

2. **Hapin:** Look at those dark clouds!

   Eon: Yes. It looks like <u>it's raining</u> / (it's going to rain) any minute.

3. **Eon:** I'd better get back to my hotel room before it starts to rain. Call me, OK?

   Hapin: OK. <u>I'm talking</u> / (I'll talk) to you later.

4. **Desk:** Dr. Eon, your son just called.

   Eon: Oh, good. I think (I'll call) / <u>I'm calling</u> him back right away.

5. **Eon:** Hi, honey. How's it going?

   Rocky: Great. And guess what? <u>I go</u> / (I'm going) fishing with Grandpa tomorrow.

6. **Eon:** Have fun, but don't forget. You still have to finish that paper.

   Rocky: I know, Mom. <u>I send</u> / (I'm sending) it to my teacher tomorrow. I already discussed it with her.

7. **Rocky:** How's the conference?

   Eon: Good. (I'm giving) / <u>I'll give</u> my talk this afternoon.

(continued on next page)

8. Rocky: Good luck. When are you / will you be here?

Eon: Tomorrow. The airship lands / will land at 7:00, so I see / I'll see you about 8:00.

9. Rocky: Great! Are we going / Do we go to the car show on my birthday?

Eon: Sure! Oh, and Will gave me something for you. I think you like / you're going to like it.

EXERCISE 3: Future Progressive

(Grammar Note 7)

Will Hapin is interviewing Nouvella Eon. Complete the interview. Use the future progressive form of the words in parentheses and short answers.

Hapin: You've been presenting a lot of papers recently. _____Will_____ you _____be going_____
1. (will / go)

to the robotics conference in Tokyo next month?

Eon: _____Yes, I will_____. But I _____won't present____ing. The Japanese are doing very innovative
2.   3. (won't / present)

things with personal robotics, and I _____am going to attend____ing every lecture possible.
4. (be going to / attend)

Hapin: Why all the excitement? What _____are____ robots _____going to do_____ for us?
5. (be going to / do)

Eon: A lot! Oh, personal robots _____are____ still _____going to help_____ the elderly
6. (be going to / help)

and people with disabilities. But the new 'bots _____will be improving_____ our lives
7. (will / improve)

in a lot of other ways too. They _____will be cooking_____ complicated recipes.
8. (will / cook)

They _____will be perfor____ming music and other creative tasks. So, _____are____ you
9. (will / perform)

_____going to buy_____ one for your family, Will?
10. (be going to / buy)

Hapin: _____Yes, I am not____. They look too much like machines to me. _____Is____ their appearance
11.

_____going to change_____?
12. (be going to / change)

Eon: _____Yes, it is_____ —and very soon. Companies are starting to meet that challenge now. In
13.

just a couple of years, they _____will be selling_____ 'bots that look just like humans—
14. (will / sell)

and show human emotions.

Hapin: Amazing! Well, thanks for the interview, Nouvella. Oh! Look at the time. This afternoon I

_____am going to test_____ the new flying car. You should see it. The technology is really
15. (be going to / test)

amazing.

Eon: I'd love to! _____Will____ you be _____driving_____ by the university?
16. (will / drive)

Hapin: Sure. Why don't I give you a lift?

EXERCISE 4: Future Progressive: Affirmative and Negative Statements *(Grammar Note 7)*

Dr. Eon's family uses a robot for household chores. Look at Asimo the Robot's schedule for tomorrow. Write sentences using the words in parentheses and the future progressive.

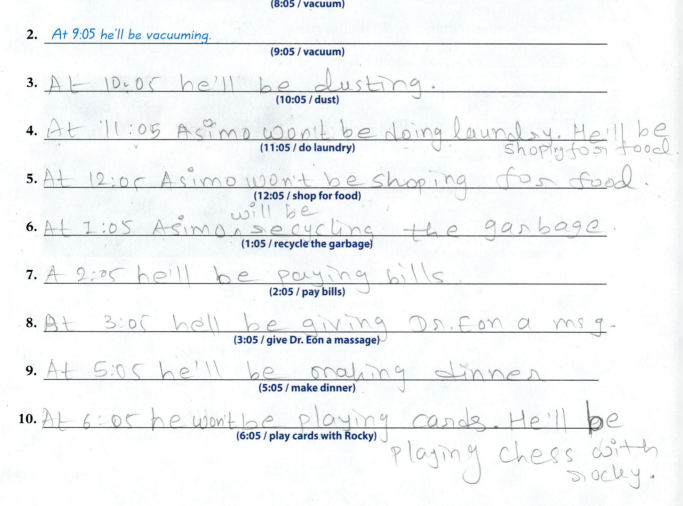

```
TOMORROW
  8:00   make breakfast
  9:00   vacuum
 10:00   dust
 11:00   shop for food
 12:00   do laundry
 12:30   make lunch
  1:00   recycle the garbage
  2:00   pay bills
  3:00   give Dr. Eon a massage
  5:00   make dinner
  6:00   play chess with Rocky
```

1. *At 8:05 Asimo won't be vacuuming. He'll be making breakfast.*
    (8:05 / vacuum)

2. *At 9:05 he'll be vacuuming.*
    (9:05 / vacuum)

3. At 10:05 he'll be dusting.
    (10:05 / dust)

4. At 11:05 Asimo won't be doing laundry. He'll be shoping for food.
    (11:05 / do laundry)

5. At 12:05 Asimo won't be shoping for food.
    (12:05 / shop for food)

6. At 1:05 Asimo will be recycling the garbage.
    (1:05 / recycle the garbage)

7. A 2:05 he'll be paying bills.
    (2:05 / pay bills)

8. At 3:05 hell be giving Dr. Eon a msg.
    (3:05 / give Dr. Eon a massage)

9. At 5:05 he'll be making dinner
    (5:05 / make dinner)

10. At 6:05 he won't be playing cards. He'll be playing chess with Rocky.
    (6:05 / play cards with Rocky)

EXERCISE 5: Future Progressive Statements and Time Clauses   *(Grammar Notes 7–8)*

Complete the ad for a getaway[1] in space with the verbs in parentheses. In sentences with time clauses, use the future progressive in the main clause. Use the simple present or the present progressive in the time clause.

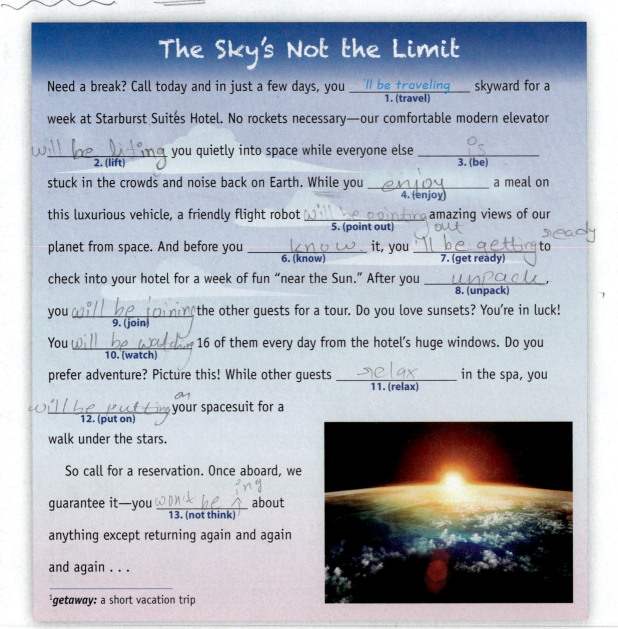

The Sky's Not the Limit

Need a break? Call today and in just a few days, you ___*'ll be traveling*___ skyward for a
                                       1. (travel)

week at Starburst Suites Hotel. No rockets necessary—our comfortable modern elevator

___*will be lifting*___ you quietly into space while everyone else _____*is*_____
  2. (lift)   **3. (be)**

stuck in the crowds and noise back on Earth. While you ___*enjoy*___ a meal on
                                       4. (enjoy)

this luxurious vehicle, a friendly flight robot *will be pointing out* amazing views of our
                                           5. (point out)

planet from space. And before you ___*know*___ it, you *'ll be getting ready* to
                                    6. (know)   **7. (get ready)**

check into your hotel for a week of fun "near the Sun." After you ___*unpack*___,
                                                8. (unpack)

you *will be joining* the other guests for a tour. Do you love sunsets? You're in luck!
    9. (join)

You *will be watching* 16 of them every day from the hotel's huge windows. Do you
    10. (watch)

prefer adventure? Picture this! While other guests ___*relax*___ in the spa, you
                                         11. (relax)

will be putting on your spacesuit for a
  12. (put on)

walk under the stars.

    So call for a reservation. Once aboard, we

guarantee it—you *won't be thinking* about
               13. (not think)

anything except returning again and again

and again . . .

_____
[1]**getaway:** a short vacation trip

EXERCISE 6: Editing

Read this article about cars of the future. There are ten mistakes in the use of the future and future progressive. The first mistake is already corrected. Find and correct nine more.

Flying Cars

The SkyCar

Your class starts in 10 minutes, but you're stuck in traffic. Don't panic. With just a press of a button, your car will ~~lifts~~ *lift* off the ground, and you'll be on your way to school. No bad roads, no stop signs, no worries!

Welcome to the future! It seems like science fiction, but it isn't. Engineers have been working on flying cars for decades, and they have already solved many of the big challenges. They predict that we'll all be use these amazing vehicles one day.

According to *Car Trends Magazine*, one model, part car and part plane, is going be on the market in the not-so-distant future. It will look like a regular car when it's on the road, but its wings will unfold when the driver will decide to take to the skies. It will runs on the same fuel for both land and air travel, and you'll be able to keep it in your garage. (But you're still going need an airport to take off and land.)

A better model will be a vertical takeoff and landing vehicle (VTOL). You won't need to go to the airport anymore, and all controls will being automatic. Imagine this: You'll be doing your homework while your car will be getting you to school safely and on time.

And what does this future dream car cost? Well, fasten your seatbelts—the price will going to be sky-high. At first it will be about a million dollars, but after a few years, you'll be able to buy one for "only" $60,000. Don't throw away your old driver's license just yet!

EXERCISE 7: Listening

A | *Four members of the Mars Association are trying to organize a conference on Venus. Read the statements. Then listen to their conversation. Listen again and check (✓)* **True** *or* **False**. *Correct the false statements.*

	True	False
1. Skyler ~~has~~ *hasn't* made all of his summer plans.	☐	☑
2. Jarek is taking a summer vacation.	☐	☐
3. Lorna needs to give her boss two or more weeks' notice before taking time off.	☐	☐
4. A lot of tourists from other planets will be visiting Earth.	☐	☐
5. Zindra is spending most of the summer at home.	☐	☐
6. Zindra won't be doing any research this summer.	☐	☐

B | *Listen again to the conversation. Mark the chart below to help you figure out when everyone will be available.*

	July				August			
Weeks:	1	2	3	4	1	2	3	4
Skyler							X	X
Jarek								
Lorna								
Zindra								

When they're all available: _____

X = not available

EXERCISE 8: Pronunciation

A | *Read and listen to the Pronunciation Note.*

Pronunciation Note

When we **contrast information**, we **stress** the words with the **information**.

EXAMPLES: I won't be **traveling** next summer. I'll be **studying**.

Noor won't be **home** on Monday. She'll be in the **office**.

Listen to the short conversations. Put a dot (●) over the words in the answers that have the most stress.

1. **A:** Will Jason be running this morning?

   B: No, he won't be running. He'll be swimming.

2. **A:** Will you be leaving for vacation next month?

   B: No, I won't be leaving for vacation, but I'll be leaving for a business trip.

3. **A:** Ana will be going into the office tomorrow. Say hi for me.

   B: Oh, she won't be going into the office tomorrow. She'll be working in the library.

4. **A:** Are you going to be working on the weekend?

   B: We'll be working Saturday, but we won't be working Sunday.

5. **A:** Will you be visiting your family in Toronto next summer?

   B: Well, I'll be visiting my sister. But my brother isn't there now.

6. **A:** Will your study group be meeting this summer?

   B: We'll be meeting in August. In July a lot of people will be on vacation.

C | *Listen again to the conversations and repeat the answers. Then practice the conversations with a partner.*

EXERCISE 9: Reaching Agreement

Complete the schedule. Write all your plans for next week. Then work with a partner. Without showing each other your schedules, find a time to get together. Then discuss your plans. Use different forms of the future.

Example: **A:** What are you doing on Tuesday morning?
B: I'm going to see the Robot Show at the Science Museum.
A: I'll go with you. I'll be free at 11:00.
B: Great. The coffee shop opens at 10:00. Want to meet for coffee first?

	MONDAY	TUESDAY	WEDNESDAY	THURSDAY	FRIDAY
9:00					
11:00					
1:00					
3:00					
5:00					
7:00					

EXERCISE 10: Discussion

Robots will be doing many things in the near future. Look at the list of activities and decide which ones you think robots will or won't be doing. In small groups, share and explain your opinions. Do you think robots will be doing too much for humans? Why?

- answer the phone
- drive cars
- find information on the Internet
- go shopping
- guide vacation tours
- have a conversation
- invent new technology
- make dinner
- paint pictures
- plant gardens
- play musical instruments
- report the news
- take a vacation
- take care of children
- teach English
- teach themselves new skills
- write letters
- write the laws

EXAMPLE: **A:** I don't think robots will be teaching English, but they will be taking care of children. Children will think they're fun—like big toys.

B: I don't agree. I think it's a bad idea. Children need human contact to help them develop emotional security.

C: Do you think robots will be driving cars?

EXERCISE 11: Information Gap: Dr. Eon's Calendar

Work in pairs (A and B). **Student B,** go to page 77 and follow the instructions there. **Student A,** complete Dr. Eon's calendar below. Get information from Student B. Ask questions and fill in the calendar. Answer Student B's questions.

EXAMPLE: **A:** What will Dr. Eon be doing on Sunday the first?
B: She'll be flying to Tokyo. What about on the second? Will she be taking the day off?
A: No, she'll be meeting with Dr. Kato.

FEBRUARY						2115
SUNDAY	MONDAY	TUESDAY	WEDNESDAY	THURSDAY	FRIDAY	SATURDAY
1 fly to Tokyo	2 meet with Dr. Kato	3	4	5	6	7
8 take Bullet Train to Osaka	9 sightseeing	10	11	12	13	14
15 fly home	16	17	18 attend energy seminar	19	20	21 shop with Rocky and Asimo
22	23	24	25	26	27	28 take shuttle to Mars

When you are finished, compare calendars. Do they have the same information?

EXERCISE 12: Writing

A | *Write a paragraph about your life 10 years from now. What will you be doing for a living? What kind of family life will you have? What hobbies will you be enjoying? What will you do to achieve these things? Use the future and future progressive.*

EXAMPLE: In 10 years, I will be working for the space program. I am going to be planning the first colony on Mars. First I'll graduate from college. . . .

B | *Check your work. Use the Editing Checklist.*

Editing Checklist

Did you use . . . ?

☐ **be going to** or **will** for facts and predictions

☐ **be going to** or the present progressive for plans

☐ the simple present for scheduled future events

☐ the future progressive for actions that will be in progress at a specific time in the future

☐ the simple present or the present progressive in time clauses

---

Student B, complete Dr. Eon's calendar below. Answer Student A's questions. Then ask Student A questions and fill in the information.

EXAMPLE: **A:** What will Dr. Eon be doing on Sunday the first?
B: She'll be flying to Tokyo. What about on the second? Will she be taking the day off?
A: No, she'll be meeting with Dr. Kato.

FEBRUARY						2115
SUNDAY	MONDAY	TUESDAY	WEDNESDAY	THURSDAY	FRIDAY	SATURDAY
1 fly to Tokyo	**2** meet with Dr. Kato	**3** attend World Future Conference	**4** ─────────	**5**	**6**	**7** ─────→
8	**9** ──────	**10** ──────→	**11**	**12** fly to Denver	**13** visit Mom and Dad	**14** ───→
15	**16** give speech at Harvard University	**17** meet with Dr. Rover	**18**	**19** ──────	**20** ──────→	**21**
22 relax!	**23** work at home	**24** ──────	**25**	**26**	**27** ──────→	**28**

When you are finished, compare calendars. Do they have the same information?

Check your answers on page UR-2.

Do you need to review anything?

A | *Circle the correct words to complete the sentences.*

1. Our daughter will turns / turn 15 next week.

2. Are / Do you going to go to work today?

3. What will you be doing / do at 3:00 this afternoon?

4. The sun will / is going to rise at 6:22 tomorrow morning.

5. Be careful! Your coffee will / is going to spill!

6. While you're / 'll be driving to work tomorrow, we'll be flying to Beijing.

7. Roboid will let us know when he finished / finishes cooking dinner.

B | *Complete the conversation with the future or future progressive form of the verbs in parentheses or with a short answer. Use the future progressive when possible.*

A: What _____ you _____ at 10:00 tomorrow morning?
1. (do)

B: 10:00? Well, let's see. My plane _____ at 9:45, so at 10:00,
2. (leave)

I _____ on the plane.
3. (sit)

A: So I guess you _____ to the office at all tomorrow.
4. (not come)

B: Doesn't look like it. Why? _____ that _____ a problem?
5. (cause)

A: _____, it _____. It _____ fine. Have a good trip.
6. **7. (be)**

B: Thanks. I _____ you in a couple of weeks.
8. (see)

C | *Find and correct five mistakes.*

A: How long are you going to staying in Beijing?

B: I'm not sure. I'll let you know you as soon as I'll find out, OK?

A: OK. It's going to be a long flight. What will you did to pass the time?

B: I'll be work a lot of the time. And I'm going to try to sleep.

A: Good idea. Have fun, and I'm emailing you all the office news. I promise.

UNIT 6

Future Perfect
and Future Perfect Progressive
MONEY AND GOALS

STEP 1 GRAMMAR IN CONTEXT

Before You Read

Look at the photos and the information for each person. Discuss the questions.

1. What are some good and bad uses of their credit cards?
2. How does money management help people reach their goals?
3. What do you think the show is about?

Read

Read the transcript of a personal finance TV show.

MONEY TALKS

Debbie Hart, age 20
Number of credit cards: 3
Used for: movies, CDs, clothes
Balance: $2,500

Sung Park, age 18
Number of credit cards: 5
Used for: textbooks, car repairs
Balance: $1,750

Jeff Hassad, age 22
Number of credit cards: 1
Used for: eating out, entertainment
Balance: $600

Trudy: Hi, everyone. I'm Trudy Norman and you're watching *Money Talks*. We've taken the show on the road —to college campuses—and by the end of tonight's *Money Talks*, we**'ll have been traveling** for a month, and we**'ll have been** in 22 cities in that time!

I love bringing the show to colleges because good money management is such an important goal for people starting out in life. In fact, it's almost as important as getting your degree. It just makes sense —if you're managing your money well, your other goals are going to be much easier to reach.

Tonight we're at Gibson College in Nebraska, and we have students Debbie Hart, Sung Park, and Jeff Hassad on our panel. Our topic is credit cards.

(continued on next page)

Future Perfect and Future Perfect Progressive   **79**

To get started, let me give you some shocking[1] statistics. A typical college freshman **will have gotten** eight credit card offers by the end of the first semester. For today's freshman, a lot of the offers will include gifts—from pizzas to iPods. So it's not surprising that many students accept at least some of those offers. In fact, by graduation, the average student in the United States **will have tripled** the number of cards in his or her wallet.

Sung: That's true. When I first got here, I only had one credit card. Then I started receiving all these emails and even phone calls with credit card offers. Finally, I thought, "Why not?" Now I have five cards.

Trudy: The national average for college students is 4.7 cards, so you're not alone. And it isn't only the number of credit cards that increases. So does the amount you owe. If you're like many students, you**'ll have doubled** your credit card debt by graduation. The average student's debt **will have grown** to $4,138 by the time he or she graduates.

Debbie: My problem is, it's too easy just to take out my card when I see something I want. Then, when I get my bill, I**'ll have charged** more than I can pay for. I'm carrying a pretty big balance right now.

Trudy: Did you know that people who always use credit cards spend more? Create a budget and start using cash—by next year you**'ll have spent** 12 percent less! And you **won't have been paying** interest on your purchases. But if you must charge, you should also start paying more than the minimum every month, even if it's only $20 more.

Debbie: How much can an extra $20 help?

Trudy: A lot. Suppose you're a freshman and you owe $1,000 on your card at 15 percent interest. Pay an extra $20 every month, and by the time you graduate, you**'ll have** already **become** debt-free! And you**'ll have been saving** interest charges the whole time. On the other hand, if you only pay the minimum, you'll be paying for 15 years, and at the end, you**'ll have spent** $1,122.78 in interest. Everything you bought on that card **will have cost** twice as much as the actual price.

Jeff: I hear what you're saying. By the end of this school year, I**'ll have been paying** interest for nine months on pizzas I ate last September! But are you saying students shouldn't use credit cards?

Trudy: That's not realistic,[2] is it? No, I'm saying one card is enough. And use it for essentials,[3] not for pizza and cool shoes.

Sung: My brother didn't have a credit card in college. When he graduated, he had a hard time getting one.

Trudy: Good point, Sung. It's hard to get credit when you have no credit history. Getting your first credit card as a student, when it's easier, can be a good idea. Use it wisely, and by graduation you**'ll have earned** a good credit rating, and that will be very useful when you're starting out.

That's all for tonight. Remember, guys, you're going to be doing a lot in the next few years. Don't let poor money management hold you back, and keep you from reaching your goals. See you next week on *Money Talks*.

---

[1] **shocking:** very upsetting and surprising
[2] **realistic:** practical or sensible
[3] **essentials:** things that are necessary

After You Read

A | Vocabulary: *Circle the letter of the word or phrase that best completes each sentence.*

1. A **budget** is a _____ for saving money.
   a. reason
   b. book
   c. plan

2. If you buy something on **credit**, you pay for it _____.
   a. now
   b. later
   c. with cash

3. A **debt** is money that you _____.
   a. save
   b. owe
   c. earn

4. If you pay the **minimum** amount, you pay the _____ amount.
   a. exact
   b. most
   c. least

5. **Statistics** are _____ that give information about people and activities.
   a. numbers
   b. students
   c. books

6. A **purchase** is something that you _____.
   a. borrow
   b. buy
   c. return

B | Comprehension: *Check (✓)* **True** *or* **False**. *Correct the false statements.*

	True	False
1. The show was traveling two months ago.	☐	☐
2. Many students get eight credit card offers in their first semester of college.	☐	☐
3. Many students have twice as much credit card debt after four years.	☐	☐
4. People who pay with credit cards spend more.	☐	☐
5. Jeff has already paid interest for nine months on pizzas he ate last September.	☐	☐
6. It's never a good idea to use a credit card when you're a student.	☐	☐

FUTURE PERFECT

Statements			
Subject	***Will (not)***	***Have* + Past Participle**	
I You He She It We They	**will (not)**	**have earned**	interest by then.

Yes / No Questions			
Will	**Subject**	***Have* + Past Participle**	
Will	I she they	**have earned**	interest by then?

Short Answers					
Affirmative			**Negative**		
Yes,	you she they	**will (have).**	**No,**	you she they	**won't (have).**

Wh- Questions				
***Wh-* Word**	***Will***	**Subject**	***Have* + Past Participle**	
How much	**will**	I she they	**have earned**	by then?

FUTURE PERFECT PROGRESSIVE

Statements			
Subject	***Will** (not)*	***Have been** + Base Form + -ing*	
I You He She It We They	**will (not)**	**have been earning**	interest for a month.

Yes / No Questions			
Will	**Subject**	***Have been** + Base Form + -ing*	
Will	I she they	**have been earning**	interest for a month?

Short Answers					
Affirmative			**Negative**		
Yes,	you she they	**will (have).**	**No,**	you she they	**won't (have).**

Wh- Questions				
***Wh-** Word*	***Will***	**Subject**	***Have been** + Base Form + -ing*	
How long	**will**	I she they	**have been earning**	interest?

1 Use the **future perfect** to show that something will happen <u>before a specific time</u> in the future.

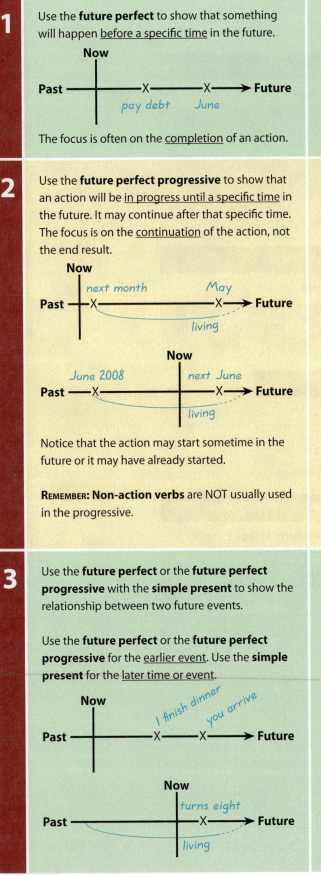

The focus is often on the <u>completion</u> of an action.

- *By June*, he **will have paid** his debt.
- She**'ll have bought** a new car *by May*.
- **I'll have been** in college for a year *by then*.
- We**'ll have saved** enough *by then*.

2 Use the **future perfect progressive** to show that an action will be <u>in progress until a specific time</u> in the future. It may continue after that specific time. The focus is on the <u>continuation</u> of the action, not the end result.

Notice that the action may start sometime in the future or it may have already started.

REMEMBER: Non-action verbs are NOT usually used in the progressive.

- **A:** You're buying a house in L.A. next month? Great! Can I visit in May?
- **B:** Sure. By then, we**'ll have been living** there for three months.

- They moved to Atlanta in June 2008. So by next June, they**'ll have been living** there for three years.

- By May, he**'ll have owned** that car for five years. NOT: By May, he'll have ~~been owning~~ that car for five years.

3 Use the **future perfect** or the **future perfect progressive** with the **simple present** to show the relationship between two future events.

Use the **future perfect** or the **future perfect progressive** for the <u>earlier event</u>. Use the **simple present** for the <u>later time or event</u>.

- By the time you **arrive**, I **will have finished** dinner. *(First I'll finish dinner. Then you'll arrive)* NOT: By the time you ~~will~~ arrive, I will have finished dinner.

- When my daughter **turns** eight, we **will have been living** here for 10 years. *(First we'll live here 10 years, then my daughter will turn eight.)*

4	We often use the **future perfect** and the **future perfect progressive** with **by** + time or event or **by the time** + time clause.	• **By 2013**, he**'ll have saved** $1,000. • He **won't have saved** $5,000 **by the time he graduates**.
	We often use **already** and **yet** with the **future perfect** to emphasize which event will <u>happen first</u>.	• By 9:00, we**'ll** **already** **have finished** dinner. • We **won't have washed** the dishes **yet**.

STEP 3 FOCUSED PRACTICE

EXERCISE 1: Discover the Grammar

Read each numbered statement. Circle the letter of the sentence that is similar in meaning.

1. By next year, Trudy will have been doing her show *Money Talks* for five years.

   a. Trudy will stop doing her show this year.

   b. Next year, Trudy can celebrate the fifth anniversary of *Money Talks*.

2. By this time tomorrow, I'll have decided which car to buy.

   a. I know which car I'm going to buy.

   b. I haven't decided yet.

3. By the time you get home, we'll have finished studying.

   a. You will get home while we are studying.

   b. You will get home after we finish studying.

4. By 2017, we'll have been working in this office for eight years.

   a. We'll move to another office before 2017.

   b. We'll be in the same office in 2017.

5. They won't have finished taping *Money Talks* by 10:00.

   a. They will still be taping at 10:00.

   b. They will finish taping at 10:00.

6. They will have finished Trudy's *Money* newsletter by 5:00.

   a. They'll be finished by 5:00.

   b. They'll still be working at 5:00.

EXERCISE 2: Future Perfect

(Grammar Notes 1, 4)

Debbie has a lot of goals. Look at the timeline. Write sentences describing what Debbie Hart
will have done *or* **won't have done** *by the year 2015.*

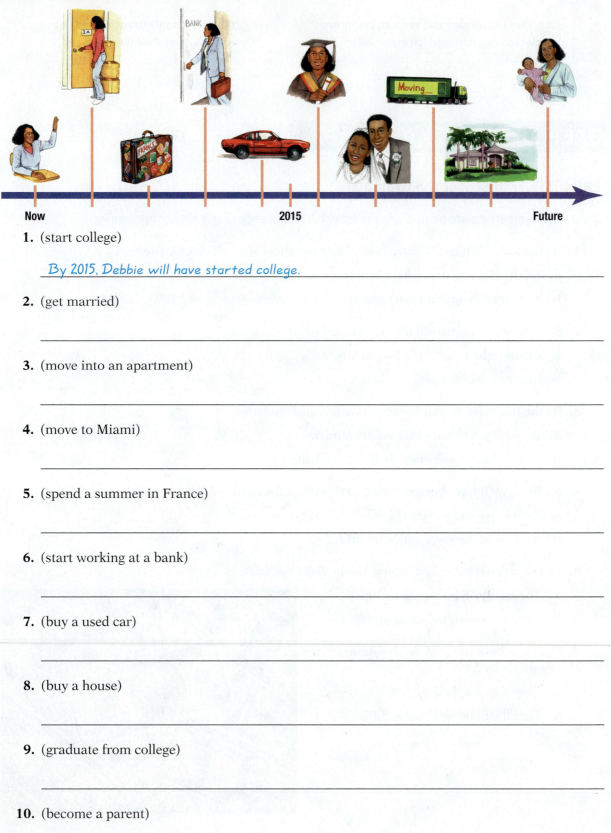

1. (start college)

By 2015, Debbie will have started college.

2. (get married)

_____

3. (move into an apartment)

_____

4. (move to Miami)

_____

5. (spend a summer in France)

_____

6. (start working at a bank)

_____

7. (buy a used car)

_____

8. (buy a house)

_____

9. (graduate from college)

_____

10. (become a parent)

_____

EXERCISE 3: Time Clauses with *Already* and *Yet*

(Grammar Notes 1, 3–4)

Read Debbie's goals. What will or won't she have achieved by the time the first event occurs?
Use the information in the timeline from Exercise 2. Write sentences using **already** *and* **yet**.

1. (move into an apartment / start college)

   By the time Debbie moves into an apartment, she'll have already started college.

2. (move into an apartment / get married)

   _____

3. (start college / buy a used car)

   _____

4. (graduate from college / move into an apartment)

   _____

5. (spend a summer in France / find a job at a bank)

   _____

6. (graduate from college / spend a summer in France)

   _____

7. (get married / graduate from college)

   _____

8. (move to Miami / buy a home)

   _____

9. (become a parent / graduate from college)

   _____

10. (buy a home / become a parent)

    _____

Ask and answer questions about these people's accomplishments. Choose between the future perfect and the future perfect progressive. Use the calendar to answer the questions.

January

S	M	T	W	T	F	S
					1	2
3	4	5	6	7	8	9
10	11	12	13	14	15	16
17	18	19	20	21	22	23
24	25	26	27	28	29	30
31						

February

S	M	T	W	T	F	S
	1	2	3	4	5	6
7	8	9	10	11	12	13
14	15	16	17	18	19	20
21	22	23	24	25	26	27
28						

March

S	M	T	W	T	F	S
	1	2	3	4	5	6
7	8	9	10	11	12	13
14	15	16	17	18	19	20
21	22	23	24	25	26	27
28	29	30	31			

April

S	M	T	W	T	F	S
				1	2	3
4	5	6	7	8	9	10
11	12	13	14	15	16	17
18	19	20	21	22	23	24
25	26	27	28	29	30	

May

S	M	T	W	T	F	S
						1
2	3	4	5	6	7	8
9	10	11	12	13	14	15
16	17	18	19	20	21	22
23	24	25	26	27	28	29
30	31					

June

S	M	T	W	T	F	S
		1	2	3	4	5
6	7	8	9	10	11	12
13	14	15	16	17	18	19
20	21	22	23	24	25	26
27	28	29	30			

1. On January 1, Debbie Hart started saving $15 a week.

QUESTION: (by February 19 / how long / save)

By February 19, how long will Debbie have been saving?

ANSWER: *By February 19, she'll have been saving for seven weeks.*

2. On March 1, Valerie Morgan started saving $5 a week.

QUESTION: (by April 19 / how much / save)

_____

ANSWER: _____

3. On March 3, Sung Park began reading a book a week.

QUESTION: (by June 16 / how many books / read)

_____

ANSWER: _____

4. On April 24, Don Caputo began running 2 miles a day.

QUESTION: (how long / run / by May 29)

_____

ANSWER: _____

5. On April 24, Tania Zakov began running 2 miles a day.

QUESTION: (how many miles / run / by May 29)

_____

ANSWER: _____

6. On February 6, Rick Gregory began saving $10 a week.

QUESTION: (save $100 / by March 27)

_____

ANSWER: _____

7. On May 8, Tim Rigg began painting two apartments a week in his building.

QUESTION: (how many apartments / paint / by May 29)

_____

ANSWER: _____

8. Tim's building has 12 apartments.

QUESTION: (finish / by June 19)

_____

ANSWER: _____

9. Talia began a fitness program on January 1. She is losing one pound a week.

QUESTION: (lose 20 pounds / by May 21)

_____

ANSWER: _____

10. Erik enrolled in a Spanish class on February 22.

QUESTION: (how long / study / by April 26)

_____

ANSWER: _____

11. In March, Jeff Hassad began paying $10.00 a month interest on a loan.

QUESTION: (how much interest / pay / by the end of June)

_____

ANSWER: _____

EXERCISE 5: Editing

Read this blog entry. There are nine mistakes in the use of the future perfect and future perfect progressive. The first mistake is already corrected. Find and correct eight more.

To My Credit

Jonathon Daly   January 1

    I have five credit cards. If nothing changes, I ~~have~~ *will* doubled the credit card debt I had as a freshman by the time I graduate. According to statistics, that makes me a typical college student. But I've decided to change. By this time next year, I'll has gotten my debt under control. I won't had become debt-free, but I'll have made a good start. Here's my debt-free timeline so far:

- I just found a part-time job, and when I start working, I'll use that money to pay debts.

- By February, I'll have been recorded all my spending for a month. Then I'll be able to make a spending plan. Only essentials—food, basic clothes, tuition—will be on this budget.

- By March 1, I'll only have two credit cards left. By that time, I'll already have been transferring all of my balances to those two cards with the lowest interest rate. And I'll have closing six accounts by then too!

- When I graduate, I've been paying more than the minimum on my cards for three months, so I might be able to get a lower interest rate. I expect a lot of financial challenges after I graduate, but by then I had experience in managing debt. I'll add goals to the timeline and record my progress during the year.

    I'd love to hear stories and suggestions from readers about getting debt-free. If you're a college student in my situation, send in your timeline and let's change the statistics together. How much progress will we "typical" college students have been making by next January 1?

STEP 4 COMMUNICATION PRACTICE

EXERCISE 6: Listening

A | *Don and Thea Caputo want to save for a summer vacation with their two children, Ned and Valerie. Read the list of things the family can do to cut back on spending. Then listen to their conversation. Listen again and check (✓) the correct boxes.*

By next summer, who will have . . . ?	Thea	Don	Ned	Valerie
1. been packing lunch	☑	☑	☐	☐
2. only bought new scarves and earrings	☐	☐	☐	☐
3. gotten some clothes at thrift shops	☐	☐	☐	☐
4. been taking the commuter van to work	☐	☐	☐	☐
5. been ordering pizza and watching DVDs at home	☐	☐	☐	☐

B | *Look at the chart. Listen again to the conversation and write the amount the family will have saved in each category by next summer.*

Amount They Will Have Saved by Next Summer	
Lunches	*$1,000*
Clothing	
Transportation	
Entertainment	
Total of all categories	

C | *With their savings, where can they go for a two-week vacation? Check (✓) the correct box(es).*

☐ 1. A car trip to British Columbia, renting camping equipment $3,000

☐ 2. A car trip to British Columbia, staying in motels $3,500

☐ 3. A trip to Disneyland $4,000

☐ 4. A trip by airplane to Mexico and two weeks in a hotel $5,000

EXERCISE 7: Pronunciation

A | *Read and listen to the Pronunciation Note.*

Pronunciation Note

In the **future perfect** and **future perfect progressive**, we often pronounce **have** like "of."

EXAMPLES: Thea **will have** left already. → "Thea **will of** left already."
I **won't have** spoken to her by then. → "I **won't of** spoken to her by then."
She**'ll have** been driving for an hour. → "She**'ll of** been driving for an hour."

B | *Listen to people talking about accomplishments. Then listen again to their conversations and complete the sentences with the verb forms that you hear.*

1. **A:** We're doing really well with our savings plan.

   B: You're right. By next summer, we _____ enough for a great vacation.

2. **A:** How are the kids?

   B: Great. In May, my daughter _____ on her degree for almost a year.

3. **A:** Uh-oh. I think this is your credit card bill.

   B: No problem! As of this month, I _____ a late payment for two years.

4. **A:** Your English is so good! How long have you been living here?

   B: Let me think . . . On December 1, I _____ in this country for three years.

5. **A:** Do you think Ned's team will win again today?

   B: I hope so. If they do, they _____ a game all year.

6. **A:** In June, Don and Thea _____ married for fifteen years.

   B: Let's throw a party for them!

7. **A:** What's up? You're looking very pleased with yourself.

   B: And I should! By 6:00 this evening, I _____ a cigarette for six months.

8. **A:** As of this Saturday, my girlfriend and I _____ each other for three years.

   B: Congratulations! What will you do to celebrate?

C | *Practice the conversations with a partner.*

EXERCISE 8: Conversation

What will some of the people in your life (including you!) have achieved by the end of this year, this month, or this week? Talk about some of these accomplishments with a partner. (Remember, even small accomplishments are important!) Use some of the ideas in the list and your own.

- making a budget
- managing time
- exercising
- learning new things
- overcoming a bad habit
- starting a good habit
- spending time with friends and family
- _____
- _____
- _____

> EXAMPLE: **A:** I'm really proud of my roommate. She's always had a problem oversleeping, but by the end of this month, she won't have missed any of her morning classes!
> **B:** That's great. How did she solve her problem?

EXERCISE 9: What About You?

A | *Think of three goals you would like to achieve in the next five years and discuss them in a small group. They can be big goals, such as buying a house, or smaller goals, such as learning a new skill.*

> EXAMPLES: **A:** I'd like to get fit and then run in a 10 km race. What about you?
> **B:** I want to save enough money to buy a digital camera and learn how to use photo editing software.
> **C:** I'd like to learn to skateboard.

B | *Arrange your goals on the timeline. Write the goals and the years you want to achieve them.*

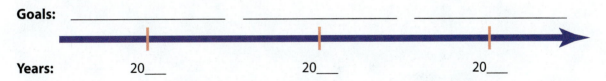

Goals: _____   _____   _____

Years: 20___   20___   20___

C | *Discuss your goals with a group. Talk about things you'll need to do before you achieve each goal. Use the future perfect and the future perfect progressive with time clauses.*

> EXAMPLES: **A:** Before I run my first 10 km race, I'll have been training for three months.
> **B:** By the holidays this year, I'll have bought a camera.

EXERCISE 10: Writing

A | *Write about the activities and goals of some of your classmates for a class website. Use information from Exercises 8 and 9, or work in small groups to exchange information. Find out the following:*

- What personal or school activities have your classmates been involved in?
- How long will they have been doing those activities by the end of the year or semester?
- What will they have achieved by the end of this year or this semester?

B | *Write three or four sentences about each student.*

> **EXAMPLE:** Dannie Munca wants to buy an iPod®. He got a part-time job in the library to help him save money. By the end of the semester, he'll have been working there for two months. He'll have saved about $200 by then, and he'll be able to get his new electronic toy. Good planning, Dannie.

C | *Check your work. Use the Editing Checklist.*

Editing Checklist

Did you use . . . ?

☐ the future perfect for actions that will already be completed by a certain time in the future

☐ the future perfect progressive for actions that will still be in progress at a specific time in the future

☐ time clauses to show the relationship between two future events

A | *Circle the correct words to complete the sentences.*

1. Kareem will <u>have saved / have been saving</u> a total of almost $1,000 by next year.

2. When we <u>get / 'll get</u> to my parents' house, they'll already have eaten dinner.

3. By the end of this week, Mia will <u>exercise / have been exercising</u> for six months.

4. When I finish this story by Sue Grafton, I <u>'ll have read / have been reading</u> all of her mysteries.

5. <u>By / Since</u> 2015, he'll have been living here for 10 years.

B | *Complete the conversation with the simple present, future perfect, or future perfect progressive form of the verbs in parentheses. Use the future perfect progressive if possible.*

A: Do you realize that in September we _____ here for two years?
1. (live)

B: Amazing! And you _____ here for four years.
2. (study)

A: I know. Next year at this time I _____ already.
3. (graduate)

B: I hope that by the time you _____, I _____ a good job.
4. (graduate)   5. (find)

A: Well, one thing is certain. By that time we _____ a lot of friends here.
6. (make)

B: Yes. And we _____ almost $400 by walking and taking the bus everywhere.
7. (save)

C | *Find and correct eight mistakes.*

I'm so excited about your news! By the time you read this, you'll have already moving into

your new house! And I have some good news too. By the end of this month, I will have been

saving $3,000. That's enough for me to buy a used car! And that means that by this time next

year, I drive to California to visit you! I have more news too. By the time I will graduate, I will

have been started my new part-time job. I hope that by this time next year, I'll also had paid off

some of my loans.

It's hard to believe that in June, we will have been being friends for 10 years. Time sure flies!

And we'll have been stayed friends even though we live 3,000 miles apart. Isn't the Internet a

great thing?

From Grammar to Writing
AVOIDING SENTENCE FRAGMENTS

Time clauses begin with **time words and phrases** such as *by the time*, *when*, *while*, *as soon as*, *before*, *after*, and *since*. A time clause by itself is not a complete sentence. When you write sentences with time clauses, avoid sentence fragments (incomplete sentences) by **connecting the time clause to a main clause**.

EXAMPLES:

Sentence Fragment	**Complete Sentence**
TIME CLAUSE	TIME CLAUSE + MAIN CLAUSE
~~As soon as I find a job.~~ →	*As soon as* I find a job, **I'll move**.
TIME CLAUSE	MAIN CLAUSE + TIME CLAUSE
~~Since I moved.~~ →	**I've been much happier** *since* I moved.

Notice that the time clause can come first or second. When it comes first, a **comma** separates the two clauses.

1 | *Read this letter. Correct the sentence fragments by connecting the time clause to a main clause. Use appropriate punctuation and capitalization.*

> December 10, 2012
>
> Hi Jamie,
>
>   As of today, I'm a working man! ~~By the time you get this letter.~~ <ins>By the time you get this letter,</ins> I'll have been taking tickets at Cine Moderne for more than a week. It's going to be hard to work and go to school full time, but you'll understand why I'm doing it. When you hear my plans.
>
>   As soon as school ends, My brother Alex and I are going to take a trip to Greece and Turkey. I plan to buy a used car, and we'll camp most of the way. By the end of January, I'll have been saving for more than a year for this trip —and I'll have enough to buy a car.
>
>   Why don't you come with us? Your exams are over on May 31, but mine don't end until June 10. That means you'll have already finished. While I'm still taking my finals. Maybe you can come early and do some sightseeing until I'm ready to leave.

Alex has some business to complete. Before he goes on vacation. He won't have finished until July 15, but he can join us then.

I'm leaving Paris on June 17. I'll drive through Italy and take the ferry from Brindisi to Greece. I'll stay in Greece, until Alex joins me. Just think, while your friends are in summer school, you could be swimming in the Aegean! We'll be leaving Greece, As soon as Alex arrives so we'll have a month in Turkey. We'll start back around August 20. Your classes won't have started by then, will they?

I hope you'll be able to join us for this trip. Alex is looking forward to seeing you again too.

Your friend,

Philippe

---

2 | *Complete the timeline with information from the letter in Exercise 1.*

December 10	*Philippe starts his new job.*
January 31	plans to areas.
May 31	exams are over.
June 10	exams are over.
June 17	leaves paris
July 15	finishes
August 20	start back

---

3 | *Before you write . . .*

1. Think about some plans you are making for the future.

2. Make a timeline about your plans like the one in Exercise 2.

3. Work with a partner. Discuss each other's plans. Use time clauses.

---

4 | *Write a letter to a friend about some plans you are making. Use information from your timeline. Remember to connect some of the events with time clauses.*

5 | *Exchange letters with a different partner. Underline the time clauses. Write a question mark (?) above any time clauses that seem wrong. Then answer the questions.*

	Yes	No
1. Are the time clauses part of complete sentences?	☐	☐
2. Are the sentences with time clauses punctuated correctly?	☐	☐
3. Are the verb forms correct in the sentences with time clauses?	☐	☐
4. Is the sequence of events clear?	☐	☐

5. What are some details you would like information about? _____

_____

_____

6 | *Work with your partner. Discuss each other's editing questions from Exercise 5. Then rewrite your own letter and make any necessary corrections.*

NEGATIVE QUESTIONS, TAG QUESTIONS, ADDITIONS AND RESPONSES

UNIT	GRAMMAR FOCUS	THEME
7	Negative *Yes* / *No* Questions and Tag Questions	Places to Live
8	Additions and Responses: *So, Too, Neither, Not either,* and *But*	Similarities and Differences

Before You Read

Look at the photos. Discuss the questions.

1. How do these places look to you?
2. Which one of these places would you like to visit or live in? Why?
3. What do you like about the town or city where you live? What don't you like?

Read

Read the on-the-street interviews reported in a travel magazine.

Life Abroad Magazine

IT'S A GREAT PLACE TO LIVE, ISN'T IT?

Our reporters around the world interviewed people living in foreign countries. Our question: How do you like living here? Here's what we learned from Lydia Sousa, Kinoro Okaya, Anton Kada, and Tessa Bradley.

Rio de Janeiro, Brazil

Reporter: Excuse me. Do you speak English?

Sousa: Yes, I do. Hey! I've seen you on TV. . . . **Aren't you** Paul Logan?

Reporter: That's right. I'm conducting a survey for *Life Abroad Magazine*. You're not from Rio, **are you**?

Sousa: No, I'm not. I'm originally from Portugal. You could tell by my accent, **couldn't you?**

Reporter: Uh-huh. You don't speak English like a Brazilian. So, how do you like living here?

Sousa: I love it. Just look around you—the beach, the bay, the mountains, the sky. It's fantastic looking! I walk along this beach every day on the way to my office.

Reporter: It's not a bad way to get to work, **is it?**

Sousa: It's not a bad place to play either! Besides this beautiful beach, there are so many restaurants and clubs. It's a great place to live, **isn't it?**

IT'S A GREAT PLACE TO LIVE, **ISN'T IT?**

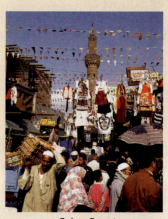

Cairo, Egypt

Reporter: This is one of the oldest markets in Cairo, **isn't it?**

Okaya: Yes, and one of the most interesting. Hey, **didn't you** buy anything?

Reporter: Not today. So, what brought you from Nairobi to Cairo?

Okaya: My job. I work for a company that provides Internet services for a lot of businesses here.

Reporter: It gets awfully hot here in the summer, **doesn't it?**

Okaya: Yes, but the winters are mild. And it almost never rains. You can't beat that,[1] **can you?**

Seoul, South Korea

Reporter: You're a student, **aren't you?**

Kada: No, actually, I'm a teacher. I'm teaching a course in architecture at the Kaywon School of Art and Design this semester.

Reporter: So, how do you like living here? **Doesn't the cold weather** bother you?

Kada: Not really. I'm from Berlin, so I'm used to it. I love this city. You can see skyscrapers right next to ancient structures. *(very old)*

Reporter: That's true. That's the old city gate over there, **isn't it?**

Kada: Yes. And there are several beautiful palaces nearby.

Reporter: You're from England, **aren't you?**

Bradley: Yes. I moved here 10 years ago.

Reporter: Was it a difficult adjustment?

Bradley: No, not really. First of all, having the same language makes things easy, **doesn't it?** And people here are very friendly.

Vancouver, Canada

Reporter: Why Canada?

Bradley: England's a very small country. I was attracted by Canada's wide-open spaces. It seems to offer endless possibilities.

---

[1] **You can't beat that:** Nothing is better than that.

After You Read

A | Vocabulary: *Circle the letter of the word or phrase that best completes each sentence.*

1. A _____ is NOT an example of a **structure**.
   a. bridge
   b. building
   c. beach

2. Foreigners living abroad often have a difficult **adjustment** because of _____.
   a. friendly people
   b. good weather
   c. a different language

3. If you're **originally** from South Korea, you _____.
   a. were born there
   b. still live there
   c. have relatives there

4. If something **bothers** you, it makes you feel _____.
   a. good
   b. bad
   c. fantastic

5. If you are **attracted** to something, you want to _____ it.
   a. avoid
   b. change
   c. get to know

6. If someone **provides** you with information, he or she _____ information.
   a. wants
   b. gives you
   c. corrects

B | Comprehension: *Check (✓)* **True** *or* **False**. *Correct the false statements.*

	True	False
she does 1. Lydia Sousa doesn't know the reporter.	☐	☑
2. The reporter thinks Sousa is from Rio.	☐	☑
3. The reporter bought a lot of things at the Cairo market.	☐	☑
4. The reporter doesn't think the cold weather bothers Kada.	☐	☑
5. The reporter thinks Tessa Bradley comes from Canada.	☐	☑
6. The move was not a difficult adjustment for Bradley.	☑	☐

NEGATIVE *YES / NO* QUESTIONS

With *Be* as the Main Verb

Questions	Short Answers	
Be + Not + Subject	**Affirmative**	**Negative**
Aren't you from Rio de Janeiro?	**Yes**, I **am**.	**No**, I'**m not**.

With All Auxiliary Verbs Except *Do*

Questions	Short Answers			
Auxiliary + *Not* + Subject + Verb	**Affirmative**		**Negative**	
Aren't you moving?		I **am**.		I'**m not**.
Hasn't he been here before?	**Yes**,	he **has**.	**No**,	he **hasn't**.
Can't they move tomorrow?		they **can**.		they **can't**.

With *Do* as the Auxiliary Verb

Questions	Short Answers			
Do + Not + Subject + Verb	**Affirmative**		**Negative**	
Doesn't he live here?	**Yes**,	he **does**.	**No**,	he **doesn't**.
Didn't they move last year?		they **did**.		they **didn't**.

always opposite

TAG QUESTIONS

With *Be* as the Main Verb

Affirmative Statement	Negative Tag
Subject + *Be*	*Be* + *Not* + Subject
You're from Rio,	aren't you?

Negative Statement	Affirmative Tag
Subject + *Be* + *Not*	*Be* + Subject
You're not from Rio,	are you?

With All Auxiliary Verbs Except *Do*

Affirmative Statement	Negative Tag
Subject + Auxiliary	Auxiliary + *Not* + Subject
You're moving,	aren't you?
He's been here before,	hasn't he?
They can move tomorrow,	can't they?

Negative Statement	Affirmative Tag
Subject + Auxiliary + *Not*	Auxiliary + Subject
You're not moving,	are you?
He hasn't been here before,	has he?
They can't move tomorrow,	can they?

With *Do* as an Auxiliary Verb

Affirmative Statement	Negative Tag
Subject + Verb	*Do* + *Not* + Subject
He lives here,	doesn't he?
They moved last year,	didn't they?

Negative Statement	Affirmative Tag
Subject + *Do* + *Not* + Verb	*Do* + Subject
He doesn't live here,	does he?
They didn't move,	did they?

GRAMMAR NOTES

1 Use **negative *yes / no* questions** and **tag questions** to:

a. **check** information you believe is true

- **Doesn't Anton** live in Seoul?
- Anton lives in Seoul, **doesn't he?**
  (The speaker believes that Anton lives in Seoul.)

b. **comment** on a situation

- **Isn't it** a nice day?
- It's a nice day, **isn't it?**
  (The speaker is commenting on the weather.)

2 Like affirmative *yes / no* questions, **negative *yes / no* questions** begin with a form of *be* or an auxiliary verb, such as *have, do, will, can,* or *should.*

- **Aren't you** Paul Logan?
- **Haven't I** seen you on TV?
- **Don't you** like the weather here?
- **Won't you** be sorry to leave?
- **Can't you** stay longer?

We almost always use **contractions** in negative questions.

- **Shouldn't we** think about moving?
  Nοτ: ~~Should we not~~ think about moving?

BE CAREFUL! Use ***are*** (not *am*) in negative questions with ***I*** and a contraction.

- **Aren't I** right?
  Nοτ: ~~Am'nt I~~ right?

3 Form **tag questions** with **statement + tag**. The statement expresses an **assumption**. The tag means *Right?* or *Isn't that true?*

STATEMENT	TAG
- You're Paul Logan, **aren't you?**
  (You're Paul Logan, right?)
- You're not from Cairo, **are you?**
  (You're not from Cairo. Isn't that true?)

a. If the statement verb is affirmative, the tag verb is negative.

AFFIRMATIVE · NEGATIVE
- You **work** on Thursdays, **don't** you?

b. If the statement verb is negative, the tag verb is affirmative.

NEGATIVE · AFFIRMATIVE
- You **don't work** on Thursdays, **do** you?

Form **the tag** with a form of *be* or an auxiliary verb, such as *have, do, will, can,* or *should.* Use the **same auxiliary** that is in the statement.

- It**'s** a nice day, **isn't** it?
- There **are** good schools here, **aren't** there?
- You**'ve** lived here a long time, **haven't** you?

If the statement does not use *be* or an auxiliary verb, use an appropriate form of ***do*** in the tag.

- You **come** from London, **don't** you?

We almost always use **contractions** in the tag.

- You **can** drive, **can't** you?
  Nοτ: You can drive, ~~can you not~~?

BE CAREFUL! In the tag, only use **pronouns**.

- ***Tom*** works here, doesn't **he?**
  Nοτ: Tom works here, doesn't ~~Tom~~?

When the subject of the statement is **this** or **that**, the subject of the tag is **it**.

- ***That's*** a good idea, isn't **it?**
  Nοτ: That's a good idea, isn't ~~that~~?

(continued on next page)

Negative *Yes / No* Questions and Tag Questions   **105**

4 Use **tag questions** in conversations when you **expect the other person to agree** with you. In this type of tag question, the <u>voice falls</u> on the tag.

Use this type of tag question to:

a. **check** information you believe is correct. You expect the other person to answer (and agree).

b. **comment** on a situation. This type of tag question is more like a statement than a question. The other person can just nod or say *uh-huh* to show that he or she is listening and agrees.

A: It's getting warmer, **isn't it?**
B: Uh-huh. Seems more like spring than winter.

A: It doesn't snow here, **does it?**
B: No, never. That's why I love it.

A: Beautiful day, **isn't it?**
B: Uh-huh. The weather here is great.

5 **Tag questions** can also be used when you want to **check information**. This type of tag question is more like a *yes / no* question. You want to confirm your information because you are not sure it is correct. Like a *yes / no* question, the <u>voice rises</u> on the tag, and you usually get an answer.

USAGE NOTE: Even though you expect an answer, these questions for information are <u>different from *yes / no* questions</u>.
a. In **yes / no questions**, you <u>have no idea of the answer</u>.
b. In **tag questions**, <u>you have an opinion</u> that you want to check.

A: You're not moving, **are you?**
    (Are you moving?)
B: Yes. I'm returning to Berlin. OR
    No. I'm staying here.

- **Do you** live in Vancouver?
  (I don't know if you live in Vancouver.)
- You live in Vancouver, **don't you?**
  (I think you live in Vancouver, but I'm not sure.)

6 Answer negative *yes / no* questions and **tag questions** the same way you answer affirmative *yes / no* questions. The answer is *yes* if the information is correct and *no* if the information is not correct.

A: **Don't you** work in Vancouver?
B: **Yes, I do.** I've worked there for years. OR
    That's right.

A: You work in Vancouver, **don't you?**
B: **No, I don't.** I work in Montreal.

EXERCISE 1: Discover the Grammar

Read this conversation between Anton Kada's mother, Petra, and a Canadian neighbor, Ken.
Underline all the negative yes / no questions and circle all the tags.

PETRA: Hi, Ken. Nice day, isn't it?

KEN: Sure is. What are you doing home today? Don't you usually work on Thursdays?

PETRA: I took the day off to help my son. He just got back to Berlin, and he's looking for an

apartment. You don't know of any vacant apartments, do you?

KEN: Isn't he going to stay with you?

PETRA: Well, he just got a new job at an architecture firm downtown, and he wants a place of his

own in a quiet neighborhood. Do you know of anything?

KEN: As a matter of fact, I do. The Edwards family lives in a nice residential neighborhood near

the river. You know them, don't you?

PETRA: Yes, I think Anton went to school with their son. But they're not moving, are they?

KEN: Yes, they're moving back to Vancouver next month.

PETRA: Are they? What kind of apartment do they have?

KEN: A one-bedroom. It's very nice. The owner is Canadian too.

PETRA: It's not furnished, is it? Anton really doesn't have any furniture.

KEN: Can't he rent some? I did that in my first apartment.

PETRA: I don't know. Isn't it less expensive to buy?

A quiet residential neighborhood in Berlin

EXERCISE 2: Affirmative and Negative Tag Questions

(Grammar Note 3)

Mr. and Mrs. Edwards are talking about their move to Vancouver. Match the statements with the tags.

	Statements		Tags
_f_	**1.** You've called the movers,	**a.**	do we?
_h_	**2.** They're coming tomorrow,	**b.**	isn't it?
_e_	**3.** This isn't going to be cheap,	**c.**	don't they?
_d_	**4.** You haven't finished packing,	**d.**	have you?
_a_	**5.** We don't need any more boxes,	**e.**	is it?
_g_	**6.** We need to disconnect the phone,	**f.**	haven't you?
_c_	**7.** The movers provide boxes for us,	**g.**	don't we?
_b_	**8.** Moving is hard,	**h.**	aren't they?

EXERCISE 3: Affirmative and Negative Tags

(Grammar Note 3)

Complete this interview with Tessa Bradley. Use appropriate tags.

HOST: You're originally from England, ___aren't you___?
1.

BRADLEY: Yes. I'm from London.

HOST: You've lived in Vancouver for many years, ___haven't you___?
2.

BRADLEY: Since I came here to teach video arts. Seems like ages ago. Looking back now, I can't

believe I just packed one suitcase and got on a plane.

HOST: You didn't know anyone here either, ___did you___?
3.

BRADLEY: No. And I didn't have a cent to my name. Just some ideas and a lot of hope. It sounds

crazy ___doesn't it___?
4.

HOST: Not when you look at all the TV shows you've done. Things have sure worked out for you,

___haven't it___? You've already worked on two big TV series, and you've done some
5.

work for the movies as well. You're working on another show now, ___aren't you___?
6.

BRADLEY: Yes. It's a comedy about some kids who become invisible.

HOST: Sounds like a good show for the whole family. I know I'll certainly take my kids to see it.

Speaking of kids, you have some of your own, ___haven't you___? / Don't you
7.

BRADLEY: Two boys and a girl—all very visible!

HOST: I know what you mean. Do you ever wish they were invisible?

BRADLEY: Hmm. That's an interesting thought, ___isn't it___?
8.

EXERCISE 4: Negative *Yes / No* Questions and Short Answers   (*Grammar Notes 2, 6*)

Anton Kada is looking at the apartment the Edwardses just left. Complete the negative
yes / no questions. Write short answers. Use the verbs that are in the sentences following
the short answers.

1. **OWNER:** Hi, you look familiar. _____*Isn't your name*_____ John Radcliffe?

   KADA: _____*No, it isn't.*_____ My name is Anton Kada.

2. **OWNER:** Oh. _____Haven't you seen_____ this apartment before?

   KADA: _____No, I haven't_____ I've never seen it before. This is the first time.

3. **KADA:** _____Are_____ the previous tenants from Vancouver?

   OWNER: _____Yes, they are_____ They just moved back there.

4. **KADA:** The apartment feels hot. _____Isn't there_____ an air conditioner?

   OWNER: _____No, there isn't_____ I don't provide one. But there is a fan.

5. **KADA:** I notice that there are marks on the walls. _____Aren't you going to paint_____ it?

   OWNER: _____Yes, I am_____ I'm going to paint it next week.

6. **OWNER:** _____Isn't it_____ a nice apartment?

   KADA: _____Yes, it is._____ It's very nice. But I'm not sure I can take it.

7. **OWNER:** _____Isn't it_____ big enough?

   KADA: _____Yes, it is_____ It's big enough, but I can't afford it.

EXERCISE 5: Negative *Yes / No* Questions and Tag Questions   (*Grammar Notes 1–3*)

Rewrite the sentences. Change the sentence in parentheses into a negative question or
a tag question.

ROLAND: Hi, Tessa. _____*Isn't it a nice day?* OR *It's a nice day, isn't it?*_____
   1. (I think it's a nice day.)

TESSA: It sure is. _____You have class today. Don't you?_____
   2. (I think you have class today.)

ROLAND: I do. But not until 3:00. _____It's only 2:30 now. Isn't it?_____
   3. (I think it's only 2:30 now.)

TESSA: You're right. You have plenty of time. _____you don't have your bike with_____
   4. (I'm surprised you don't have your bike with you.) you? Do u?

ROLAND: I lost it. That's why I'm walking.

TESSA: Well, it's a nice day for a walk. _____Vancouver is a beautiful city. Isn't_____
   5. (I think Vancouver is a beautiful city.) it?

ROLAND: Yes. And a great city for video artists. _____wouldn't you?_____
   6. (I'm pretty sure you're coming to see my film tonight.)

TESSA: I wouldn't miss it. Hey, _____your class isn't that_____? We took the wrong path.
   7. (I'm pretty sure your class is that way.) way

EXERCISE 6: Negative *Yes / No* Questions and Tag Questions

(Grammar Notes 1–3)

Read this information about video artist Nam-June Paik. Imagine you are going to interview his agent, and you are not sure of the information in parentheses. Write negative **yes / no** *questions or tag questions to check that information.*

1. born July 1932 in Korea (in Seoul?)
2. at age 14, studied music (took piano lessons?)
3. family left Korea in 1950 (moved to Tokyo?)
4. moved to Germany in 1956 (originally studied music composition there?)
5. attracted to electronic music (wrote traditional music?)
6. during the 1960s created a new art form with TV screens and video (painted on paper?)
7. produced a huge art installation for 1988 Seoul Olympics (the structure used 1,003 TV monitors?)
8. after an illness in 1996 started painting on flat surfaces (did installations after that?)
9. lived in New York (became a U.S. citizen?)
10. died in January 2006 in Florida (was 75 years old?)

Nam-June Paik with his video art

1. _Wasn't he born in Seoul?_ OR _He was born in Seoul, wasn't he?_ _____

2. _____

3. _____

4. Didn't he study music composition ?

5. Didn't he write traditinal music?

6. Didn't he paint on paper ?

7. Didn't he produce a huge art installation?

8. Didn't he

9. Didn't you become a U.s citizen?

10. Didn't he die when he was 75 years old?

EXERCISE 7: Editing

*Tessa Bradley is working on a script for a movie that takes place in Vancouver. There are ten mistakes in the use of negative **yes** / **no** questions, tag questions, and short answers. The first mistake is already corrected. Find and correct nine more.*

BEN: It's been a long time, Joe, ~~haven't~~ *hasn't* it?

JOE: That depends on what you mean by a long time, doesn't ~~that~~ *it*?

BEN: ~~Are not~~ *Aren't* you afraid to show your face here in Vancouver?

JOE: I can take care of myself. I'm still alive, ~~amn't I~~ *Aren't I*?

BEN: Until someone recognizes you. You're still wanted by the police, are*n't* you? Don't that bother you?

JOE: I'll be gone by morning. Look, I need a place to stay. Just for one night.

BEN: I have to think about my wife and kid. Don't you have *any* ~~any~~ place else to go?

JOE: Yes, I do. There's no one to turn to but you. You have to help me.

BEN: I've already helped you plenty. I went to jail for you, haven't I? And didn't I kept my mouth shut the whole time?

JOE: Yeah, OK, Ben. Don't you remember what happened in Vegas, do you?

BEN: Don't ever think I'll forget that! OK, OK. I can make a call.

EXERCISE 8: Pronunciation

A | *Read and listen to the Pronunciation Note.*

Pronunciation Note

In **tag questions**:

The **voice rises** at the end when the speaker **expects the other person to give information**.

EXAMPLE: **A:** He's a student, **isn't he?**
               B: Yes, he goes to my college.

The **voice falls** at the end when the speaker is making a comment and **expects the other person to agree**.

EXAMPLE: **A:** Seoul's interesting, **isn't it?**
               B: Uh-huh.

B | *Read the tag questions. Then listen to them and decide if the voice rises (→) or falls (→) at the end of the tag. Draw the correct arrow over the tag.*

1. You're originally from Vancouver, aren't you?

2. It's a beautiful city, isn't it?

3. It's been a big adjustment, hasn't it?

4. That building isn't new, is it?

5. It doesn't have any vacancies, does it?

6. You haven't lived there very long, have you?

7. You don't know Anne, do you?

8. She works around here, doesn't she?

9. It's near the river, isn't it?

10. It's a great place to live, isn't it?

C | *Listen again to the tag questions and repeat.*

EXERCISE 9: Listening

A | *Listen to the people ask questions. Notice if their voices rise or fall at the end of each question. Then listen again and decide if the speaker expects the other person to give information or just expects the other person to agree. Check (✓) the correct column.*

	Expects Information	Expects Agreement
1.	✓	☐
2.	☐	☐
3.	☐	☐
4.	☐	☐
5.	☐	☐
6.	☐	☐
7.	☐	☐
8.	☐	☐
9.	☐	☐
10.	☐	☐

B | *Read the statements. Listen again to the conversations and decide if the statements are* **True** *or* **False**. *Check (✓) the correct boxes.*

		True	False
1.	The man wants to know if Rio is the capital of Brazil.	✓	☐
2.	The man thinks Rio has an exciting night life.	☐	☐
3.	The woman wants to know if Anton was teaching a course in Korea.	☐	☐
4.	The woman wants to know if it is hard to find an apartment in Berlin.	☐	☐
5.	The first man wants to know if the second man speaks Arabic.	☐	☐
6.	The second man is asking about the traffic.	☐	☐
7.	The woman thinks Anne is from Vancouver.	☐	☐
8.	The woman wants to know if the man is from Vancouver.	☐	☐
9.	The man is commenting on the weather.	☐	☐
10.	The man is surprised that the woman was in Scotland.	☐	☐

EXERCISE 10: Information Gap: London and Vancouver

Work in pairs (A and B). **Student B,** *go to page 116 and follow the instructions there.* **Student A,** *look at the questions below. What do you know about London? Complete the questions by circling the correct words and writing the tags.*

1. London is / isn't the largest city in the United Kingdom, _____isn't it_____ ?

2. It is / isn't the capital of the United Kingdom, __Isn't it__ ?

3. London lies on a river / the ocean, __Doesn't it__ ?

4. It consists of two / thirty-two "boroughs," or parts, __Doesn't it__ ?

5. It has / doesn't have a lot of theaters, __Hasn't it__ ?

6. Many / Not many tourists visit London, __Don't they__ ?

7. It is / isn't a very safe city, __It is__ ?

Ask Student B the questions. Student B will read a paragraph about London and tell you if your information is correct or not.

> **EXAMPLE:** **A:** London is the largest city in the United Kingdom, isn't it?
> **B:** That's right.

Now read about Vancouver and answer Student B's questions.

VANCOUVER

Vancouver is the third largest city in Canada. Lying on the Pacific coast, it is surrounded on three sides by water and has the largest and busiest seaport in the country. It is also home to Stanley Park, one of the largest city parks in North America. Because of its great natural and architectural beauty and its moderate climate, Vancouver is a very popular place to live. It also attracts millions of tourists each year. It is a very international city, and more than 50 percent of its residents do not speak English as their first language. Today Vancouver is called the "Hollywood of the North" because of the number of films made in this exciting city.

> **EXAMPLE:** **B:** Vancouver isn't the largest city in Canada, is it?
> **A:** No, it isn't. It's the third largest city.

EXERCISE 11: Conversation

How well do you know your classmates? Work with a partner. Complete the questions with information about your partner that you think is correct. Then ask the questions to check your information. Check (✓) each question that has the correct information. Which one of you knows the other one better?

EXAMPLES: **A:** You're from Venezuela, aren't you?
   B: That's right. OR No, I'm from Colombia.

A 1. _____, aren't you?

B 2. Don't you _____?

A 3. _____, haven't you?

B 4. _____, did you?

A 5. _____, do you?

B 6. Aren't you _____?

A 7. _____, will you?

B 8. Didn't you _____?

EXERCISE 12: Writing

A | *You are going to interview a classmate about his or her city. Write eight questions. Use negative* **yes** / **no** *questions and tag questions. Ask your questions and take notes on your classmate's answers.*

EXAMPLE: You're originally from Venezuela, aren't you? *yes—Caracas*
   Isn't that the capital? *yes*

B | *Write up the interview.*

EXAMPLE: **INTERVIEWER:** You're originally from Venezuela, aren't you?
   MIGUEL: Yes, I am. I'm from Caracas.
   INTERVIEWER: Isn't that the capital?
   MIGUEL: Yes, it is.

C | *Check your work. Use the Editing Checklist.*

Editing Checklist

Did you use . . . ?
- [ ] contractions in negative *yes* / *no* questions
- [ ] contractions in tags
- [ ] negative tags with affirmative statements
- [ ] affirmative tags with negative statements
- [ ] the same auxiliary in the tag and in the statement
- [ ] *it* in the tag when the statement used **this** or **that**

Student B, read about London and answer Student A's questions.

LONDON

London is the capital and largest city of the United Kingdom. It is also one of the oldest and largest cities in the world. Located in southeastern England, the city lies on the River Thames, which links it to shipping routes throughout the world. Because of its size, the city is divided into 32 "boroughs" or parts. With its many museums, palaces, parks, and theaters, tourism is a major industry. In fact, millions of tourists visit the city every year to take advantage of its many cultural and historical offerings. Unfortunately, like many great urban centers, London has problems such as traffic congestion, crime, and homelessness.

EXAMPLE: **A:** London is the largest city in the United Kingdom, isn't it?
   B: That's right.

Now look at the questions below. What do you know about Vancouver? Circle the correct words and complete the tag questions.

1. Vancouver is / (isn't) the largest city in Canada, _____ *is it* _____?

2. It lies / (doesn't lie) on the Atlantic Coast, does it ?

3. It (has) / doesn't have a very large port, Hasn't it ?

4. It (is) / isn't a very beautiful city, Isn't it ?

5. (Many) / Not many tourists visit the city, Don't they ?

6. You can / can't hear many different languages there, _____?

7. Movie production is / isn't an important industry in Vancouver, _____?

Ask Student A the questions. Student A will read a paragraph about Vancouver and tell you if your information is correct or not.

EXAMPLE: **B:** Vancouver isn't the largest city in Canada, is it?
   A: No, it isn't. It's the third largest city.

UNIT 7 Review

Check your answers on page UR-2.

Do you need to review anything?

A | *Circle the correct words to complete the sentences.*

1. It's a beautiful day, <u>isn't</u> / is it?

2. <u>Didn't</u> / Aren't you order coffee?

3. You'<u>ve</u> / haven't heard from Raoul recently, haven't you?

4. That was a great movie, wasn't that / <u>it</u>?

5. <u>Hasn't</u> / Didn't he lived in Vancouver for several years?

6. Lara can't move out of her apartment yet, can Lara / <u>she</u>?

7. <u>Shouldn't</u> / Should not we leave soon? It's getting late.

B | *Complete the conversation with negative* **yes / no** *questions and tag questions. Use the correct verbs and short answers.*

A: You _____ lived in Vancouver for very long, have you?
1.

B: _____. Only for a month. _____ you tell by the way I'm dressed?
2. 3.

A: I sure can. But it's warm today! You're not really *that* cold, _____ you?
4.

B: _____! But I'm originally from Rio de Janeiro. I'll get used to this,
5.

_____ I?
6.

A: _____. It won't take long, and winter here isn't very cold. This is a great city.
7.

C | *Find and correct six mistakes.*

A: Ken hasn't come back from Korea yet, has Ken?

B: No, he has. He got back last week. Didn't he call you when he got back?

A: No, he didn't. He's probably busy. There are a lot of things to do when you move, isn't it?

B: Definitely. And I guess his family wanted to spend a lot of time with him, won't they?

A: I'm sure they will. You know, I think I'll just call him. You have his phone number, have you?

B: Yes, I do. Could you wait while I get it off my computer? You're not in a hurry, aren't you?

same meaning

Additions and Responses:
So, *Too*, *Neither*, *Not either*, and *But*
SIMILARITIES AND DIFFERENCES

(negative)

STEP 1 GRAMMAR IN CONTEXT

Before You Read

Look at the photos of twins. Discuss these questions.

1. What is different about them? What is the same?
2. How are you similar to family members? How are you different?

Read

Read the article about identical twins.

The TWIN Question:
Nature or Nurture?

by Ruth Sanborn, *Family Life* Editor

MARK AND GERALD are identical twins. Mirror images of each other, they also share many similarities in lifestyle. Mark was a firefighter, and **so was Gerald**. Mark has never been married, and **neither has Gerald**. Mark likes hunting, fishing, and old movies. **Gerald does too**.

These similarities might not be unusual in identical twins, except that Mark and Gerald were separated when they were five days old. They grew up in different states with different families. Neither one knew that he had a twin until they found each other at age 31.

Average people are fascinated by twins, and **so are scientists**. Identical twins share the same genes. Therefore, they offer researchers the chance to study the effect of genetic heredity on health and personality.

MARK AND GERALD

However, when identical twins grow up together, they also experience the same social environment.[1] How can researchers separate these environmental factors from genetic factors? By looking at identical twins who were separated at birth!

---

[1] **social environment:** the social conditions in which people live, for example: family members, religion, education, financial situation, location

The TWIN Question

JIM AND JIM

Twins with completely different childhoods give researchers the chance to study the age-old question: Which has more effect on our lives—heredity (the genes we receive from our parents) or environment (the social influences on our childhood)? In other words: nature or nurture?

Some startling coincidences have turned up in these studies. One astonishing pair is the Springer and Lewis brothers, who were adopted by different families soon after birth. The Springer family named their adopted son Jim. **So did the Lewis family**. When the two Jims met for the first time as adults, they discovered more surprising similarities. Jim Lewis had worked as a gas station attendant and a police officer. **So had Jim Springer**. Both men had owned dogs. Lewis had named his Toy; **so had Springer**. And believe it or not, Lewis had married a woman named Linda, divorced her, and later married a woman named Betty. **So had Springer**.

Do our genes really determine our names, our spouses, our jobs, even our pets? The lives of other twins indicate that the question of nature or nurture is even more complicated.

Identical twins Tamara Rabi and Adriana Scott, for example, were born in Mexico and separated at birth. Each girl was adopted by a different family from New York. Tamara grew up in the city with a Jewish family, but Adriana was raised Catholic in the suburbs. It wasn't until the age of 20 that the two sisters learned about each other and met for the very first time. The similarities were amazing. Apart from a light birthmark over Tamara's right eyebrow and the fact that Adriana had colored her hair lighter, the girls looked exactly the same. They even talked the same and had had the same nightmare since childhood.

TAMARA AND ADRIANA

There were other differences beyond the small physical ones, however. Tamara loves Chinese food, **but Adriana doesn't**. More importantly, Tamara is a very outgoing person, **but Adriana isn't**. She's very shy, despite her identical heredity. And although both girls grew up as only children, Adriana was more eager to get to know her sister after they first met. (Now, however, they consider each other a gift.)

Clearly, our heredity doesn't completely control our lives. Our **environment doesn't either**. The lives of twins separated at birth suggest that we have a lot to learn about the complex[2] role these two powerful forces play in shaping human lives.

---

2 **complex:** difficult to understand because of its many connected parts

After You Read

A | Vocabulary: *Complete the sentences with the words from the box.*

coincidence	despite	factor	identical	image	outgoing

1. Some parents like to dress their twins in _____ clothes. Others prefer to focus

   on differences.

2. What an amazing _____! My twin and I bought the same kind of car in the

   same color, on the same day.

3. When Don saw the _____ of his twin in the photo, he thought at first that he

   was looking at himself.

4. Karyn's sister is friendly and _____, but Karyn is quite shy.

5. _____ their similarities, the twins have very different personalities.

6. Mia's education was an important _____ in her success.

B | Comprehension: *Check (✓) the boxes to complete the sentences. Check **all** the true information from the article.*

1. Mark and Gerald have had the same _____.
   - ☐ marriage histories
   - ☐ types of jobs
   - ☐ hobbies

2. By studying separated twins, scientists hope to discover the _____ twins.
   - ☐ best environment for
   - ☐ effects of nature and nurture on
   - ☐ similarities between

3. The Springer and Lewis brothers have the same _____.
   - ☐ first names
   - ☐ marriage histories
   - ☐ job histories

4. The question of nature or nurture is _____ to answer.
   - ☐ easy
   - ☐ difficult
   - ☐ impossible

5. Tamara and Adriana do NOT have the same _____.
   - ☐ food preferences
   - ☐ hair color
   - ☐ language

6. Heredity _____ our lives.
   - ☐ partly controls
   - ☐ completely controls
   - ☐ has a weak effect on

(handwritten notes in margin)

Auxiliary	modal.
Be	can
Do	could
Have	should
will	would

Peter will go home soon, so will Amy.

Peter can go to scl, neither can Amy

SIMILARITY: *SO* AND *NEITHER*

Affirmative

Statement		Addition
Subject + Verb	***And so***	***Verb* + Subject***
Amy *is* a twin,		*am* I.
She *has* **traveled**,	**and so**	*have* we.
She *can* **ski**,		*can* they.
She *likes* dogs,		*does* Bill.

*The verb in the addition is a form of *be*, an auxiliary, or a modal.

Negative

Statement		Addition
Subject + Verb + *Not*	***And neither***	**Verb + Subject**
Amy *isn't* a twin,		*am* I.
She *hasn't* **traveled**,	**and neither**	*have* we.
She *can't* **ski**,		*can* they.
She *doesn't* **like** dogs,		*does* Bill.

SIMILARITY: *TOO* AND *NOT EITHER*

Affirmative

Statement		Addition
Subject + Verb	***And***	**Subject + Verb + *Too***
Amy *is* a twin,		I *am* **too**.
She *has* **traveled**,	**and**	we *have* **too**.
She *can* **ski**,		they *can* **too**.
She *likes* dogs,		Bill *does* **too**.

Negative

Statement		Addition
Subject + Verb + *Not*	***And***	**Subject + Verb + *Not either***
Amy *isn't* a twin		I'*m not* **either**.
She *hasn't* **traveled**,	**and**	we *haven't* **either**.
She *can't* **ski**,		they *can't* **either**.
She *doesn't* **like** dogs,		Bill *doesn't* **either**.

DIFFERENCE: BUT

Affirmative + Negative

Statement		Addition	
Subject + Verb	*But*		**Subject + Verb + *Not***
Amy *is* a twin,			I'*m not*.
She *has* traveled,	but	we *haven't*.
She *can* ski,		they *can't*.
She *likes* dogs,		Bill *doesn't*.

Negative + Affirmative

Statement		Addition	
Subject + Verb + *Not*	*But*		**Subject + Verb**
Amy *isn't* a twin,			I *am*.
She *can't* ski,	but	we *can*.
She *hasn't* traveled,		they *have*.
She *doesn't* like dogs,		Bill *does*.

[verb comes b4 the subject]

Aff: Jeni can speak spanish
Neg: Julie can't.
↝ Jeni can speak spanish,
   but Julie can't.

Neg: Juli doesn't like to
     travel.
Aff: Jeni does
↝ Juli doesn't like to
   travel, but Jeni does.

* similarity:
Jeni is a teacher. Juli is a teacher.
– Jeni is a teacher, and so is Juli.

* Difference:
Juli doesn't like to travel. Jeni likes to travel
– Juli doesn't like to travel, but Jeni does.

* Julie is a teacher and so is Jeni.
Julie is a " , and Jeni is too.

negative {
* Julie isn't married, and neither is Jeni.
Julie isn't married, and Jeni isn't either.

GRAMMAR NOTES

1 | **Additions** are clauses or short sentences that follow a statement. They express **similarity** or **difference** with the information in the statement. We use additions to <u>avoid repeating</u> information.

SIMILARITY:
- Bill bites his fingernails, **and so does Ed**.
  (Bill bites his fingernails. Ed bites his fingernails.)

DIFFERENCE:
- Ana lived in the city, **but Eva didn't**.
  (Ana lived in the city. Eva didn't live there.)

---

2 | Use **so**, **too**, **neither**, or **not either** to express **similarity**. Additions of similarity can be **clauses** starting with *and*.

Additions of similarity can also be separate **sentences**.

a. Use **so** or **too** if the addition follows an <u>affirmative</u> statement.

b. Use **neither** or **not either** if the addition follows a <u>negative</u> statement.

BE CAREFUL! Notice the **word order** after **so** and **neither**. The verb comes before the subject.

CLAUSE
- Mark is a firefighter, **and *so* is Gerald**. OR
- Mark is a firefighter, **and Gerald is *too***.
  (Mark is a firefighter. Gerald is a firefighter.)

SENTENCE
- Mark isn't married. ***Neither* is Gerald**. OR
- Mark isn't married. **Gerald *isn't either***.
  (Mark isn't married. Gerald isn't married.)

AFFIRMATIVE STATEMENT
- Mark **is** a firefighter, and **so is** Gerald.
- Mark **is** a firefighter, and Gerald **is *too***.

NEGATIVE STATEMENT
- Mark **didn't** marry. ***Neither* did** Gerald.
- Mark **didn't** marry. Gerald **did*n't either***.

- So **is** Gerald. NOT: So ~~Gerald is~~.
- Neither **did Gerald**. NOT: Neither ~~Gerald did~~.

---

3 | Use **but** in additions that show **difference**.
a. If the statement is <u>affirmative</u>, the addition is <u>negative</u>.

b. If the statement is <u>negative</u>, the addition is <u>affirmative</u>.

AFFIRMATIVE　　　**NEGATIVE**
- Ana **has** a birthmark, **but** Eva **doesn't**.
- Ana **lived** in Mexico, **but** Eva **didn't**.

NEGATIVE　　　**AFFIRMATIVE**
- Ana **doesn't like** to read, **but** Eva **does**.
- Ana **didn't** speak English, **but** Eva **did**.

---

4 | **Additions** always use a form of *be*, an auxiliary verb, or a modal.
a. If the statement uses *be*, use **be** in the addition.
b. If the statement uses an auxiliary verb (*be*, *have*, *do*, or *will*), or a modal (*can*, *could*, *should*, *would*) use the **same auxiliary verb or modal** in the addition.
c. If the statement doesn't use *be* or an auxiliary verb, use an appropriate form of **do** in the addition.

BE CAREFUL! The verb in the addition agrees with the subject of the addition.

- I'**m** a twin, and so **is** my cousin.
- Jim Lewis **had** worked in a gas station, and so **had** Jim Springer.
- I **can't** drive, and neither **can** my twin.

- Bill **bought** a Chevrolet, and so **did** Ed.
- Bill **owns** a dog, and so **does** Ed.

- They'**ve learned** Spanish, and so **has** she.
  NOT: They've learned Spanish, and so ~~have~~ she.

(continued on next page)

5 In conversation, you can use **short responses** with *so*, *too*, *neither*, *not either*, and *but*.

a. Use *so*, *too*, *neither*, and *not either* to express **agreement** with another speaker.

A: **I like** sports.
B: ***So do I.*** OR **I do** *too*.

A: **I don't like** sports.
B: ***Neither do I.*** OR **I** *don't either*.

USAGE NOTE: In **informal speech**, people say *Me too* to express agreement with an affirmative statement and *Me neither* to express agreement with a negative statement.

A: **I think** twin studies are fascinating.
B: ***Me too.***
A: **I've never heard** of the Jim twins.
B: ***Me neither.***

b. Use *but* to express **disagreement** with another speaker. You can often leave out *but*.

A: **I wouldn't like** to have a twin.
B: Oh, *(but)* **I would.**

STEP 3 FOCUSED PRACTICE

EXERCISE 1: Discover the Grammar

Read these short conversations between reunited twins. Decide if the statement that follows is True (T) or False (F).

1. **MARK:** I like Chinese food.

    GERALD: So do I.

    _T_ Gerald likes Chinese food.

2. **ADRIANA:** I don't want to go out tonight.

    TAMARA: Neither do I.

    _____ Tamara wants to go out tonight.

3. **AMY:** I didn't understand that article.

    KERRIE: Oh, I did.

    _____ Kerrie understood the article.

4. **JEAN:** I'm not hungry.

    JOAN: Me neither.

    _____ Jean and Joan are hungry.

5. **TAMARA:** I was nervous about our meeting.

    ADRIANA: So was I.

    _____ Tamara and Adriana were both nervous about their meeting.

6. **AMY:** I've always felt lonely.

    KERRIE: So have I.

    _____ Kerrie has felt lonely.

7. **MARK:** I'm pretty outgoing.

    GERALD: I'm not.

    _____ Gerald is outgoing.

8. **DAVE:** I can meet at eight o'clock.

    PETE: I can too.

    _____ Pete can meet at eight o'clock.

9. **JIM:** I have a headache.

    JIM: So do I.

    _____ Both Jims have headaches.

10. **DAVE:** I'm not looking forward to the TV interview.

    PETE: Oh, I am.

    _____ Pete isn't looking forward to the TV interview.

EXERCISE 2: Additions

(Grammar Notes 1–4)

Circle the correct words to complete the paragraph about being a twin.

Sometimes being a twin can cause trouble. In high school, I was in Mr. Jacobs's history class.

Neither / (So) was Joe. One day we took a test. The results were identical. I got questions 18 and 20
    1.

wrong. Joe did so / too.
    2.

I didn't spell *Constantinople* correctly, and either / neither did Joe. The teacher was sure we had
    3.

cheated. As a result, I got an F on the test, and so did / got Joe. We tried to convince Mr. Jacobs
    4.

that it was just a coincidence. After all, I had sat on the left side of the room, but Joe didn't / hadn't.
    5.

As always, he sat on the right. But Mr. Jacobs just thought we had developed some complex

way of sharing answers across the room. Our parents believed we were honest, but Mr. Jacobs

didn't / weren't. The principal didn't either / too. We finally convinced them to give us another test.
    6.   **7.**

Despite the fact that we were in separate rooms so cheating *couldn't* be a factor, I got questions 3

and 10 wrong. Guess what? Neither / So did Joe. Our teacher was astounded, and / but we weren't.
    8.   **9.**

EXERCISE 3: Short Responses

(Grammar Note 5)

Two twins are talking. They agree on everything. Complete their conversation with short responses.

MARTA: I'm so happy we finally found each other.

CARLA: So _____*am I*_____. I always felt like something was missing from my life.
    1.

MARTA: So _____. I always knew I had a double somewhere out there.
    2.

CARLA: I can't believe how alike we look!

MARTA: Neither _____.
    3.

CARLA: And we like and dislike all the same things.

MARTA: Right. I hate lettuce.

CARLA: I _____. And I detest liver.
    4.

MARTA: So _____. I love pizza, though.
    5.

CARLA: So _____. Especially with mushrooms. But I can't stand pepperoni.
    6.

MARTA: Neither _____.
    7.

CARLA: This is amazing! I'd like to find out if our husbands have a lot in common too.

MARTA: So _____! That would be quite a coincidence!
    8.

EXERCISE 4: Additions: Similarity or Difference

(Grammar Notes 1–4)

Look at this chart about the twins' husbands. Then complete the sentences about them. Add statements with **so, too, neither, not either,** *and* **but**.

	Bob	**Randy**
AGE	32	32
HEIGHT	6'2"	6'
WEIGHT	160 lb	160 lb
HAIR COLOR	blond	blond
EYE COLOR	blue	brown
HOBBIES	tennis	tennis
FAVORITE FOOD	steak	steak
MILITARY SERVICE	yes	no
EDUCATION	graduate degree	graduate degree
LANGUAGES	English, Spanish	English, French
JOB	lawyer	engineer
BROTHERS OR SISTERS	none	none

1. Bob is 32, *and so is Randy*. OR *and Randy is too.* _____

2. Bob is 6'2", _____

3. Bob weighs 160 pounds, _____

4. Bob has blond hair, _____

5. Bob doesn't have green eyes, _____

6. Bob plays tennis, _____

7. Bob likes steak, _____

8. Bob served in the military, _____

9. Bob has attended graduate school, _____

10. Bob doesn't speak French, _____

11. Bob became a lawyer, _____

12. Bob doesn't have any brothers or sisters, _____

EXERCISE 5: Editing

Read Ryan's composition. There are five mistakes in the use of sentence additions. The first mistake is already corrected. Find and correct four more.

> # My Brother and I
>
> My brother is just a year older than I am. (I'm 18.) We have a lot of things in common. We look alike. In fact, sometimes people ask us if we're twins. I am 5'10", and so ~~he is~~ *is he*. I have straight black hair and dark brown eyes. So does he. We share some of the same interests too. I love to play soccer, and he too. Both of us swim every day, but I can't dive, and either can he.
>
> Although there are a lot of similarities between us, there are also many differences. For example, he likes eating all kinds of food, but I don't. Give me hamburgers and fries every day! My brother doesn't want to go to college, but I don't. I believe it's important to get as much education as possible, but he wants to get real-life experience. I think our personalities are an important factor in these choices. I am quiet and easygoing, but he doesn't. He's very outgoing and talks a lot. When I think about it, despite the many things we have in common, we really are more different than similar.

EXERCISE 6: Understanding Additions

(Grammar Notes 1–4)

Look at Exercise 5. Complete the chart by checking (✓) the correct column(s).

	Ryan	Ryan's Brother
1. is 18 years old	✓	☐
2. is 5'10" tall	☐	☐
3. has black hair	☐	☐
4. has dark brown eyes	☐	☐
5. loves soccer	☐	☐
6. swims	☐	☐
7. dives	☐	☐
8. prefers hamburgers and fries	☐	☐
9. wants to go to college	☐	☐
10. prefers real-life experience	☐	☐
11. is quiet and easygoing	☐	☐

EXERCISE 7: Listening

A | *A couple is on a date. Read the sentences. Then listen to their conversation. Listen again and circle the correct words to complete each statement.*

1. The man and woman know / (don't know) each other very well.

2. They're eating dinner at the woman's home / in a restaurant.

3. She likes to cook the same / new recipes.

4. Both people probably prefer to read mystery stories / history.

5. They probably won't play tennis / go on another date together.

6. They're going to watch a movie / TV show at eight o'clock.

B | *Look at the information. Listen again to the couple's conversation. Check (✓) the correct box(es).*

	Man	Woman		Man	Woman
1. loves Italian food	✓	✓	6. enjoys fiction	☐	☐
2. cooks	☐	☐	7. plays sports	☐	☐
3. eats out a lot	☐	☐	8. watches sports on TV	☐	☐
4. enjoys old movies	☐	☐	9. watches news programs	☐	☐
5. reads biographies	☐	☐	10. wants to see the documentary	☐	☐

EXERCISE 8: Pronunciation

A | *Read and listen to the Pronunciation Note.*

> **Pronunciation Note**
>
> In **additions** and **short responses** of **similarity**, we usually **stress *so, neither, too, either*** and the **subject** of the addition. We do NOT stress the verb.
>
> EXAMPLES: A: Maya is a student, **and so am I.**
>
> B: She doesn't spend much time studying.
>
> A: **I don't either.**
>
> In **additions** and **short responses** that show **difference**, we usually **stress** the **subject** and the **verb**. We do NOT stress *but*.
>
> EXAMPLES: A: My brother loves baseball, **but I don't.**
>
> B: And you love to swim.
>
> A: **But he doesn't.**

B | *Listen to the short conversations. Put a dot (•) over the stressed words or parts of words in the additions and short responses.*

1. **A:** I really enjoyed the show.

   B: So did I.

2. **A:** My friends haven't seen it yet.

   B: Mine haven't either.

3. **A:** Did you go dancing with Sue and Kate last night?

   B: Just with Sue. Sue loves to dance, **but Kate doesn't**.

4. **A:** I don't like to watch TV for very long.

   B: Neither do I. Want to take a walk?

5. **A:** Your friend Bob's a twin, **and I am too**.

   B: You're a twin? I didn't know that.

6. **A:** My twin isn't identical.

   B: Oh, **Bob's is**. His name is Steve.

7. **A:** They both love music. Bob plays the piano.

   B: So does Steve.

8. **A:** It's getting late. I should go home pretty soon.

   B: I should too. Let's get together again sometime.

C | *Listen again and repeat the short responses and additions. Then practice the conversations with a partner.*

EXERCISE 9: Discussion

Work in small groups. Look at Exercise 7. Do you think that the man and woman are a good match? Is it important for couples to have a lot in common? What other factors are important in a good match?

EXAMPLE: **A:** The man and woman have a lot in common.
B: He loves Italian food, and so does she. I think they're a good match.
C: Oh, but I don't. The woman doesn't . . .

EXERCISE 10:   Picture Discussion

Work with a partner. Look at the picture of reunited twins. Imagine their conversations. You can use these topics or your own.

- abilities
- appearance
- childhood
- clothes
- education
- food preferences
- health
- hobbies
- language
- marriage history
- occupation
- personality

EXAMPLE: **A:** I drink a lot of soda.
B: So do I.

EXERCISE 11:   Find Someone Who . . .

A | *Complete these statements. Then read your statements to a classmate. He or she will give you a short response. Check (✓) the items the two of you have in common. Then do the same with another classmate.*

EXAMPLE: **A:** I like to walk in the rain.
B: So do I.   OR   Oh, I don't. I like to stay home and watch TV.

I have these things in common with:

	(Classmate 1)	(Classmate 2)
1. I like to _____.	☐	☐
2. I never _____.	☐	☐
3. I love _____. (name of food)	☐	☐
4. I can't _____.	☐	☐
5. I would like to _____.	☐	☐
6. I've never _____.	☐	☐
7. When I was younger, I didn't _____.	☐	☐
8. I'll never _____.	☐	☐

B | *Count the number of checkmarks for each of the two classmates. Which classmate do you have more in common with?*

EXERCISE 12: Compare and Contrast

Work with a partner. Look at the pictures of these twins. How many things do they have in common? How many differences can you find? You have eight minutes to write your answers. Then compare your answers with those of another pair.

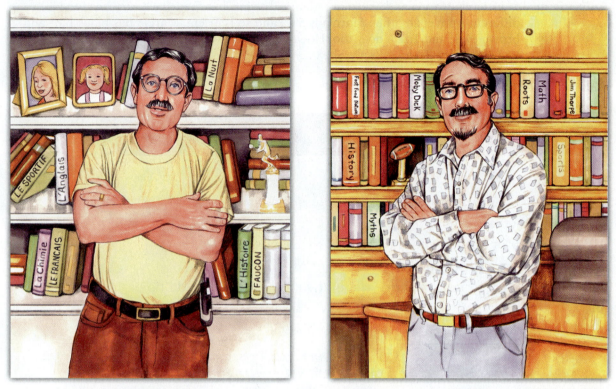

Michael   Matthew

EXAMPLE: Michael has a mustache, and so does Matthew.

EXERCISE 13: What Do You Think?

Reread the article beginning on page 118. What do you think is more important, nature or nurture? Tell the class. Give examples to support your views.

EXAMPLE: In my opinion, nature is more important than nurture. For example, despite the fact that my brother and I grew up together, we're very different. He could throw a ball when he was only three, but I couldn't. I hate sports . . .

EXERCISE 14: Writing

A | *Write two paragraphs about two people who are close (twins or other siblings, cousins, friends, spouses, etc.). What do they have in common? What are their differences? Use* **so, too, neither, not either,** *and* **but.** *You can use Exercise 5 on page 127 as a model.*

EXAMPLE: My friends Marcia and Tricia are identical twins, but they work very hard to look different from each other. Marcia is 5'3", and so is Tricia. Marcia has black hair and brown eyes, and Tricia does too. However, Marcia wears her hair very short and loves lots of jewelry. Tricia doesn't. She . . .

B | *Check your work. Use the Editing Checklist.*

Editing Checklist

Did you use . . . ?

☐ *so*, *too*, *neither*, or *not either* to express similarity

☐ *so* or *too* after an affirmative statement

☐ *neither* or *not either* after a negative statement

☐ *but* to show difference

☐ the correct form of *be*, *have*, *do*, *will*, or a modal in the additions

A | *Circle the correct words to complete the sentences.*

1. Mary lives in Houston, and so <u>lives / does</u> Jan.

2. Doug moved to Florida. <u>So / Neither</u> did his brother.

3. Mia isn't married. Her sister <u>is too / isn't either</u>.

4. My friends play tennis, <u>but / so</u> I don't.

5. They speak French, but she <u>does / doesn't</u>.

6. Dan plays tennis, and I do <u>so / too</u>.

B | *Combine each pair of sentences. Use an addition with* **so, too, neither, not either,** *or* **but.**

1. I speak Spanish. My brother speaks Spanish.

   _____

2. Jaime lives in Chicago. His brother lives in New York.

   _____

3. Chicago is an exciting city. New York is an exciting city.

   _____

4. Chen doesn't play tennis. His sister plays tennis.

   _____

5. Diego doesn't eat meat. Lila doesn't eat meat.

   _____

C | *Find and correct nine mistakes.*

My friend Alicia and I have a lot in common. She comes from Los Angeles, and so I do.

She speaks Spanish. I speak too. Her parents are both teachers, but mine are too. (My mother

teaches math, and her father do too.) I don't have any brothers or sisters. Either does she. There

are some differences too. Alicia is very outgoing, and I'm not. I like to spend more time alone.

I don't enjoy sports, but she doesn't. She's on several school teams, but not I'm. I just think our

differences make things more interesting, and so my friend does!

From Grammar to Writing
AVOIDING REPETITION WITH SENTENCE ADDITIONS

When you write, one way to **avoid repetition** is to use **sentence additions**.

EXAMPLES: Brasília is a capital city. Washington, D.C. is a capital city. ➔
Brasília is a capital city, *and so* is Washington, D.C.

Brasília's shape is modern. Washington's shape isn't modern. ➔
Brasília's shape is modern, *but* Washington's isn't.

1 | *Read this student's essay comparing and contrasting Brasília and Washington, D.C.
Underline once additions that express similarity. Underline twice additions that express
contrast.*

BRASÍLIA AND WASHINGTON, D.C.

Citizens of Brasília and citizens of Washington, D.C. live on
different continents, but their cities still have a lot in common.
Brasília is its nation's capital, and so is Washington. Brasília did
not exist before it was planned and built as the national capital.
Neither did Washington. Both cities were designed by a single
person, and both have a definite shape. However, 20th-century
Brasília's shape is modern—that of an airplane—but the shape
of 18th-century Washington isn't. Its streets form a wheel.

The cities reflect their differences in location and age. Brasília
is located in a dry area in the highlands, while Washington was
built on wet, swampy land. As a result, Brasília has moderate
temperatures all year, but Washington doesn't. Washington is
famous for its cold winters and hot, humid summers. Brasília
was built 600 miles from the Atlantic coast in order to attract
people to an unpopulated area. Washington, near the Atlantic
coast, includes old towns that had already existed. Brasília is
home to many famous theaters and museums, and so is the city
of Washington. However, as a new city, Brasília has not yet
become its nation's real cultural center. Washington hasn't
either. Washington is its country's capital, but it is not its
country's most popular city. Neither is Brasília. Many people
still prefer the excitement of Rio and New York.

2 | *Before writing the essay in Exercise 1, the student made a Venn diagram showing the things that Brasília and Washington, D.C., have in common, and the things that are different. Complete the student's diagram.*

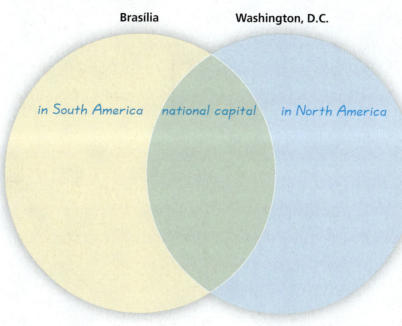

Brasília   Washington, D.C.

in South America   *national capital*   *in North America*

3 | *Before you write . . .*

1. Work with a partner. Agree on a topic for an essay of comparison and contrast. For example, you can compare two places, two people, two types of food, or two TV programs.

2. Brainstorm ideas and complete a Venn diagram like the one in Exercise 2.

4 | *Write an essay of comparison and contrast using your diagram in Exercise 3.*

5 | *Exchange essays with a different partner. Underline once additions that show similarity. Underline twice additions that show difference. Write a question mark (?) above the places where something seems wrong. Then answer the following questions.*

	Yes	No
1. Did the writer use the correct auxiliary verbs in the additions?	☐	☐
2. Did the writer use correct word order?	☐	☐
3. Do the examples show important similarities and differences?	☐	☐

4. What are some details you would like to know about the two things the writer compared?

_____

_____

6 | *Work with your partner. Discuss each other's editing questions from Exercise 5. Then rewrite your own paragraph and make any necessary corrections.*

GERUNDS AND INFINITIVES

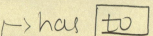

UNIT 9

Gerunds and Infinitives: Review and Expansion

FAST FOOD

STEP 1 GRAMMAR IN CONTEXT

Before You Read

Look at the title of the article and the photos. Discuss the questions.

1. Why do you think the title is *McWorld*?
2. What do you think of fast-food restaurants like McDonald's?
3. Do you eat in fast-food restaurants? Why or why not?

Read

Read the article about the largest fast-food restaurant chain in the world.

"I'll have a Big Mac, a large fries, and a medium soda." The language may change, but you can **expect to hear** this order in more than 115 countries all over the world. Fast food has become almost synonymous[1] with McDonald's, the best known of all the multinational fast-food restaurant chains. At the moment, Antarctica is the only continent that doesn't (yet!) have one. And the numbers **keep growing**. In the United States, most McDonald's customers **need to travel** less than four minutes **to arrive** at the next pair of golden arches.

Dining on fast food has become a way of life for millions and millions of people from Illinois, U.S.A. (the very first McDonald's), to Colombo, Sri Lanka (a more recent one). What is it **about eating** on the run that so many people find appealing? Of course, the most obvious answer is that, true to its name, fast food is fast. In today's hectic society, people **don't want to waste** time. But apart from the speed **of ordering** and **getting** served, satisfied customers often talk about convenience, price, and, yes, even good taste.

Many people also like the reliability that fast-food chains provide. You can **count on getting** the same thing every time, every place. McDonald's **has started to introduce** some local variety, though. For example, in

---

[1]*synonymous: having the same meaning*

New Delhi, India

the New England region of the United States, you can get a lobster roll; in Japan, you can order a teriyaki McBurger; and in India, you can have a Maharaja Mac or a vegetable burger. And although most McDonald's restaurants resemble one another, some **try to adjust** to the surroundings. In Freiburg, Germany, one McDonald's is housed in an historic building more than 700 years old, and in Sweden, there's even a McSki lodge.

Not everyone is **in favor of** fast-food restaurants' **spreading** over the globe. In fact, a lot of people are **fed up with seeing** the same restaurants wherever they go. "**Walking** down the Champs Elysées just isn't as romantic as it once was. When I see McDonald's or KFC (Kentucky Fried Chicken) everywhere I go, I feel that the world is shrinking too much," complained one traveler. But there are more serious objections too.

Nutritionists[2] point to the health consequences **of eating** fast foods since they are generally high in calories, fat, and salt, but low in fiber and nutrients. They blame the world-wide problem of obesity,[3] in part, **on eating** fast food. Sociologists[4] complain that fast-food restaurants may prevent

families **from spending** quality time together around the dinner table. Social critics condemn fast-food chains **for introducing** these unhealthy foods to other countries and **for underpaying** their workers. Then there is the question of pollution. Those Big Macs and Quarter Pounders come wrapped in a lot of paper and plastic, which create waste that pollutes the air and water. It's a high **price to pay** for convenience.

But like it or not, it's **easy to see** that fast-food restaurants like McDonald's are **here to stay**. From Rovaniemi, Finland, in the north; Invercargill, New Zealand, in the south; Tokyo, Japan, in the east; and Vancouver, Canada, in the west, the sun never sets on the golden arches.

Tokyo, Japan

[2]*nutritionist:* an expert on what people should eat
[3]*obesity:* the condition of being extremely fat
[4]*sociologist:* an expert on how people behave in groups

Fast Facts

- The average adult in the United States visits a fast-food restaurant six times a month.
- Hamburgers are the most popular fast food in the United States.
- Tacos are the second most popular fast-food choice in the United States, followed by pizza and chicken.
- Men are more **likely** than women **to order** a hamburger.
- Lunch is the most popular meal at a fast-food restaurant.

After You Read

A | Vocabulary: *Complete the sentences with the words from the box.*

appealing	consequence	globe	objection	region	reliability

1. As a newspaper reporter, Ozawa travels all over the _____. In fact, last year she was in 40 countries.

2. I have no _____ to the report. It's excellent.

3. There are only two Japanese restaurants in the _____, but another one is opening up soon.

4. People like the newspaper's _____. They know that the information is correct.

5. One _____ of the nutrition report was that some people stopped eating fast food.

6. The idea of low-cost, healthy food choices is very _____.

B | Comprehension: *Circle the letter of the word or phrase that best completes each sentence.*

1. The number of McDonald's restaurants is _____.

   a. decreasing   **b.** remaining the same   **c.** increasing

2. The article does NOT mention _____ as a reason for McDonald's popularity.

   a. cost   **b.** attractiveness   **c.** quick service

3. All McDonald's serve _____.

   a. soda   **b.** vegetable burgers   **c.** teriyaki McBurgers

4. _____ happy to see fast-food chains all around the globe.

   a. Some people are   **b.** Everyone is   **c.** Nobody is

5. One big objection to fast food is that it is _____.

   a. cheap   **b.** unhealthy   **c.** bad-tasting

6. According to the article, workers at fast-food chains don't _____.

   a. eat well   **b.** make enough money   **c.** spend time with their families

*Joe stopped exercising
(doesn't exercise
anymore)*

*Joe stopped to exe.
(He will do it again)*

STEP 2 GRAMMAR PRESENTATION

GERUNDS AND INFINITIVES

Gerunds	Infinitives
Gerund as Subject	***It* + Infinitive**
Eating fast foods is convenient.	***It*'s** convenient **to eat** fast foods.
Verb + Gerund	**Verb + Infinitive**
They *recommend* **reducing** fats in the food.	They *plan* **to reduce** fats in the food.
Verb + Gerund or Infinitive	**Verb + Gerund or Infinitive**
She *started* **buying** McBreakfast every day.	She *started* **to buy** McBreakfast every day.
Preposition + Gerund	**Adjective + Infinitive**
We're tired **of reading** calorie counts.	We were *surprised* **to read** the number of calories.
Possessive + Gerund	**Object Pronoun + Infinitive**
I didn't like **his ordering** fries.	I urged **him to order** fries.

GRAMMAR NOTES

1

A **gerund** (base form + **-ing**) is a verb used as a noun. We often use a **gerund** as the **subject** of a sentence.

- **Cooking** *is* a lot of fun.

REMEMBER: A gerund can have a <u>negative</u> form (**not** + base form + **-ing**), and it is always <u>singular</u> (**gerund** + **third-person singular** form of verb).

- **Not exercising** *leads* to health problems.

A gerund is often part of a phrase. When a **gerund phrase** is the **subject** of a sentence, make sure the following verb is in the <u>singular</u>.

- **Eating too many fries** *is* unhealthy.
  NOT: Eating too many fries ~~are~~ unhealthy.
- **Not caring about calories** *is* a mistake.

2

A **gerund** often follows certain verbs as the **object** of the verb.

- I *dislike* **eating** fast food every day.
- Julio *considered* **not eating** fast foods.

You can use a **possessive** (*Anne's, the boy's, my, your, his, her, its, our, their*) before a gerund.

- I dislike ***Julio's*** **eating** fast foods.
- I dislike ***his*** **eating** fast foods.

USAGE NOTE: In informal spoken English, many people use **nouns** or **object pronouns** instead of possessives before a gerund.

- I dislike ***Julio*** **eating** fast foods.
- I dislike ***him*** **eating** fast foods.

(continued on next page)

Gerunds and Infinitives: Review and Expansion   **141**

3 Some verbs can be followed by an **infinitive** (**to** + base form). These verbs fall into three groups:

- **verb** + **infinitive**

- **verb** + **object** + **infinitive**

- **verb** + **infinitive**
  OR
  verb + **object** + **infinitive**

- They **hope to open** a new McDonald's.
- She **chose not to give up** meat.

- I **urge you to try** that new restaurant.
- She **convinced him not to order** fries.

- I **want to try** that new restaurant.

- I **want her to try** it too.

4 Some verbs can be followed by either a **gerund** or an **infinitive**. The <u>meanings are the same</u>.

BE CAREFUL! A few verbs (for example, **stop**, **remember**, and **forget**) can be followed by either a gerund or an infinitive, but the <u>meanings are very different</u>.

- I **started bringing** my own lunch. OR
- I **started to bring** my own lunch.

- She **stopped eating** pizza.
  (She doesn't eat pizza anymore.)
- She **stopped to eat** pizza.
  (She stopped another activity in order to eat pizza.)

- He **remembered meeting** her.
  (He remembered that he had already met her in the past.)
- He **remembered to meet** her.
  (First he arranged a meeting with her. Then he remembered to go to the meeting.)

- I never **forgot eating** lunch at McDonald's.
  (I ate lunch at McDonald's, and I didn't forget the experience.)
- I never **forgot to eat** lunch.
  (I always ate lunch.)

5 A **gerund** is the only verb form that can follow a **preposition**.

There are many common **verb** + **preposition** and **adjective** + **preposition** combinations that must be followed by a gerund and not an infinitive.

BE CAREFUL! **To** can be part of an infinitive or it can be a preposition. Use a <u>gerund after the preposition **to**</u>.

- I read an article **about counting** calories.

- I don't **approve of eating** fast food.
- We're very **interested in trying** different types of food.

- We look forward **to having** dinner with you.
  Not: We look forward ~~to have~~ dinner with you.

6	An **infinitive** often follows:	
	a. an **adjective** Many of these adjectives express feelings or attitudes about the action in the infinitive.	• They were *eager* **to try** the new taco. • She was *glad* **to hear** that it was low in calories. • We're *ready* **to have** something different.
	b. an **adverb**	• It's too *soon* **to eat**. • The restaurant is *here* **to stay**.
	c. certain **nouns**	• It's *time* **to take** a break. • I have the *right* **to eat** what I want. • They made a *decision* **to lose** weight. • It's a high *price* **to pay**. • He has *permission* **to stay** out late.
7	Use an **infinitive** to explain the **purpose** of an action.	• Doug eats fast food **to save** time.

8	To make **general statements** you can use:
	
	     gerund as subject
	     OR
	     It + **infinitive**
		• **Cooking** is fun.
		 OR
		 • *It*'s fun **to cook**.

REFERENCE NOTES

For a list of **verbs that can be followed by gerunds**, see Appendix 3 on page A-2.

For lists of **verbs that can be followed by infinitives**, see Appendices 4 and 5 on page A-3.

For a list of **verbs that can be followed by either gerunds or infinitives**, see Appendix 6 on page A-3.

For a list of **verb + preposition combinations**, see Appendix 7 on page A-3.

For a list of **adjective + preposition expressions**, see Appendix 8 on page A-3.

For a list of **adjectives that can be followed by infinitives**, see Appendix 9 on page A-4.

For a list of **nouns that can be followed by infinitives**, see Appendix 10 on page A-4.

EXERCISE 1: Discover the Grammar

Read this questionnaire about fast-food restaurants. Underline the gerunds and circle the infinitives.

FAST-FOOD QUESTIONNAIRE

Please take a few minutes (to complete) this questionnaire about fast-food restaurants. Check (✓) all the answers that are appropriate for you.

1. In your opinion, eating fast food is _____.
☐ convenient ☑ fast ☐ healthy ☑ cheap ☐ fun

2. Which meals are you used to eating at a fast-food restaurant?
☐ breakfast ☑ lunch ☐ dinner ☐ snacks ☐ None

3. Which types of fast food do you like to eat?
☐ hamburgers ☑ pizza ☐ fried chicken ☐ tacos ☐ sushi
☐ Other: _____ ☐ None

4. What is the most important issue to you in selecting a fast-food restaurant?
☑ choice of food ☐ quality of food
☐ fast service ☐ low prices
☐ reliability ☐ Other: _____

5. How often are you likely to eat at a fast-food restaurant?
☑ 1–3 times a week ☐ more than 6 times a week
☐ 4–6 times a week ☐ Never

6. How much do you enjoy going to fast-food restaurants?
☐ I like it very much. ☐ I don't enjoy it.
☑ It's just OK. ☐ I never go.

7. How do you feel about seeing the same fast-food restaurants all over the world?
☐ I like it. ☐ I have no objections. ☑ I don't like it.

8. Do you think the government should require fast-food restaurants to include healthy choices?
☑ Yes ☐ No

EXERCISE 2: Gerund or Infinitive

(Grammar Notes 1–6, 8)

Complete the statements with the correct form—gerund or infinitive—of the verbs in parentheses. Use the bar graph to find the number of calories.

People are starting ___*to think*___ about the consequences of ___*eating*___ in

1. (think)　　　　　　　　　　　　　　　　　　　　　　**2 (eat)**

fast-food restaurants. Here are some facts ___*to consider*___ before you order.

3. (consider)

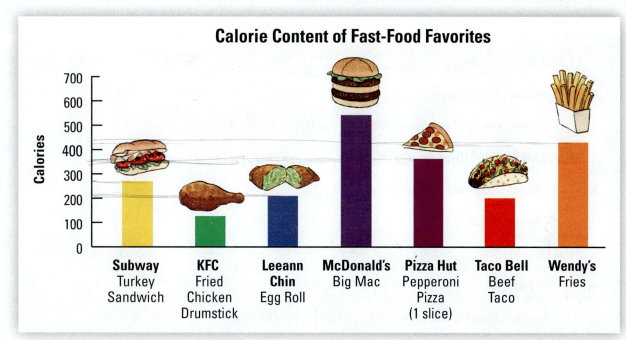

Calorie Content of Fast-Food Favorites

Source: www.calorieking.com

- ___*Ordering*___ a Big Mac will "cost" you about ___550___ calories.

  4. (order)

- ___*Having*___ a Taco Bell taco is much less fattening. One taco has only about

  5. (have)

  ___200___ calories.

- If you want ___*to lose*___ weight, you should also consider ___*eating*___ a

  6. (lose)　　　　　　　　　　　　　　　　　　**7. (eat)**

  Subway turkey sandwich. It contains around ___270___ calories.

- You're likely ___*to gain*___ weight if you eat half of a medium pepperoni pizza. A single

  8. (gain)

  slice at Pizza Hut has about ___350___ calories.

- Stop ___*eating*___ so many French fries! An order at Wendy's contains about

  9. (eat)

  ___440___ calories.

- Think about ___*choosing*___ an egg roll instead of fries. Leeann Chin's has just a little over

  10. (choose)

  ___200___ calories.

- Nutritionists advise people ___*to stay away*___ from fried chicken. A drumstick at KFC

  11. (stay away)

  contains about ___150___ calories—but people usually eat much more!

EXERCISE 3: Verb + Gerund or Infinitive

(Grammar Notes 2–4)

Complete each summary with the appropriate form of a verb from the box plus the gerund or infinitive form of the verb in parentheses. Go to Appendices 3 and 4 on pages A-2 and A-3 for help.

admit	deserve	~~forget~~	recommend	remember	~~stop~~	try	~~volunteer~~

1. **CUSTOMER:** Uh, didn't I order a large fries too?

   SERVER: That's right, you did. I'll bring them right away.

   SUMMARY: The server _____*forgot to bring*_____ the fries.
   (bring)

2. **FATHER:** That Happy Meal isn't enough for you anymore. Have a Big Mac, OK?

   CHILD: OK, but I really wanted the toy in the Happy Meal.

   SUMMARY: The father _recommended ordering_ a Big Mac.
   (order)

3. **MOM:** This car is a mess! Somebody throw out all those fast-food containers!

   STAN: I'll do it, Mom.

   SUMMARY: Stan _volunteered to throw out_ the fast-food containers.
   (throw out)

4. **PAT:** Hi, Renee. Want to go to Pizza Hut with us?

   RENEE: Thanks, but I can't eat fast food now. I'm training for the swim team.

   SUMMARY: Renee _stopped eating_ fast food.
   (eat)

5. **EMPLOYEE:** Thanks for the raise. I can really use it.

   MANAGER: You've earned it. You're our best drive-through server.

   SUMMARY: The employee _deserved to receive_ a raise.
   (receive)

6. **MOTHER:** I think you should quit that fast-food job. Your grades are suffering.

   CAROL: It's hard to decide. I need to save for college, but if my grades are bad . . .

   SUMMARY: Carol _tried to decide_ whether to keep her job.
   (decide)

7. **MOM:** You're not eating dinner. You had some fast food on the way home, didn't you?

   CHRIS: Well . . . Actually, I stopped at Arby's, but I only had a large fries.

   SUMMARY: Chris _admitted stoping_ at Arby's after school.
   (stop)

8. **TIM:** I used to stay in the McDonald's playground for hours when I was little.

   WANG: Yeah, me too. My mother couldn't get me to leave.

   SUMMARY: The boys _remembered playing_ in the McDonald's playground.
   (play)

EXERCISE 4: Gerund or Infinitive with and without Object

chose

(Grammar Notes 2–4)

Use the correct forms of the words in parentheses to complete the letters to the editor of a school newspaper. Go to Appendices 3–10 on pages A-2—A-4 for help.

To the Editor,

Yesterday, my roommate Andre _____wanted me to have_____ lunch with him in the dining hall.
1. (want / I / have)

I was surprised about _____Andre choose to go_____ there because last year he'd completely
2. (Andre / choose / go)

_____stopped using_____ the dining hall. It just wasn't appealing to him. But when we went
3. (stop / use)

in yesterday, instead of _____finding_____ the usual greasy fries and mystery meat,
4. (find)

I was happy _____to see_____ the colorful Taco Bell sign. In my opinion,
5. (see)

_____changing_____ to fast foods is the thing _____to do_____ . The
6. (change) **7. (do)**

administration made a great choice. I _____supported them to sell_____ fast food, and I really
8. (support / they / sell)

_____appreciate my frnd to encourage_____ me to give campus food another try.
9. (appreciate / my friend / encourage)

M. Rodriguez

To the Editor,

I'm writing this letter _____to express_____ my anger and great disappointment at
10. (express)

_____having_____ fast-food chains in the dining halls. When a classmate and I went
11. (have)

to eat yesterday, I _____expected to find_____ the usual healthy choices of vegetables and
12. (expect / find)

salads. I _____didn't expecte to see_____ a fast-food court. In my opinion, it's simply wrong
13. (not expect / see)

_____to bring_____ fast food into the college dining hall. The consequence of
14. (bring)

_____eating_____ fast food is bad health. As a commuter, I absolutely
15. (eat)

_____need to have_____ a healthy meal every evening before class, so I usually
16. (need / have)

_____try to stay away_____ from fast foods. I _____urged the administration to set up_____ a salad bar so
17. (try / stay away) **18. (urge / the administration / set up)**

that students like me can _____keep on buying_____ meals on campus. I'm sure other
19. (keep on / buy)

commuters will agree with my objections.

B. Chen

EXERCISE 5: Editing

Read these posts to an international online discussion group. There are fifteen mistakes in the use of gerunds and infinitives. The first mistake is already corrected. Find and correct fourteen more.

Re: love those tacos

eating OR *to eat*

I love ~~eat~~ tacos for my lunch. I think they are delicious, convenient, nutritious, and inexpensive. I don't mind to have the same thing every day! And I'm not worried about any health consequences. What do you think?

Re: vegetarian travel

I'm a vegetarian. I stopped to eat meat two years ago. I feel a little nervous about traveling to other countries. I'm going to Ghana in September. Is to find meatless dishes there easy?

Re: takoyaki

Hi! I am Paulo, and I come from Brazil. I travel a lot, and I enjoy trying different foods from all over the globe. I hope I have a chance trying takoyaki (fish balls made with octopus) when I go to Japan. Is there a takoyaki shop you can recommend my going to? I look forward to hear from you.

Re: recipe exchange

My name is Natasha. I'm interested in exchange recipes with people from other countries. If you

Would

want to know about Russian food, I'd be glad sending you some information.

Re: calamari

Hi! I was in Italy last month. The region I was visiting is famous for seafood. I don't usually like

to find

eating seafood, so I was not eager trying calamari (squid). I was surprised ~~finding~~ that I liked it! I

to be

expected it ~~being~~ tough, but it's actually quite tender if prepared well.

Re: cheap and delicious in Taiwan

trying

Are you going to Taiwan? If so, I suggest ~~to try~~ the appealing little restaurants around the National

ing   *to*

University in Taipei. ~~Eat~~ there is cheap, and it's easy find the neighborhood. The dumpling shops

to stop

are great—once you eat at one, you won't want ~~stopping.~~

EXERCISE 6: Listening

A | *Read the statements. Then listen to two college students discuss their responses to a food service survey. Listen again and circle the correct answers.*

1. Lily and Victor are in <u>class / a fast-food restaurant / the school dining hall</u>.

2. Lily thinks the meatloaf is <u>disgusting / appealing / unhealthy</u>.

3. Victor asks to borrow a <u>pen / pencil / survey</u>.

4. Victor thinks you can't prevent students from eating <u>fast food / quickly / fat</u>.

5. Victor and Lily both think the school food is pretty <u>good / cheap / healthy</u>.

6. Lily wants the cafeteria to hire someone to <u>plan menus / clean tables / cook Chinese food</u>.

7. Victor says he doesn't want to <u>get up earlier / miss breakfast / go for a run</u> in the morning.

B | *Listen again to the conversation. Check (✓) the suggestions that each student agrees with.*

School Food Service Survey

We're changing and you can help! Please complete the survey by checking (✓) the changes you want to see.

		Lily	Victor
1. Introducing Burger Queen fast foods	☐	☐	✓
2. Showing fat and calorie contents of each serving	☐	☐	☐
3. Providing more healthy choices	☐	☐	☐
4. Lowering prices	☐	☐	☐
5. Improving food quality	☐	☐	☐
6. Offering Chinese food	☐	☐	☐
7. Starting breakfast at 6:30 A.M.	☐	☐	☐

EXERCISE 7: Pronunciation

 A | *Read and listen to the Pronunciation Note.*

> ### Pronunciation Note
>
> The **way we say something** can express our **feelings** about it. For example:
>
> We can say *That's great!* and mean that we really think something is great. When we mean what we say, we are being **sincere**.
>
> But we can also say *That's great!* and mean *That's terrible!* When we mean the opposite of what we say, we are being **sarcastic**.
>
> When we are being **sincere**, our voice often starts **high** and then **drops**.
>
> **EXAMPLE:**   That's great!
>
> When we are being **sarcastic**, our voice starts much **lower**, and stays **flat**. The words are often **drawn out**.
>
> **EXAMPLE:**   That's great!

B | *Listen to the short conversations. Notice how the speaker says the last sentence in each conversation. Decide if the speaker is being **sincere** or **sarcastic**. Check (✓) the correct box.*

The speaker is being . . .	Sincere	Sarcastic
1. A: What's for dinner tonight?		
B: Liver.		
A: That's great!	☐	☐
2. A: Another fast-food restaurant is opening on Main Street.		
B: Really?		
A: Yeah. **Great, huh?**	☐	☐
3. A: What's that thing on your plate?		
B: Meatloaf!		
A: Oh. **That looks appealing.**	☐	☐
4. A: The cafeteria is going to start opening at 6:30 A.M.		
B: 6:30 A.M. **Great idea!**	☐	☐
5. A: What did you think of Ana's suggestion?		
B: Another great idea!	☐	☐
6. A: Bye. I'm leaving now. How's the weather?		
B: Take a look outside.		
A: Nice day!	☐	☐

C | *Listen again and repeat the last sentence in each conversation. Then practice the conversations with a partner.*

EXERCISE 8: Information Gap: The Right Job?

Work in pairs (A and B). **Student B**, go to page 154 and follow the instructions there.
Student A, ask Student B questions to complete the quiz. Answer Student B's questions.

EXAMPLE: **A:** What does Jennifer enjoy doing?
   B: She enjoys working with others. What does Jennifer expect to do?
   A: She expects to make a lot of money.

JOB / PERSONALITY QUIZ

Before you start looking at job ads, take this quiz to find out about your job preferences. Complete the statements with information about yourself.

Name: _____ Jennifer Johnson _____

1. I enjoy _____ *working with others* _____.
2. I expect _____ to make a lot of money _____.
3. I'm good at _____.
4. I dislike _____ working inside _____.
5. I don't mind _____.
6. I'm willing _____ to learn new skills _____.
7. I never complain about _____.
8. I'm eager _____ to meet new people _____.
9. I plan _____ next year.
10. I dream about owning my own business one day.
11. I can't stand _____.
12. I expect people _____ to be friendly _____.

JOB CENTER

Volunteering can lead to a high-paying job
Be a Park Volunteer!
Learn about plants and wildlife
Lead tours through the park

Word Processor
in busy 2-person office
~ 3 days/week
~ must type 60 wpm
~ reliability important—
   must meet deadlines
~ $10/hr

Athletic Department
Office Assistant
– answer phones
– assist students during registration
– file papers
– $7.25/hr

BURGER QUEEN
Server Wanted
evenings
$7.25/hr

When you are finished, compare quizzes. Are they the same?

Now look at the job notices to the right of the quiz. Which jobs do you think would be good for Jennifer? Which jobs wouldn't be good for her? Explain your choices.

Gerunds and Infinitives: Review and Expansion   **151**

EXERCISE 9: Questionnaire

A | *Complete the fast-food questionnaire on page 144.*

B | *Work with a partner. Compare your answers on the questionnaire with your partner's.*

> **EXAMPLE:** **A:** What's your answer to number 1?
> **B:** In my opinion, eating fast food is convenient, fast, and cheap. What do you think?
> **A:** I agree. And, it's not healthy, but it is fun!

C | *Have a class discussion about your answers. Tally the results.*

> **EXAMPLE:** Fifteen students agree that eating fast food is convenient and fast.

EXERCISE 10: Cross-Cultural Comparison

A | *Work in small groups. Describe a food from your culture that you would like to introduce to others. Is it a fast food? Do you remember eating it at special times? If so, when? Who used to make it for you? Listen to other students' favorite foods. Which ones do you want to try?*

> **EXAMPLE:** I'm from Colombia. My favorite food is *ajiaco*, a kind of potato soup. It is definitely not a fast food! I remember eating it . . .

B | *Imagine that you are planning an international food festival. Which foods from your country would you like to see there? Which foods from other countries would you enjoy trying? Make a list. Compare your list with other groups' lists.*

> **EXAMPLE:** I'm from Japan, and my favorite food is *takoyaki*. I'd like to introduce this food to other people. For myself, I'm interested in trying Turkish food, such as . . .

EXERCISE 11: Problem Solving

A | *Work in small groups. For each of the social problems below, brainstorm as many solutions as you can in five minutes. (You can also add a problem not listed.) Take notes. You can use some of the expressions from the list.*

I'm in favor of . . .	I'm opposed to . . .
I support . . .	I'm against . . .
I suggest . . .	What about . . .
I go along with . . .	We need . . .
I advise . . .	I recommend . . .
We should start / stop . . .	I urge . . .

1. In many countries, a lot of people are overweight. What can people do about this problem?

> **EXAMPLE:** **A:** What about improving physical education programs in schools?
> **B:** I'm in favor of offering healthier meals in schools.
> **C:** We need to educate people about the role of exercise.

2. Heavy traffic is a big problem in both cities and suburbs. What can we do about it?

3. Many adults can't read or write well enough to function in society. What can be done about this problem?

4. There are millions of homeless people living in the streets and parks. How can we help solve this problem?

5. Another social problem: _____

B | *Compare your answers with those of another group.*

EXERCISE 12: Writing

A | *Write a short editorial in response to one of the statements below or another issue involving food. Express your opinions and give reasons for your ideas. Use gerunds and infinitives and some of the expressions from the list in Exercise 11.*

- There ought to be a law requiring restaurants to list the number of calories for each dish.
- Schools and hospitals shouldn't be allowed to sell fast food.
- There should be a tax on soft drinks, candy, and other foods that contain a lot of sugar.
- Schools should expand their physical education programs to help prevent obesity.
- Candy and soft drink advertising on children's TV programs should be banned or limited.

> **EXAMPLE:** I'm in favor of requiring restaurants to list the calorie content of the foods on their menu. If diners have that information they can consider . . .

B | *Exchange editorials with a classmate. After you read your classmate's editorial, write a letter to the editor explaining why you agree or disagree with your classmate's opinions.*

> **EXAMPLE:** To the Editor:
> I go along with requiring restaurants to list the number of calories in each dish, but I don't think that is enough. To make good decisions, diners also need to know . . .

C | *Check your work. Use the Editing Checklist.*

Editing Checklist

Did you use . . . ?
- ☐ gerunds as subjects
- ☐ correct **verbs** + **gerunds**
- ☐ correct **verbs** + **infinitives**
- ☐ **prepositions** + **gerunds**
- ☐ infinitives after adjectives, adverbs, and certain nouns
- ☐ *it* + **infinitive** for general statements

Student B, answer Student A's questions. Then ask Student A questions to complete the quiz.

EXAMPLE: **A:** What does Jennifer enjoy doing?
B: She enjoys working with others. What does Jennifer expect to do?
A: She expects to make a lot of money.

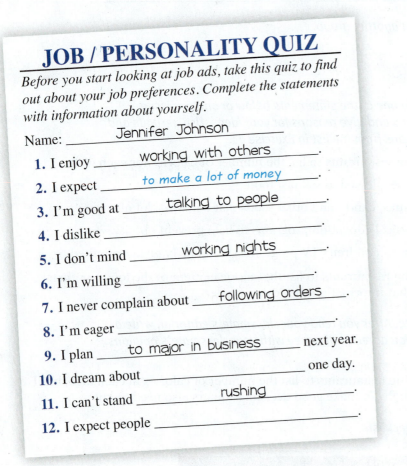

JOB / PERSONALITY QUIZ

Before you start looking at job ads, take this quiz to find out about your job preferences. Complete the statements with information about yourself.

Name: _____Jennifer Johnson_____

1. I enjoy _____working with others_____.
2. I expect _____to make a lot of money_____.
3. I'm good at _____talking to people_____.
4. I dislike _____.
5. I don't mind _____working nights_____.
6. I'm willing _____.
7. I never complain about _____following orders_____.
8. I'm eager _____.
9. I plan _____to major in business_____ next year.
10. I dream about _____ one day.
11. I can't stand _____rushing_____.
12. I expect people _____.

JOB CENTER

Volunteering can lead to a high-paying job
Be a Park Volunteer!
Learn about plants and wildlife
Lead tours through the park

Word Processor
in busy 2-person office
~ 3 days/week
~ must type 60 wpm
~ reliability important
    must meet deadlines
~ $10/hr

BURGER QUEEN
Server Wanted
evenings
$7.25/hr

Athletic Department
Office Assistant
– answer phones
– assist students during registration
– file papers
– $7.25/hr

When you are finished, compare quizzes. Are they the same?

Now look at the job notices to the right of the quiz. Which jobs do you think would be good for Jennifer? Which jobs wouldn't be good for her? Explain your choices.

Check your answers on page UR-3.

Do you need to review anything?

A | Complete the paragraph with the gerund or infinitive form of the verbs in parentheses.

Cost and convenience often persuade people _to use_ fast-food restaurants. If
1. (use)

you're eating a fast-food lunch _to save_ money, think about _ordering_
2. (save) **3. (order)**

from the dollar menu. A fast-food dinner can leave you free _to relax_ or
4. (relax)

to study instead of _preparing_ food. _stopping_ for fast food is a
5. (study) **6. (prepare)** **7. (stop)**

cheap and convenient way _to eat_. But you should avoid _having_ fast
8. (eat) **9. (have)**

food too often. _cooking_ at home provides better quality food for less money.
10. (cook)

B | Read the conversations. Complete each summary (**S**) with the correct form of the words
in parentheses.

1. **DAD:** You used to love Taco Bell as a kid.

   LYDIA: I *did*? Did you take me there a lot?

   S: Lydia _did not remember eating_
   (remember / eat)
   at Taco Bell.

2. **IVAN:** I'm sick of eating fast food.

   NIKA: You should take a cooking class.

   S: Nika _wanted him to take_
   (want / Ivan / take)
   a cooking class.

3. **CHU:** I ate in the cafeteria today.

   ANYA: That's strange. You hate that food.

   S: Anya _wondered about Chu's eating_
   (wonder about / Chu / eat)
   in the cafeteria.

4. **DINA:** I made lasagna. Would you like some?

   ERIKA: Sure! I haven't eaten since breakfast.

   S: Erika _stopped up to have_
   (stop / have)
   some lunch.

5. **PAULO:** Did you mail that letter I gave you?

   TANYA: Oops. Sorry. I'll mail it tomorrow.

   S: Tanya _forgot to mail_
   (forget / mail)
   Paulo's letter.

C | Find and correct five mistakes.

A: I was happy to hear that the cafeteria is serving salads now. I'm eager ~~trying~~ to try them.

B: Me too. Someone recommended eating more salads in order for ~~losing~~ to lose weight.

A: It was that TV doctor, right? He's always urging ~~we~~ us to exercise more too.

B: That's the one. He's actually convinced me to stop ~~to eat~~ eating meat.

A: Interesting! It would be a hard decision for us ~~making~~ to make, though. We love to barbecue.

UNIT 10
Make, Have, Let, Help, and *Get*
ZOOS AND WATER PARKS

Before You Read

Look at the photos. Discuss the questions.

1. How do you think these animals learned to perform like this?
2. Do you think people should use animals for entertainment?

Read

Read the article about performance animals.

That's
Entertainment?

"Ooooh!" cries the audience as the orcas leap from the water in perfect formation. "Aaaah!" they shout as the trainer rides across the pool on the nose of one of the graceful giants.

For years, dolphins, orcas, and other sea mammals have been **making** *audiences* **say** *ooooh* and *aaaah* at water parks like Sea World. But how do trainers **get** *nine-ton whales* **to do** acrobatic tricks[1] or **make** *them* "dance"?

It's not easy. Traditional animal trainers controlled animals with collars and leashes and **made** *them* **perform** by using cruel[2] punishments. Then, in the 1940s, water parks wanted to **have** *dolphins* **do** tricks. The first trainers faced big problems. You can't **get** *a dolphin* **to wear** a collar. And you can't punish a dolphin—it will just swim away from you! This challenge **made** *the trainers* **develop** a kinder, more humane method to teach animals.

"Ooooh!"

[1]**acrobatic trick:** the kind of act that animals and people do at the circus (example: walking on a wire)
[2]**cruel:** causing pain

That's Entertainment?

This method, positive reinforcement, uses rewards rather than punishments for training. To begin teaching, a trainer **lets** *an animal* act freely. When the trainer sees the "correct" behavior, he or she rewards the animal immediately, usually with food. The animal quickly learns that a reward follows the behavior.

Elephant performing in circus

For complicated acts, the trainer breaks the act into many smaller parts and **has** *the animal* learn each part separately.

Positive reinforcement has completely changed our treatment of animals in zoos. Elephants, for example, need a lot of physical care. However, traditional trainers used force to **make** *elephants* **"behave."** Elephants sometimes rebelled[3] and hurt or even killed their keepers. Through positive reinforcement, elephants at modern zoos have learned to stand at the bars of their cage and **let** *keepers* **draw** blood for tests and **take care of** their feet. Trainers even **get** *primates* (monkeys and apes) **to bring** their own bedding to the keepers for washing. Gary Priest, a former orca trainer, **helped** *the keepers* **train** the elephants at the San Diego Zoo. Do the elephants like the new system? "They love it! They'll do anything we ask. They'd fly for us if they could," Priest said.

Unfortunately, not all trainers use positive reinforcement. Animal rights organizations have found abuses[4] of animal actors by circuses and other entertainment companies. And the question remains: Even with kind treatment, should we keep these animals captive[5] and **have** *them* **perform** just for our entertainment? In the wild, orcas may travel 100 miles a day. Is it really kind to **make** *them* **live** in small pools of chemically treated water? Today, more and more people say the only real kindness is to **let** *these captive animals* **live** natural lives.

[3]*rebel:* to fight against someone in authority (for example a trainer, a parent, the president of a country)
[4]*abuse:* cruel or violent treatment
[5]*captive:* kept in a place that you are not allowed to leave

After You Read

A | Vocabulary: *Circle the letter of the word or phrase that best completes each sentence.*

1. _____ is NOT an example of a **reward**.
   a. Money
   b. Homework *(circled)*
   c. Ice cream

2. As a **punishment**, the child couldn't _____.
   a. go to school
   b. clean her room
   c. watch TV *(circled)*

3. The opposite of **complicated** is _____.
   a. easy *(circled)*
   b. cheap
   c. small

4. A **physical** problem is a problem with your _____.
   a. job
   b. body *(circled)*
   c. home

5. **Humane** treatment of animals _____.
   a. shows kindness *(circled)*
   b. uses power
   c. is full of mistakes

6. If someone is a **former** teacher, he or she _____.
   a. is famous
   b. teaches art
   c. used to teach *(circled)*

B | Comprehension: *Check (✓)* **True** *or* **False**. *Correct the false statements.*

	True	False
1. It's easy to train orcas and dolphins.	☐	☑
2. Many dolphins wear collars.	☐	☑
3. Methods of animal training have changed a lot since the 1940s.	☑	☐
4. Today most elephants and their trainers have a better relationship than in the past.	☑	☐
5. Many people think it is wrong to keep animals in zoos and water parks.	☑	☐

MAKE, HAVE, LET, HELP, AND GET

Make, Have, Let, Help				
Subject	**Make / Have / Let / Help**	**Object**	**Base Form**	
They	(don't)	**make** **have** **let** **help***	animals them	**learn**	tricks.

* *Help* can also be followed by an infinitive.

Get, Help				
Subject	**Get / Help**	**Object**	**Infinitive**	
They	(don't)	**get** **help**	animals them	**to learn**	tricks.

GRAMMAR NOTES

1 Use **make**, **have**, and **get** to talk about things that someone causes another person (or an animal) to do. These verbs show how much choice the other person or animal has about doing the action.

a. **make** + **object** + **base form of the verb** means to force a person or animal to do something. There is no choice.

b. **have** + **object** + **base form of the verb** often means to cause a person or animal to do a task. There is some choice.

c. **get** + **object** + **infinitive** often means to persuade a person or animal to do something by giving rewards or reasons. There is a choice.

BE CAREFUL! *Get* is always followed by **object** + **infinitive**, NOT base form of the verb.

Make can also mean to have an effect on someone or something.

- The trainer **made *the elephant* do** tricks for the audience.

- On one TV show, pet owners **have *their pets* perform** tricks.

- Jan **got *her parents* to take** her to the zoo for a school assignment.

LESS CHOICE

MORE CHOICE

Not: Jan got her parents ~~take~~ her . . .

- The monkeys always **make *me* laugh**. (*They have this effect on me.*)

2 *Let* + **object** + **base form of the verb** means to allow a person or animal to do something.

- Our teacher **let *us* leave** early after the test.
- Some zoos **let *animals* interact** with humans.

3 *Help* means to make something easier for a person or an animal. *Help* can be followed by: **object** + **base form of the verb** OR **object** + **infinitive** The meaning is the same.

- She **helped *me* do** the homework. OR
- She **helped *me* to do** the homework. (*She made it easier for me to do the homework.*)

EXERCISE 1: Discover the Grammar

Read each numbered statement. Circle the letter of the sentence that is similar in meaning.

1. Ms. Bates got the principal to arrange a class trip to the zoo.

   a. Ms. Bates arranged the class trip.

   (b.) The principal arranged the class trip.

2. Mr. Goldberg had us do research about animals.

   a. Mr. Goldberg did the research for us.

   (b.) We did the research.

3. My teacher made me rewrite the report.

   (a.) I wrote the report again.

   b. I didn't write the report again.

4. She got me to do research on sea mammals.

   (a.) I agreed to do the research.

   b. I didn't agree to do the research.

5. The zoo lets small birds and animals wander freely inside the habitat.[1]

   (a.) They can choose where they go.

   b. They have to stay in cages.

6. I was sick, so my mother didn't let me go on the trip to the zoo.

   (a.) I stayed home.

   b. I went on the trip.

7. The homework was complicated, but Paulo helped Maria finish it.

   a. Paulo did Maria's homework for her.

   (b.) Both Paulo and Maria worked on her homework.

8. Their trip to the zoo made the students really appreciate animals.

   a. The trip forced the students to appreciate animals.

   (b.) The trip changed the students' opinions of animals.

---

[1] *habitat:* in a zoo, a place outdoors or in a building that is like the natural environment of the animals

EXERCISE 2: Meaning: *Make, Have, Let, Help,* and *Get*

(Grammar Notes 1–3)

Students in a conversation class are talking about their experiences with authority figures. Complete the sentences by circling the correct verb. Then match each situation with the person in authority.

Situation

Person in Authority

___c___ **1.** The elephant was tired, so she didn't <u>help</u> / (have) it perform.

a. my teacher

___h___ **2.** I didn't really want to work overtime this week, but she (made) / let me work late because some of my co-workers were sick.

b. my doctor

c. the trainer

___e___ **3.** I forgot to turn on my headlights before I left the parking lot a few nights ago. She (made) / let me pull over to the side of the road and asked to see my license.

d. my father

e. a police officer

___a___ **4.** At first, we didn't really want to write in our journals. He explained that it would help us. Finally, he <u>had</u> / (got) us to try it.

f. the judge

g. my landlord

___g___ **5.** My check was delayed in the mail. I told him what had happened, and he <u>had</u> / (let) me pay the rent two weeks late.

h. my boss

i. my mother

___b___ **6.** I needed to get a blood test for my physical exam. He <u>got</u> / (had) me roll up my sleeve and make a fist.

___i___ **7.** We're a big family, and we all have our own chores. While she washed the dishes, she (helped) / <u>had</u> me dry. My brother, a former high school wrestling star, swept the floor!

___d___ **8.** I'm an only child, and when I was young I felt lonely. He (let) / got me sleep over at my friend's house.

___f___ **9.** I wasn't paying attention, and I hit a parked car. He (let) / <u>made</u> me tell the court what happened.

EXERCISE 3: Affirmative and Negative Statements

(Grammar Notes 1, 3)

Complete each summary. Use the correct form of the verbs in parentheses. Choose between affirmative and negative.

1.

PABLO: Ms. Allen, do I have to rewrite this paper on elephants?

MS. ALLEN: Only if you want to.

SUMMARY: Ms. Allen *didn't make Pablo rewrite* OR *didn't make him rewrite* his paper.
(make / rewrite)

2.

ANA: Could I work alone? I really don't like to work in a group.

MS. ALLEN: You need to work in a group today. Don't look so sad. It's not a punishment!

SUMMARY: She _made_ _Ana_ _work_ in a group.
(make / work)

(continued on next page)

3. **Ms. Allen:** Fernando, could you do me a favor and clean the board before you leave?

Fernando: Sure.

SUMMARY: She _had Fernando_ clean _the board._
(have / clean)

4. **Ms. Allen:** Uri, I know you're busy, but I'd like you and Greta to research orcas. You're both so good at Internet research.

Uri: Oh, OK!

SUMMARY: She got us _to research_ orcas on the Internet.
(get / research)

5. **Uri:** We need some really great orca photos, and I can't find any.

Greta: Try the *National Geographic* site. They have fantastic nature photographs.

SUMMARY: Greta _helped Uri to find_ photographs of orcas.
(help / find)

6. **Hector:** What does *positive reinforcement* mean?

Ms. Allen: Why don't you see if one of your classmates can explain it to you?

SUMMARY: Ms. Allen _had asked_ his classmates for help.
(have / ask)

EXERCISE 4: Affirmative and Negative Statements

(Grammar Notes 1–3)

*Complete each summary. Use **make, have, let, help,** or **get** plus the correct form of the verbs in parentheses. Choose between affirmative and negative.*

1. **Masami:** Can we use our dictionaries during the test?

Ms. Allen: No. You should be able to guess the meaning of the words from the context.

SUMMARY: She _____didn't let them use_____ their dictionaries.
(use)

2. **María:** Mom, can I borrow the car?

Mom: Only if you drive your sister to soccer.

SUMMARY: María's mother _mad her drive_ her sister to soccer.
(drive)

3. **John:** Can I borrow your camera for our class trip to the zoo?

Dad: Sure. I know you'll take good care of it.

SUMMARY: John's father _let him borrow_ his camera.
(borrow)

4. **John:** Excuse me, could I take pictures in here?

Worker: Yes, but don't use the flash. Light bothers these animals.

SUMMARY: The zoo worker _didn't let him use_ the flash on his camera.
(use)

5.   **PAUL:**   Ms. Allen, which movie on this list do you think we should watch?

      MS. ALLEN: You might like *Free Willy*. It's about a captive orca.

      SUMMARY: Ms. Allen <u>helped   her chose</u> a movie to watch.
                                    (choose)

6.   **MARÍA:**   John, the group wants you to read your report to the class.

      JOHN: No way! Sorry, but speaking in front of the class makes me nervous.

      SUMMARY: María <u>didn't have John</u> ^{to read} the report to the class.
                              (read)

EXERCISE 5: Editing

Read this email petition about orcas. There are eight mistakes in the use of **make, have, let, help,** *and* **get.** *The first mistake is already corrected. Find and correct seven more.*

LET THEM GO!

    Orcas are beautiful and intelligent, so aquariums easily get audiences ^{to buy} ~~buy~~ tickets for orca shows. What does this mean for the orcas? In the wild, an orca may swim up to 100 miles a day and dive hundreds of feet below the surface of the ocean. In captivity, an orca can't have normal physical or emotional health. We make this animal lives in a small, chemically-treated pool where it may get sick and die of an infection. Is that humane? Some people argue that captive orcas have helped us learned about these animals. However, orcas cannot behave naturally in an aquarium. In captivity, trainers make them to perform embarrassing tricks for a "reward." In the wild, these animals have rich and complicated social lives in families. How can watching tricks help we learn about their lives? Orcas don't belong in aquariums!

    Don't let these beautiful animals suffering in order to entertain us! First, help us stop aquarium shows. Stop going to these shows, and get your friends and family stop also. Next, we must make aquariums stop buying orcas. Write to your mayor and tell him or her how you feel. Can former captives live in the wild? It's a difficult question, but aquariums must let others retrained these animals and try to release them to a normal life.

    Help us help the orcas! It's the humane thing to do. Sign this e-letter and send it to your friends.

EXERCISE 6: Listening

A | *Read the statements. Then listen to a student talk to his teacher about a writing assignment. Listen again and circle the correct words to complete the statements.*

1. Simon wrote an essay about his uncle / **animals in zoos**.

2. Simon and his uncle used to go to the wildlife park / **zoo** together to look at animals.

3. Ms. Jacobson gets Simon to answer some *yes / no* questions / ***wh-* questions** to make his essay more interesting.

4. Simon is having trouble using the **gerund** / simple past.

5. Simon would like to make an appointment for a physical exam / **another conference** on Wednesday.

B | *Read the statements. Then listen again and check (✓)* **True** *or* **False**. *Correct the false statements.*

	True	False
1. Ms. Jacobson ~~made~~ *let* Simon write about animals in zoos.	☐	☑
2. She let him change the topic of his essay.	☐	☐
3. She had him remove some details from his second paragraph.	☐	☐
4. She got him to talk about his uncle.	☐	☐
5. She helped him correct a grammar mistake.	☐	☐
6. Simon got Ms. Jacobson to correct the gerunds in his essay.	☐	☐
7. Ms. Jacobson made Simon look for the gerunds in his essay.	☐	☐
8. She let Simon make an appointment for another conference.	☐	☐

EXERCISE 7: Pronunciation

A | *Read and listen to the Pronunciation Note.*

> **Pronunciation Note**
>
> In conversation, we often **don't pronounce the first sound** of the pronouns *him*, *her*, and *them* and we **connect the pronoun to the word** that comes before it.
>
> **EXAMPLES:**   let **her** go   →   "let**'er** go"
> made **him** work   →   "made**'im** work"
> got **them** to come →   "got**'em** to come"
>
> Notice that **'im** and **'em** sound the same: /əm/.
>
> You can **understand** if /əm/ means *him* or *them* **from the context** (other words the speaker says). For example, if you hear "Bob's mother made'im do his homework," you know that "im" is "him" because of *Bob* and *his*.

B | *Listen to the short conversations. Complete the sentences. Use the full forms.*

1. **A:** Was she happy with the essay topic?

   B: Yes, her teacher _____ _____ write about pets.

2. **A:** Where did they go for their class trip?

   B: The teacher _____ _____ to the children's zoo.

3. **A:** Did he enjoy the trip?

   B: Yes. They _____ _____ feed the rabbits.

4. **A:** What are the elephants doing?

   B: The trainer _____ _____ to stand on one foot!

5. **A:** Is Ellie walking the dog?

   B: Yes, we finally _____ _____ to do it.

6. **A:** Why does Jack look so angry?

   B: They _____ _____ stop taking pictures of the monkey.

C | *Listen again to the conversations and repeat the responses. Then practice the conversations with a partner. Use the short forms.*

EXERCISE 8: Discussion

Work with a partner. Talk about someone who helped you learn something (for example, a parent, other relative, teacher, friend). Answer the following questions. You can also choose to write about how you learned something from taking care of or observing an animal. Use **make, have, let, help,** *and* **get.**

- What did the person get you to do that you never did before?

- How did this person help you?

- Did he or she let you make mistakes in order to learn?

EXAMPLE: **A:** My older brother was a big help to me when I was a teenager.
                 B: Oh? What did he do?
                 A: Well, he got me to try a lot of new things. He even taught me to dance. And he never laughed at my mistakes or made me feel stupid.

EXERCISE 9: For or Against

Is it humane to keep animals captive for human entertainment and research? What are some reasons for and against keeping animals in zoos and water parks? You can check the Internet for ideas (search **zoos good or bad.***) Discuss your ideas in small groups. Use* **make, have, let, help,** *and* **get.**

EXAMPLE: **A:** I think it's cruel to make wild animals live in small habitats.
                 B: I'm not sure. But having them perform . . .
                 C: I think zoos can help us . . .

EXERCISE 10: Writing

A | *Write a three-paragraph essay for and against keeping animals in zoos and water parks. Give the arguments* **for** *in your first paragraph. Give the arguments* **against** *in your second. Give your own opinion in the third paragraph. You can use information from Exercise 9.*

EXAMPLE: Many people believe that it is good to keep animals in zoos and water parks. They say that people can . . .
                  Others argue that it is bad. Animals in zoos and water parks cannot . . .
                  I believe that . . . .

B | *Check your work. Use the Editing Checklist.*

Editing Checklist

Did you use . . . ?

- ☐ **object** + **base form** of the verb after *make*, *have*, and *let*
- ☐ **object** + **base form or infinitive** after *help*
- ☐ **object** + **infinitive** after *get*
- ☐ the correct verb to express your meaning

UNIT 10 Review

Check your answers on page UR-3.

Do you need to review anything?

A | *Circle the correct words to complete the sentences.*

1. I didn't know what to write about, so my teacher <u>helped / made</u> me choose a topic by suggesting ideas.

2. Before we began to write, she <u>had / got</u> us research the topic online.

3. At first I was annoyed when my teacher <u>let / made</u> me rewrite the report.

4. She was very helpful. She always <u>let / helped</u> me ask her questions.

5. It was a good assignment. It really <u>made / got</u> me to think a lot.

B | *Complete the sentences with the correct form of the verbs in parentheses. Choose between affirmative and negative and use pronoun objects.*

1. When I was little, my parents _____ a pet. They said I was too young.
   (let / have)

2. When I was 10, I finally _____ me a dog. His name was Buttons.
   (get / give)

3. It was a lot of responsibility. My parents _____ him every day.
   (make / walk)

4. They _____ him too. He ate a lot!
   (have / feed)

5. I was annoyed at my older brother. He _____ care of Buttons very much.
   (help / take)

6. Sometimes I _____ Buttons a bath. Both my brother and Buttons enjoyed it.
   (get / give)

7. When I have children, I plan to _____ a pet. It's a great learning experience.
   (let / have)

C | *Find and correct eight mistakes.*

Lately I've been thinking a lot about all the people who helped me adjusting to moving here when I was a kid. My parents got me join some school clubs so that I met other kids. Then my dad helped me improves my soccer game so I could join the team. And my mom never let me to stay home. She made me to get out and do things. My parents also spoke to my new teacher, and they had her called on me a lot so the other kids got to know me quickly. The neighbors helped too. They got I to walk their dog Red, and Red introduced me to all her human friends! The fact that so many people wanted to help me made me to realize that I was not alone. Before long I felt part of my new school, my new neighborhood, and my new life.

From Grammar to Writing

USING PARALLEL FORMS: GERUNDS AND INFINITIVES

When you write a **list using gerunds or infinitives**, make sure the items are in **parallel form**. If a list starts with a gerund, all items in that list should be gerunds. If it starts with an infinitive, all items in the list should be infinitives.

> **EXAMPLE:** Homer loved hunting, fishing, and ~~to hike~~. →
> Homer loved **hunting**, **fishing**, and **hiking**.
> **OR**
> Homer loved **to hunt**, **fish**, and **hike**. → one *to*

Notice that in a list of infinitives it is not necessary to repeat *to*.

1 | *Read this movie summary. Correct any gerunds or infinitives that are not parallel.*

OCTOBER SKY
Directed by Joe Johnston

Present tense.

It's October 1957, and the Soviet Union has just launched *Sputnik*. Homer, a teenage boy (played by Jake Gyllenhaal), watches the satellite fly over his poor coal-mining town in West Virginia and dreams of building and ~~to launch~~ *launching* his own rocket. He teams up with three friends, and "The Rocket Boys" start to put together and firing their homemade missiles. The boys' goal is to win the regional science fair. First prize will bring college scholarships and a way out of Coalwood. The school science teacher, Miss Riley, encourages him, but Homer's father (played by Chris Cooper) is angry about the boys' project. He wants Homer to follow in his footsteps and working at the mine. Nevertheless, the boys continue launching rockets, failing in different ways, and to learn with each failure. People begin changing their minds and to admire the Rocket Boys. Some even help them.

However, success does not come easily in Coalwood. When a forest fire starts nearby, a rocket is blamed, and the boys must give up their project. Then Homer's father is injured, and Homer quits school to support his family as a miner. His father is proud of him, but Homer can't stand giving up his dream and to work in the mine.

He uses mathematics to prove a rocket did not start the fire. Then he tells his father he plans to leave the mine and returning to school.

The Rocket Boys win first prize at the science fair, and all four of them receive scholarships. The whole town celebrates, and Homer wins another very valuable prize—his father attends the science fair and launches the rocket. It's clear that father and son will try to make peace and respecting each other.

2 | *Complete the story map with information from Exercise 1.*

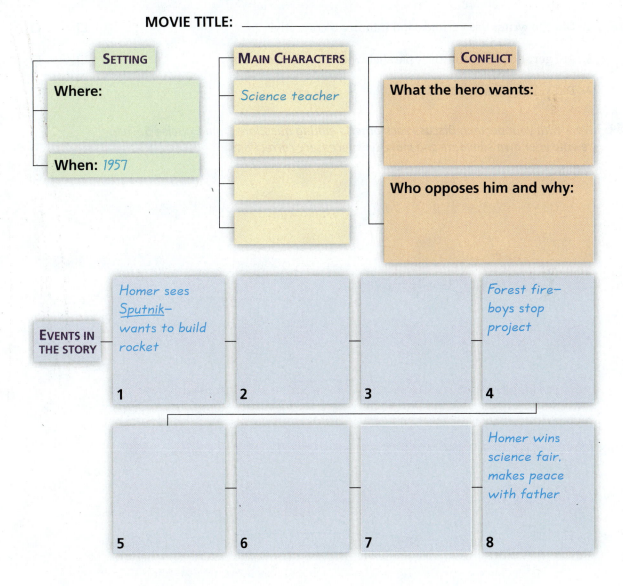

MOVIE TITLE: _____

SETTING

Where:

When: *1957*

MAIN CHARACTERS

Science teacher

CONFLICT

What the hero wants:

Who opposes him and why:

EVENTS IN THE STORY

1. *Homer sees Sputnik— wants to build rocket*
2.
3.
4. *Forest fire— boys stop project*
5.
6.
7.
8. *Homer wins science fair, makes peace with father*

3 | *Before you write . . .*

1. Work with a partner. Choose a movie or TV show that you have both seen or a story that you have both read.

2. Create a story map like the one in Exercise 2.

4 | *Write a summary about the movie, TV show, or story you chose in Exercise 3. Use your story map for information. Remember to use gerunds and infinitives.*

5 | *Exchange your writing with a different partner. Underline gerunds once. Underline infinitives twice. Write a question mark (?) over anything that seems wrong in your partner's summary. Answer the following questions.*

	Yes	No
1. Did the writer use gerunds and infinitives?	☐	☐
2. Did the writer use gerunds and infinitives correctly?	☐	☐
3. Are gerunds and infinitives parallel when they are in a list?	☐	☐
4. Did you understand the story?	☐	☐

6 | *Work with your partner. Discuss each other's editing questions from Exercise 5. Then rewrite your own summary and make any necessary corrections.*

PHRASAL VERBS

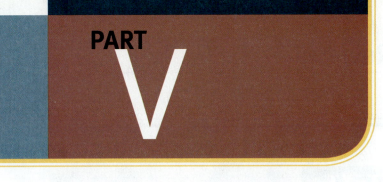

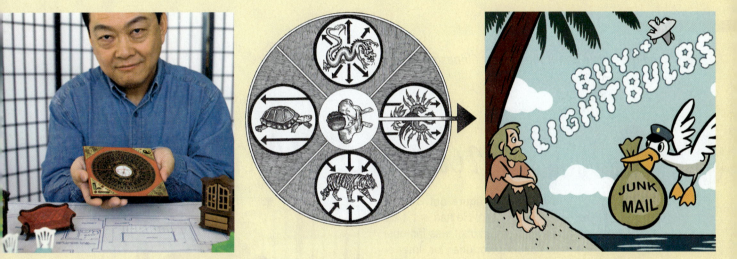

STEP 1 GRAMMAR IN CONTEXT

Before You Read

Look at the photo and read the caption. Discuss the questions.

1. What kind of advice do you think a feng shui consultant gives about people's homes?
2. Do you think the furniture and colors in your home affect your life? If yes, how?

Read

Read the article about the ancient Chinese art of feng shui.

Wind and Water

Ho Da-ming couldn't **figure out** why his restaurant was failing. He had **set it up** on a busy street. His chef was famous. He had paid a fortune for interior design.[1] But customers rarely **came back**. Why? Mr. Ho **called in** a feng shui consultant to **find out**. Feng shui (meaning "wind and water" and pronounced FUNG SHWAY) is the ancient Chinese art of placing things in the environment. According to this art, the arrangement of furniture, doors, and windows affects our health, wealth, and happiness.

The consultant used a *loupan* (a feng shui compass) to **look into** the patterns of energy in the restaurant. He told Mr. Ho that the entrance was **letting** prosperity[2] **out**. The desperate owner quickly **tore down** the old entrance and **put up** a new one. His action **paid off**. Soon business **picked up**, and Mr. Ho became rich.

A feng shui consultant on the job with his *loupan*

---

[1] ***interior design:*** the selection and arrangement of furniture and other objects in a room
[2] ***prosperity:*** having money and other things needed for a good life

Wind and Water

Feng shui has **caught on** with modern architects and homeowners everywhere. Although the complex charts of feng shui are hard to **work out**, the theory is simple: We are part of nature, and we must adjust to its natural energies. To be healthy and prosperous, we must **lay out** our homes and workplaces to allow *chi* (good energy) to circulate gently and to **cut off** *sha* (harmful energy).

Try this activity **out** in your home, dorm room, or office. First **sit down** and think about how you feel in this room. Now look around. Try to **pick out** the things that make you feel good or bad. To **find out** more, **look up** the topic online or go to your library or bookstore and **pick up** a book on basic feng shui. You'll be surprised at what you learn.

After You Read

A | Vocabulary: *Complete the sentences with the words from the box.*

complex	consultant	environment	harmful	theory

1. If you need advice, you can hire a(n) _____.

2. What is the _____ behind feng shui?

3. It's not an easy question. In fact, it's very _____.

4. It's very important to have a nice _____ to live and work in.

5. What's wrong with having a window there? Why is that _____?

B | Comprehension: *Check (✓)* **True** *or* **False**. *Correct the false statements.*

	True	False
1. Mr. Ho called in a consultant because his chef needed help.	☐	☑
2. Mr. Ho hadn't spent much on the restaurant's appearance.	☐	☑
3. The restaurant's customers usually didn't return.	☑	☐
4. Feng shui has been used for a very long time.	☑	☐
5. Mr. Ho changed the location of his restaurant.	☐	☑
6. Today, many architects use the ideas of feng shui.	☑	☐
7. To find out more about feng shui, you need to hire a consultant.	☐	☑

PHRASAL VERBS: REVIEW

Transitive Phrasal Verbs

Not Separated			
Subject	Verb	Particle	Direct Object
She He	called	in	a consultant.
	figured	out	the problem.

Separated			
Subject	Verb	Direct Object	Particle
She He	called	a consultant him	in.
	figured	the problem it	out.

Intransitive Phrasal Verbs

Not Separated			
Subject	Verb	Particle	
They It	came	back	quickly.
	caught	on	everywhere.

GRAMMAR NOTES

1 A **phrasal verb** (also called a *two-word verb*) has two parts: a verb and a particle.

        verb + particle = phrasal verb

Particles look like prepositions, but they act differently.

  a. Prepositions <u>do not change the meaning</u> of the verb.

  b. Particles often <u>change the meaning</u> of the verb.

VERB + PARTICLE
- Let's **figure out** this problem now.

VERB + PARTICLE
- Ho **called in** a consultant.

VERB + PREPOSITION
- He **looked into** the room.
  *(He was outside the room and **looked** in.)*

VERB + PARTICLE
- He **looked into** the problem.
  *(He **researched** the problem.)*

2 A **phrasal verb** has a **special meaning**, often very different from the meanings of its parts.

PHRASAL VERB	MEANING
call in	hire
figure out	understand
find out	discover
look into	research
pick up	improve

USAGE NOTE: Phrasal verbs are more **informal** than one-word verbs with similar meaning. They are very **common in everyday speech**. You have to learn the meaning of phrasal verbs to understand spoken English.

BE CAREFUL! Like other verbs, phrasal verbs often have **more than one meaning**.

- Let's **call in** an expert to help.
- We had to **figure out** the problem.
- Did you **find out** what was wrong?
- We **looked into** feng shui.
- Business has **picked up**.

- We're **putting up** signs for our business.
  (We're erecting signs for our business.)

- Please **turn down** the radio. It's too loud.
  (Please lower the volume.)
- Bill didn't get the job. They **turned down** his application.
  (They rejected his application.)

(continued on next page)

3 Many phrasal verbs are **transitive**. They have **objects**.

Phrasal Verb	Meaning
call off something	cancel
pick out something	choose
take away something	remove
think up something	invent
work out something	solve

PHRASAL VERB + OBJECT

- Let's **call off** *the meeting.*
- **Pick out** *the chair* you like best.
- **Take away** *the dishes*.
- He **thought up** *good answers*.
- He **worked out** *the problem*.

Most transitive phrasal verbs are **separable**. This means that **noun objects** can go:
- **after** the particle OR

- **between** the verb and the particle

VERB + PARTICLE + OBJECT

- They **tore down** *the entrance*. OR

VERB + OBJECT + PARTICLE

- They **tore** *the entrance* down.

BE CAREFUL! If the direct object is a **pronoun**, it must go <u>between</u> the verb and the particle.

- I didn't understand the word, so I **looked** *it* up in the dictionary.
  NOT: I ~~looked up it~~

USAGE NOTE: When the noun object is part of a **long phrase**, we usually <u>do not separate</u> the verb and particle of a phrasal verb.

- Ho **tried out** *the many complex theories of feng shui*.
  Not: Ho ~~tried the many complex theories of feng shui out~~.

4 Some phrasal verbs are **intransitive**. They do **NOT** have an object. They are always **inseparable**.

Phrasal Verb	Meaning
catch on	become popular
get ahead	make progress
show up	appear
sit down	take a seat

- Feng shui has **caught on** all over.
- Tina is **getting ahead** in her career.
- The consultant **showed up** early.
- **Sit down** over there.

BE CAREFUL! Do **NOT** separate an intransitive phrasal verb.

Not: Sit ~~over there down~~.

REFERENCE NOTES
For a list of **transitive phrasal verbs**, see Appendix 18 on page A-6.
For information about **transitive verbs that are inseparable**, see Unit 12.
For a list of **intransitive phrasal verbs**, see Appendix 19 on page A-8.

EXERCISE 1: Discover the Grammar

A | *Read the article about feng shui. Underline all the phrasal verbs and circle the direct objects of the transitive phrasal verbs. Go to Appendices 18 and 19 on pages A-6 and A-8 for help.*

Everyday Feng Shui

Have you noticed that some spaces cheer you up and give you energy, while others bring you down? This feng shui diagram uses mythological animals[1] to explain why. Look it over, and then imagine yourself in the center. According to feng shui theory, a phoenix takes off in front of you and gives you inspiration.[2] Behind you, a tortoise guards you from harmful things you cannot see. On your left and right, a dragon and a tiger balance each other. The dragon floats above the floor and helps you take in the big picture, not just small details. The tiger's energy gives you courage.

These symbols can be important in setting up a work environment. Dana, for example, needed ideas and energy in order to get ahead. Unfortunately, her undecorated, windowless cubicle[3] took away most of her powers. After she hung up a scenic poster in the phoenix area in front of her desk, she began to feel more inspired. She gave her tiger some power by picking out plants to put on the file cabinet to her right. For her dragon, she hung a cheerful mobile from the top of the left wall of her cubicle. Try these ideas out in your own work area and see what happens!

---

[1] **mythological animals:** animals in ancient stories about natural or historical events
[2] **inspiration:** something that causes you to produce good or beautiful things
[3] **cubicle:** a small part of a room, especially in an office, that is separated from the rest of the room by low walls

B | *Read the statements and check (✓)* **True** *or* **False**. *Correct the false statements.*

		True	False
1.	Your environment ~~can't~~ *can* bring about changes in your mood.	☐	☑
2.	The phoenix remains sitting in the space ahead of you.	☐	☐
3.	The dragon's energy helps you understand an overall plan.	☑	☐
4.	Dana wanted a promotion.	☑	☐
5.	From the beginning, Dana's work area *didn't* inspired her.	☐	☑
6.	She removed a poster from the area in front of her desk.	☐	☑
7.	There ~~were no~~ *is* plants in her cubicle at first.	☐	☑

EXERCISE 2: Particles

(Grammar Note 1)

Circle the correct particles to complete these questions and answers from an online feng shui message board. Go to Appendix 18 on page A-6 for help.

Q: I've been having a lot of trouble sleeping. My bed faces north. Is that *really* harmful?

A: Yes. Turn it (around) / up so that your head is to the north and your feet to the south.
     1.

Q: Our building owner has cut down / up all the trees in our garden. Now he's going to put (on) / up
     2.   **3.**

a tall building there! This will block away / (out) all our light. What can we do?
                                             4.

A: I don't know if you can work this problem (off) / out. You may need to think about moving.
                                               5.

Q: I am opening a new restaurant in Los Angeles. I would like to have a feng shui consultant look it

(over) / up to see if the energy is positive. Could you recommend someone?
6.

A: We don't give out / up names online. Email me, and I will put (together) / off a list for you.
              7.   **8.**

Q: I hung (up) / out a beautiful mirror on my bedroom wall. Then I read that mirrors bring too much
           9.

energy into a bedroom. I don't want to take it out / (down)! What can I do?
                                             10.

A: Before you go to sleep, put a scarf over the mirror. That will keep on / (out) the "bad energy."
                                                                          11.

Q: I don't know much about feng shui. How can I find after / (out) more about the theory behind it?
                                                             12.

A: There are hundreds of books about feng shui. Go to your local library and take some (out) / up.
                                                                                      13.

Or look after / (up) feng shui on an online bookstore website to get a list of titles.
     14.

EXERCISE 3: Meaning of Phrasal Verbs

(Grammar Notes 2–3)

Read about one of the most famous modern architects. Complete the information with the
correct forms of the phrasal verbs from the boxes. Go to Appendices 18 and 19 on pages
A-6 and A-8 for help.

| ~~grow up~~ | put up | settle on | turn out |

Born in 1917, Ieoh Ming Pei (better known as I. M.

Pei) _____grew up_____ in Canton, China. As a child,
        1.

Pei watched workers _putting up_ large new
                    2.

buildings. When he was 17, he went to the United States

to learn about building. He considered becoming an

engineer or an architect. However, he didn't finally

settle on his career until after he enrolled in
  3.

I. M. Pei in front of the Louvre pyramid

college. As it _turned out_, Pei became one of the most famous modern architects in
              4.

the world.

| figure out | go up | let in | put on | tear down |

Pei is famous for his strong geometric forms made of steel, glass, concrete, and stone.

One of his most controversial projects was his glass pyramid at the Louvre in Paris. The old

museum was dark, confusing, and crowded, but no one wanted to _tear down_ the
                                                              5.

old structure. Pei had to _figured out_ a solution to the Louvre's complex problems
                        6.

and still be sensitive to the famous old building and its surroundings. When he proposed his

71-foot-high glass pyramid as a new entrance to the museum, many Parisians were shocked,

and they _put on_ buttons asking "Why the pyramid?" However, the glass _put_
        7.

pyramid _went up_ anyway, blending with the environment, reflecting the sky,
        8.

and _let in_ the sunlight. Today, many people say that it is a good example of
    9.

the principles of feng shui.

(continued on next page)

Phrasal Verbs: Review   **179**

give up	go back		keep on	set up

In spite of harsh criticism, Pei _kept on_
10.
building structures that reflected their environment—

from the 70-story Bank of China skyscraper in Hong

Kong to the Rock 'n' Roll Hall of Fame in Cleveland,

Ohio. He has received many prizes and has become very

prosperous. He has used some of the prize money to

Inside the Louvre pyramid

set up a scholarship fund for Chinese
11.

students to study architecture in the United States and then to _go back_ to China
12.

to work as architects.

Pei is both creative and persistent. Throughout his career, many people have criticized

his work, but Pei strongly believes that "you have to identify the important things and press

for them and not _give up_."
13.

EXERCISE 4: Pronoun Objects

(Grammar Note 2)

Complete the conversations. Use the correct form of the phrasal verb in the first line of the conversation. Include a pronoun object.

1. **A:** Could I borrow your truck? I need to pick up some chairs this week.

   B: Sure. When are you _____ going to pick them up _____?

2. **A:** Hey! Who took down my feng shui posters?

   B: Sorry. I _____. I thought you didn't like them anymore.

3. **A:** I need to cheer up my roommate. He just flunked a big test.

   B: Why don't you straighten up the room? That will _____.

4. **A:** This room is depressing. Let's try out some of these feng shui ideas.

   B: I agree. Let's _____ this weekend.

5. **A:** We need something to light up that corner. It's awfully dark.

   B: I have an extra lamp. This will _____ nicely.

6. **A:** Can someone touch up the paint in my dorm room? It's cracked in several places.

   B: Sure. We'll send someone to _____ next week.

EXERCISE 5: Editing

Read this student's journal entry. There are ten mistakes in the use of phrasal verbs. The first mistake is already corrected. Find and correct nine more. Go to Appendices 18 and 19 on pages A-6 and A-8 for help.

> I just read an article about feng shui. The author suggests sitting ~~up~~ *down* in your home and thinking about how your environment makes you feel. I tried out it.
>
> My apartment is bright and sunny. This cheers me out. At night, it's very dark, but I've figured up what to do. I'm going to buy another lamp to light the apartment at night up. I'll leave it on when I go out at night so I can see light as soon as I come in. I also like the light green walls in my bedroom, but the chipped paint has been bringing down me. I'm going to touch it over soon.
>
> My apartment is too small, but I can't tear up the walls. I think it'll look more spacious if I just straighten it up. I'll try to put books back after I take them off the shelves and hang away my clothes at night. With just a few small changes, I'll end up feeling happier in my home. It's worth trying on. And I won't even need a consultant!

STEP 4 COMMUNICATION PRACTICE

EXERCISE 6: Listening

A | *Read the statements. Then listen to the short conversations. Listen again and check (✓)* **True** *or* **False.** *Correct the false statements.*

	True	False
1. Amy and Ben are talking about the ~~noise~~ *temperature* in their apartment.	☐	☑
2. Amy is interested in trying out feng shui.	☐	☐
3. Ben has finished redecorating his office.	☐	☐
4. Ben is a student.	☐	☐
5. Amy and Ben agree about the curtains.	☐	☐
6. The mattress is very comfortable.	☐	☐
7. Amy and Ben are going to paint the kitchen.	☐	☐

B | *Listen again to the conversations. Complete the sentences with the words that you hear. Then listen again and check your answers.*

1. It's a little too cold for me. Do you mind if I turn the air conditioner _____*down*_____?

2. I haven't had the chance to look it _____ yet.

3. I'm going to the furniture store today to pick _____ a new couch.

4. I'll put them _____ as soon as I'm done with my homework.

5. I'm going to take them _____ tomorrow.

6. I think we need to turn it _____.

7. Let's look _____ some colors online.

EXERCISE 7: Pronunciation

A | *Read and listen to the Pronunciation Note.*

Pronunciation Note
For many **phrasal verbs**, the verb ends in a consonant sound and the particle begins with a vowel sound.   In conversation, we often **link** the **final consonant** sound to the **beginning vowel** sound.   **EXAMPLES:** Could you **pick up** a book about feng shui?   I'm going to **turn on** the heat.

B | *Listen to the short conversations. Draw linking lines (‿) from the final consonant in the verb to the beginning vowel in the particle.*

1. **A:** Did you **find out** anything more about feng shui?

   B: No. I'm going to **look over** some information now.

2. **A:** Have you **made up** your mind about the paint color?

   B: Not yet. But I'm sure I'll **come up** with something.

3. **A:** So, do you think we should **hang up** some paintings on that wall?

   B: Maybe we can just **pick up** a few posters from the store.

4. **A:** We need a better lamp to **light up** this room.

   B: I know. Maybe we can **pick out** one from this website.

5. A: This room is a mess. Can you **put away** some of your stuff?

   B: No problem. As soon as I **clean out** this closet.

6. A: Hey, it's dark in here. Let's **turn on** some lights.

   B: OK. And I'll **turn off** the heat too. It's hot in here.

C | *Listen again to the conversations. Then practice them with a partner.*

EXERCISE 8: Problem Solving

Work in small groups. How would you like to change your classroom or your school? What would you like to remain the same? Use some of these phrasal verbs in your discussion.

cover up	light up	put away	throw away
do over	make up	put up	touch up
hang up	move around	straighten up	turn around
leave on	pick out	tear down	turn on / off

EXAMPLE: **A:** I think we should hang up some posters.
B: It would be nice to hang some photographs up too.
C: We could hang some paintings up too.

EXERCISE 9: Compare and Contrast

*Work with a partner. Look at the **Before** and **After** pictures of Amy's room for two minutes. Write down all the differences you can find. Then compare your list with another pair's list.*

Before   After

EXAMPLE: **A:** She took the curtains down.
B: Right. And she also . . .

EXERCISE 10: Writing

A | *Write two paragraphs about how you feel in your home, office, dorm, or classroom. What makes you feel good? What makes you feel bad? What would you like to change? Use phrasal verbs. You can use the journal entry in Exercise 5 on page 181 as a model.*

EXAMPLE: My dorm room is bright and sunny. The room always cheers me up when I get back from a hard day at school. My roommate and I picked out the curtains together. We also put up some new posters on the walls . . .

B | *Check your work. Use the Editing Checklist.*

Editing Checklist
Did you . . . ?   ☐ use phrasal verbs   ☐ use the correct particles   ☐ put pronoun objects between the verb and the particle of separable phrasal verbs

A | *Circle the correct words to complete the sentences.*

1. We called <u>up / off</u> the meeting because so many people were on vacation.

2. The house was badly damaged by the storm. They're planning to tear <u>down it / it down</u>.

3. Ina is really getting <u>ahead / away</u> in her career. She's just gotten another promotion.

4. I hadn't heard of I. M. Pei, so I looked him <u>out / up</u> online.

5. Let's straighten this room up. I'll start by putting <u>away / over</u> my books.

6. I really don't like the new lamp. Let's take it <u>over / back</u> to the store and get another one.

7. I just bought a new couch. I'm going to pick <u>it up / up it</u> tomorrow.

B | *Complete the conversations with the correct form of the phrasal verbs from the box.*

figure out	leave on	show up	touch up
find out	settle on	take down	turn off

- **A:** Why did you _____ my poster?
  1.
  B: I needed to _____ the paint on that wall.
  2.
- **A:** Will Ana ever _____ a career? She changes her mind every month.
  3.
  B: It's a problem, but I think she'll _____ it _____ herself.
  4.
- **A:** The plumber was supposed to come today, but he didn't _____.
  5.
  B: Why don't you call and _____ what happened?
  6.
- **A:** We _____ the light _____ in the car. I can see it from here.
  7.
  B: You're right. I'll go _____ it _____.
  8.

C | *Find and correct five mistakes.*

A: This apartment is bringing me down. Let's do over it.

B: It *is* depressing. Let's put around a list and figure out what to do first.

A: OK. Write this down: Pick on new paint colors. We can look at some online.

B: The new streetlight shines into the bedroom. We need to block up the light somehow.

A: We could put on some dark curtains in that room. That should take care of the problem.

STEP 1 GRAMMAR IN CONTEXT

Before You Read

Look at the cartoon. Discuss the questions.

1. Who do you think is calling the man? How does the man feel about the call?
2. Do you receive unwanted calls? How do you feel about them?

Read

Read the magazine article about telemarketers.

WELCOME HOME!

You just **got back** from a long, hard day at the office. You're exhausted. All you want to do is **take off** your jacket, **put down** your briefcase, and relax over a great dinner. Then, just as you're about to **sit down** at the table, the phone rings. You hesitate to **pick** it **up**. It's probably just another telemarketer trying to **talk** you **into** buying something you really don't need. But, what if it's not? It could be important. Maybe there's a family emergency. You have to **find out**!

"Hello?" you answer nervously.

"Hello, is this Mr. Groaner?" a strange voice asks. You know right away that it's a telemarketer. Your last name is Groden.

"I just got home. Can you call back tomorrow when I'm still at work?"

"We have great news for you! You've been chosen to receive an all-expense-paid trip to the Bahamas! It's an offer you can't afford to **turn down**!"

Telemarketing—the practice of selling products and services by phone—is rapidly spreading throughout the world as the number of household phones **goes up** and phone rates **come down**. To most people, these annoying calls are about as welcome as a bad case of the flu.

What can be done about this invasion of privacy?[1] Look at the next page for several tactics you can **try out**.

[1]*invasion of privacy:* interrupting or getting involved in another's personal life in an unwelcome way

WELCOME HOME!

☎ **Sign up** to have your phone number placed on "Do Not Call" lists. Many countries are **setting up** lists of people who do not want to be called by telemarketers. These lists actually make it against the law for telemarketers to call you. If you still receive these calls, **write down** the date and time of the call. **Find out** the name of the organization calling you. You can then report the illegal call to the proper authorities.

☎ Use Caller ID to help identify telemarketers. If an unfamiliar number **shows up** on your ID screen, don't **pick up** the phone.

☎ If you *have* answered the phone, say (firmly but politely!): "I'm **hanging up** now," and **get off** the phone.

☎ Ask the telemarketing company to **take** you **off** their list. But don't **count on** this happening immediately. You may have to ask several times before it takes effect.

None of these measures will eliminate all unwanted telephone solicitations,[2] but they should help **cut down** the number of calls that you receive.

Telemarketing, however, is just part of the larger problem. We are constantly being flooded with unwanted offers and requests. "Junk mail" **fills up** our mailboxes (and later our trash cans when we **throw** it **out**).

And the invasion is, of course, not limited to paper. When you **turn on** your computer to check your email, you are greeted by dozens of commercial messages. Known as *spam*, it's the electronic equivalent of junk mail.

What's the solution? Leave home? Move to a desert island? Maybe not. They'll probably **get to** you there too!

---

[2]*solicitation:* asking someone for something such as money or help

---

After You Read

A | **Vocabulary:** *Circle the word or phrase that best completes each sentence.*

1. If Jason **constantly** calls you, he <u>always / sometimes / never</u> calls you.

2. The **authorities** are people that <u>buy / control / write</u> about things.

3. If you **eliminate** a problem, the problem <u>disappears / gets better / gets worse</u>.

4. If two things are **equivalent**, they are <u>the same / different / expensive</u>.

5. Telemarketers' **tactics** are their <u>products / sales methods / prices</u>.

6. If you can **identify** someone, you <u>ask / know / like</u> the person's name.

B | Comprehension: *Check (✓)* **True** *or* **False.** *Correct the false statements.*

	True	False
1. Mr. Groden got a call from a telemarketer in the morning.	☐	☐
2. The telemarketer didn't pronounce his name correctly.	☐	☐
3. Most people welcome these calls.	☐	☐
4. If your name is on a Do Not Call list, it is illegal for a telemarketer to call you.	☐	☐
5. You can do something to stop *all* of these unwanted calls.	☐	☐
6. Telemarketing is just one example of an invasion of privacy.	☐	☐

STEP 2 GRAMMAR PRESENTATION

PHRASAL VERBS: SEPARABLE AND INSEPARABLE

Separable Transitive			
Subject	Verb	Particle	Direct Object
She	picked	up	the phone.

Separable Transitive			
Subject	Verb	Direct Object	Particle
She	picked	the phone it	up.

Inseparable Transitive			
Subject	Verb	Particle	Direct Object
He	counts	on	your calls. them.

Intransitive		
Subject	Verb	Particle
They	sat	down.

GRAMMAR NOTES

1

As you learned in Unit 11, **phrasal verbs** have two parts: a verb and a particle.

verb + **particle** = **phrasal verb**

Particles look like prepositions, but they act differently.

Particles often **change the meaning** of the verb, but prepositions do not.

VERB + PARTICLE
• I **got off** the phone quickly.

VERB + PREPOSITION
• I **looked up** and saw a large bird.
  (*I looked toward the sky.*)

VERB + PARTICLE
• I **looked up** his number online.
  (*I tried to find his number.*)

2

Many phrasal verbs are **transitive**: they take an **object**. And most transitive phrasal verbs are **separable**. This means that **noun objects** can go <u>after</u> the particle <u>or between</u> the verb and the particle.

BE CAREFUL! If the direct object is a **pronoun**, it must go <u>between</u> the verb and the particle.

USAGE NOTE: When the noun object is part of a **long phrase**, we usually <u>do not separate</u> the verb and particle of a phrasal verb.

A small group of transitive phrasal verbs **must be separated**.

PHRASAL VERB	MEANING
keep something **on**	not remove
ask someone **over**	invite to one's home

VERB + PARTICLE + OBJECT
• I just **took off** *my coat*. OR

VERB + OBJECT + PARTICLE
• I just **took** *my coat* **off**.

• I **wrote** *it* **down**.
  NOT: I wrote ~~down it~~.

• I **filled out** *the form from the Do Not Call service*.
  NOT: ~~I filled the form from the Do Not Call service out.~~

• **Keep** *your coat* **on**. NOT: Keep ~~on your coat~~.
• **Ask** *Ian* **over**. NOT: Ask ~~over Ian~~.

3

Some **transitive** phrasal verbs are **inseparable**. This means that both noun and pronoun objects always go <u>after</u> the particle. You cannot separate the verb from its particle.

REMEMBER: Some phrasal verbs are **intransitive**: They do not take an object.

Like other verbs, some phrasal verbs can be **both transitive and intransitive**. The meaning is often the same.

BE CAREFUL! Some phrasal verbs have a completely **different meaning** when they are transitive or intransitive.

• I **ran into** *Karim* at work.
  NOT: I ~~ran Karim into~~ at work.
• I **ran into** *him* at work.
  NOT: I ~~ran him into~~.

• He's been away and just **got back**.
• They don't **give up**. They keep calling.

• He **called** *me* **back**.
• He **called back**.

• We **made up** a story. (*=invented*)
• We **made up**. (*=ended a disagreement*)

(continued on next page)

4 Some **transitive phrasal verbs** are used in combination with **prepositions** such as *of*, *to*, *with*, *at*, and *for*.

A **phrasal verb** + **preposition** combination (also called a *three-word verb*) is usually **inseparable**.

PHRASAL VERB	MEANING
come up *with* something	invent
drop out *of* something	quit
keep up *with* something/someone	go as fast as

- She **came up** *with* a way to stop junk mail.
- I **dropped out** *of* school and got a job.
- He couldn't **keep up** *with* his email. There was too much to read.

REFERENCE NOTES

For a list of **separable phrasal verbs**, see Appendix 18 on page A-6.
For a list of **inseparable transitive phrasal verbs**, see Appendix 18 on page A-6.
For a list of **phrasal verbs that must be separated**, see Appendix 18 on page A-6.
For a list of **phrasal verb + preposition combinations**, see Appendix 18 on page A-6.
For a list of **intransitive phrasal verbs**, see Appendix 19 on page A-8.

STEP 3 FOCUSED PRACTICE

EXERCISE 1: Discover the Grammar

A | *Read this article about ways of dealing with telemarketers. Underline the phrasal verbs.*

<u>HOLD ON</u>, PLEASE! Your phone number is on the Do Not Call list, but you keep on receiving telemarketing calls. Constantly. Why not have some fun with them? We came up with these amusing tactics:

- When the telemarketer asks, "How are you today?"—tell her! Don't leave anything out. Say, "I have a headache you wouldn't believe, and my back is acting up again. Now I can't figure out the instructions for my DVD player . . ."

- When a telemarketer calls during dinner, request his home telephone number so you can call him back. When he refuses, ask him to hold on. Put the phone down and continue eating until you hear the dial tone.

- Ask the telemarketer to spell her first and last name and the name of the company. Tell her to speak slowly—you're taking notes. Ask questions until she hangs up.

- To credit card offers, say, "Thanks a lot! My company just laid me off, and I really need the money!"

B | Write down each phrasal verb from the article next to its meaning.

1. _____ causing problems

2. _____ continue

3. _____ ends a phone call

4. _____ fired from a job

5. _____ invented

6. ___hold on___ not end a phone call

7. _____ omit

8. _____ return a call

9. _____ stop holding something

10. _____ understand

EXERCISE 2: Meaning

(Grammar Note 1)

A scam is a dishonest plan, usually to get money. Read about how to avoid some common scams. Complete the information with the correct forms of the phrasal verbs from the boxes. Go to Appendices 18 and 19 on pages A-6 and A-8 for help.

end up with	**hang up**	**let down**	~~**threw out**~~

I just ___threw out___ my first issue of *Motorcycle Mama*. I'm nobody's mama, and I
         1.

don't own a motorcycle, so how did I _____ this subscription? Well, my neighbor's
                                              2.

son was raising money for his soccer team, and I didn't want to _____ him

_____. It's easy to _____ on telemarketers, but it's hard to say *no* to
       3.   **4.**

your friends and neighbors.

fall for	**get to**	**help out**	**watch out for**

The magazine company _____ me through a friendship. It's one of the ways
                             5.

"persuasion professionals" get us to say *yes*. Of course it's OK to _____ the local soccer
                                                                         6.

team. But a lot of people _____ scams because of similar techniques. Learn to identify
                              7.

and _____ these common scams.
       8.

find out	**give back**	**go along with**	**turn down**

When someone gives you something, you want to _____ something

_____. This desire to return a favor can cost you money when a telemarketer
       9.

announces you've won a vacation or a new car. These offers aren't free. When people

_____ them, they always _____ that there's a tax or a fee to
       10.   **11.**

collect the "free" prize. Since they've accepted the offer, they feel obligated to pay. You should

_____ these offers _____. These are scams and they are illegal.
                                  12.

(continued on next page)

count on	fill out	pick out	put on	turn up

A TV actor will _____ **13.** a doctor's white jacket and talk about cough medicine. In a magazine ad, a woman in a business suit will help you _____ **14.** the best investment firm. Ads with fake "authority figures" are quite easy to identify, but there's an Internet scam called *phishing* that's harder to recognize. The scammer sends emails that seem to be from well-known banks. They tell you that a problem with your account has _____ **15.** . Then they send you to an Internet site to _____ **16.** forms with your account information and password. The site looks like the real thing, but a real bank will NEVER ask for your information over the Internet. You can _____ **17.** that! Tell the authorities right away about any phishing scams.

EXERCISE 3: Separable Phrasal Verbs and Pronoun Objects (Grammar Note 2)

Complete the conversations. Use phrasal verbs and pronouns.

1. **A:** Tell Ana not to pick up the phone. It's probably a telemarketer. They call constantly.

   B: Too late. She's already _____ *picked it up* _____ .

2. **A:** You can't turn down this great offer for cat food!

   B: I'm afraid I have to _____. I don't *have* a cat.

3. **A:** Did you fill out the online Do Not Call form?

   B: I _____ yesterday. I hope this will take care of the

   problem. I'm tired of these calls.

4. **A:** I left out my office phone and fax numbers on that form.

   B: Why did you _____?

5. **A:** Remember to call your mother back.

   B: I _____ last night.

6. **A:** Did you write down the dates of the calls?

   B: I _____, but then I lost the piece of paper.

7. **A:** Can you take my mother's name off your calling list?

   B: Sure. We'll _____ right away.

8. **A:** Let's turn the phone off and have dinner.

   B: I can't _____. I'm expecting an important call.

EXERCISE 4: Separable and Inseparable Phrasal Verbs

(Grammar Notes 2–4)

Complete the ads from spam emails. Use the correct forms of the phrasal verbs and objects in parentheses. Place the object between the verb and the particle when possible. Go to Appendices 18 and 19 on pages A-6 and A-8 for help.

Lose Weight!

Take those extra pounds off fast! Love bread and cake? Don't _____.
1. (take off / those extra pounds)   **2. (give up / them)**

No diet! No pills! No exercise! Our delicious drinks will _____ while you
3. (fill up / you)

lose weight. _____ at no cost. It's FREE for one month!
4. (try out / our plan)

Our weight loss secrets can be yours today. _____ as soon as you
5. (find out / them)

_____. Want to know more? Click <u>here</u> for our information request form.
6. (sign up for / our plan)

_____ to get our brochure. Just _____ and watch
7. (fill out / it)   **8. (stick to / our plan)**

those pounds come off! If you do not want to receive email from us, we will be more than happy to

_____ our list.
9. (take off / you)

💰 Make $$$$ working from home! 💰

_____ cash and increase your savings without leaving your home!
1. (turn into / your hobby)

My home-based business constantly _____ a day. That's right—and I
2. (take in / $2,000)

_____ every week. Sure, I could _____, but I'd
3. (turn down / work)   **4. (take on / employees)**

rather teach **you** how to _____. This is an easy business, and you can
5. (go after / those jobs)

_____ in a few days. Click on the <u>$</u>, and I'll _____
6. (set up / it)   **7. (send out / the materials)**

right away. _____. If you don't like them, _____.
8. (check out / them)   **9. (send back / them)**

It's as simple as that! Don't _____! This offer is a money machine, so
10. (put off / it)

don't _____. Start to _____ by next week!
11. (pass up / it)   **12. (cash in on / this great opportunity)**

EXERCISE 5: Editing

*Read the transcript of a phone call between a telemarketer (**TM**) and Janis Linder (**JL**). There are fourteen mistakes in the use of phrasal verbs. The first mistake is already corrected. Find and correct thirteen more.*

TM: Hello, Ms. Linder?

JL: Yes. Who's this?

TM: This is Bob Watson from *Motorcycle Mama*. I'm calling to offer you a 12-month subscription for the low price of just $15 a year. Can I sign ~~up you~~ *you up*?

JL: No thanks. I'm trying to eliminate clutter, so I'm not interested in signing in for any more magazine subscriptions. Besides, I just sat up for dinner.

TM: Why don't you at least try out it for six months? Don't pass this great opportunity down! It's a once in a lifetime chance.

JL: Sorry, I'm really not interested. I don't even have a motorcycle.

TM: Well then, this is a great opportunity to find all about them out! We'll send you a free copy, and you can look over it.

JL: You're not going to talk me in it! In fact, I'm going to hang the phone down right now. And please take my name out your list. If you keep calling, I'll notify the authorities.

TM: No, hold out! Don't go away! Don't turn this great offer down! You'll be sorry if you do. Chances like this don't come around every day! Don't miss it out on!

JL: OK. I have an idea. Why don't you give me your phone number, and I'll call back you during YOUR dinner?

[*The telemarketer hangs the phone.*]

JL: Hello? Hello?

EXERCISE 6: Listening

A | *Look at Mr. Chen's notes from a telemarketing call. Then listen to the call. Listen again and complete the notes.*

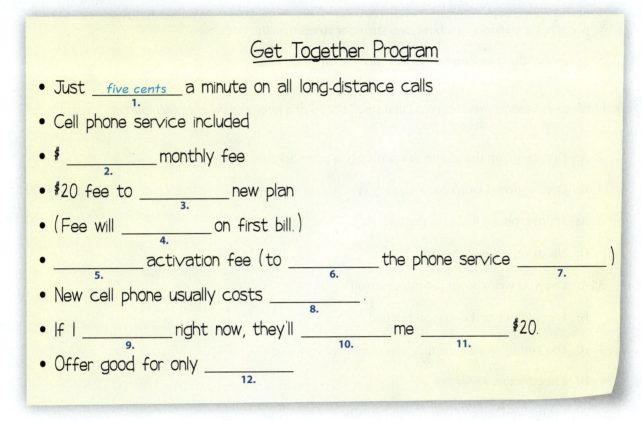

> ### Get Together Program
>
> - Just ___five cents___ a minute on all long-distance calls
>   1.
> - Cell phone service included
> - $ _____ monthly fee
>   2.
> - $20 fee to _____ new plan
>   3.
> - (Fee will _____ on first bill.)
>   4.
> - _____ activation fee (to _____ the phone service _____)
>   5.   6.   7.
> - New cell phone usually costs _____ .
>   8.
> - If I _____ right now, they'll _____ me _____ $20.
>   9.   10.   11.
> - Offer good for only _____
>   12.

B | *Listen again to the call. Check (✓) **True** or **False**. Correct the false statements.*

	True	False
Mr. 1. ~~Mrs.~~ Chen picks up the phone.	☐	☑
2. The telemarketer says she wants to help Mr. Chen out with his phone rates.	☐	☐
3. With the new program, Mr. Chen will run out of cell phone minutes after 20 hours a month.	☐	☐
4. There's a charge for setting up the new plan.	☐	☐
5. The cell phone is free.	☐	☐
6. The telemarketer is going to give Mr. Chen some time to think over the plan.	☐	☐
7. Mr. Chen is going to sign up for the service.	☐	☐

EXERCISE 7: Pronunciation

A | *Read and listen to the Pronunciation Note.*

> **Pronunciation Note**
>
> When a phrasal verb is **not separated**, the **verb and particle** usually have **equal stress**.
>
> But, when the **object** of a phrasal verb is a **pronoun** that comes between the verb and its **particle**, the **particle** usually receives **stronger stress** than the verb.
>
> EXAMPLES: Don't **pick up** the phone. BUT Don't **pick** it **up**.

B | *Listen to the short conversations. Put a small dot (•) or a large dot (●) over each part of the phrasal verbs to show stress.*

1. **A:** Don't pick up the phone. It's probably a telemarketer.

   B: Don't worry. I won't pick it up.

2. **A:** Did the phone wake up the baby?

   B: No. It didn't wake her up.

3. **A:** Can you write down the information?

   B: Sure. I'll write it down on the pad.

4. **A:** Did you fill out the form?

   B: I filled it out yesterday.

5. **A:** I think you left out your phone number.

   B: I didn't leave it out. Here it is.

6. **A:** Did you turn down the offer?

   B: Yes. I turned it down.

7. **A:** Let's turn off the phone and have dinner.

   B: I already turned it off.

C | *Listen again to the conversations and repeat each sentence. Then practice the conversations with a partner.*

EXERCISE 8: For or Against

A | *Work in a small group. Talk about these questions.*

• What do you think of telemarketing? Does it offer consumers anything positive? Or is it equivalent to junk mail?

• Should telemarketing be illegal? Do you go along with the idea of Do Not Call lists? Should some organizations be allowed to keep on calling you? If yes, what kind?

• Do you get a lot of calls from telemarketers? How do you handle them? Do you think people should just hang up? Or should they put them off with a polite excuse, such as, "Thanks. I'll think it over."?

EXAMPLE: **A:** I think telemarketing is a terrible idea.
B: Me too. I've never gotten anything useful out of a telemarketing call.
C: I just politely say I have to hang up, and then I get off the phone.

B | *Compare your answers with those of the rest of the class.*

EXERCISE 9: Discussion

Bring in an ad from a magazine, a piece of junk mail, spam, or an offer from the Internet. Discuss these ads in a group. Talk about these questions. Try to use some of the phrasal verbs in the list in your discussion. Go to Appendices 18 and 19 on pages A-6 and A-8 for help.

• What group of people might want this product or service (children, teenagers, older people, men, women)?

• What tactics does the ad use to get people to want this product or service?

• Is this an honest offer or a scam? What makes you think so?

cash in on s.t.	fall for s.t.	get to s.o.	miss out
catch on	fill s.t. out	go after s.o.	miss out on s.t.
count on s.t.	find s.t. out	help s.o. out	pay off
end up	get ahead	leave s.t. out	send s.t. back
end up with s.t.	get s.t. out of s.t.	make s.t. up	turn s.t. down

EXAMPLE: **A:** I think this ad is trying to get to teenagers.
B: I agree. It shows a group of teens fooling around and having a good time while they're drinking soda.
C: Right, but I don't think many teens will fall for this.

EXERCISE 10: Writing

A | *Write a paragraph about an experience you have had on the phone. It could be a conversation with a friend, a wrong number, or a telemarketing call. Use some of these phrasal verbs:*

call back	fall for	go on	keep on	think over
check out	figure out	go over	pick up	turn down
come up	find out	hang up	sign up	turn out
end up	give up	hold on	talk into	wake up

EXAMPLE: When I first got to this country, I had difficulty understanding English speakers on the phone. I often couldn't figure out what people were saying to me. I kept on asking the person to repeat. Sometimes I had to give up, say "Sorry," and hang up.

B | *Check your work. Use the Editing Checklist.*

Editing Checklist

Did you . . . ?
- ☐ use phrasal verbs
- ☐ use the correct particles
- ☐ put pronoun objects between the verb and the particle of separable phrasal verbs

UNIT 12 Review

Check your answers on page UR-3.

Do you need to review anything?

A | *Match each phrasal verb with its meaning.*

_____ **1.** pick up   **a.** remove

_____ **2.** look up   **b.** meet by accident

_____ **3.** take off   **c.** complete

_____ **4.** fill out   **d.** return

_____ **5.** run into   **e.** find in a dictionary

_____ **6.** get back   **f.** lift

_____ **7.** give up   **g.** quit

B | *Complete each sentence with the correct form of the phrasal verb and object in parentheses. Place the object between the verb and particle when possible.*

1. The phone rang at 11:00 P.M. It _____.
                                          (wake up / Jason)

2. I didn't want to _____, but I did.
                                 (pick up / it)

3. It was Ada. I can always _____ to call too late!
                                 (count on / her)

4. I asked her to _____ in the morning.
                                 (call back / me)

5. Then I _____.
                                 (get off / the phone)

6. I _____ and went to bed.
                                 (put on / my nightshirt)

7. Then I _____ and fell asleep.
                                 (turn off / the lights)

C | *Find and correct six mistakes.*

I'm so tired of telemarketers calling me up as soon as I get from work back or just when I sit up for a relaxing dinner! It's gotten to the point that I've stopped picking the phone when it rings between 6:00 to 8:00 P.M. up. I know I can count on it being a telemarketer who will try to talk me into spending money on something I don't want. But it's still annoying to hear the phone ring, so sometimes I turn off it. Then, of course, I worry that it may be someone important. So I end up checking caller ID to find out. I think the Do Not Call list is a great idea. Who thought up it? I'm going to sign for it up tomorrow!

From Grammar to Writing

USING THE APPROPRIATE LEVEL OF FORMALITY

Phrasal verbs are very common in **informal writing**. In more **formal writing**, however, we often use **one-word verbs or phrases** with similar meanings in place of some phrasal verbs.

EXAMPLES: I **threw away** your address by mistake. Can you resend it? (*less formal*)
I **discarded** your address by mistake. Could you resend it please? (*more formal*)

1 | *Match the phrasal verbs on the left with the more formal verbs and phrases on the right.*

Less Informal	More Formal
_f_ **1.** check out	**a.** appear
____ **2.** fix up	**b.** awaken
____ **3.** get on	**c.** assemble
____ **4.** get together with	**d.** board
____ **5.** give up	**e.** discard
____ **6.** go along with	**f.** examine
____ **7.** light up	**g.** illuminate
____ **8.** look into	**h.** indicate
____ **9.** pick up	**i.** meet
____ **10.** point out	**j.** purchase
____ **11.** put together	**k.** quit
____ **12.** show up	**l.** redecorate
____ **13.** sign up	**m.** register
____ **14.** throw away	**n.** research
____ **15.** wake up	**o.** support

2 | *Read the two notes. Complete them with the correct form of the verbs and phrases from Exercise 1. Use the appropriate level of formality.*

Hi Van,

I just moved into my new apartment, and I'm only half an hour from school! This morning I _____woke up_____ at 6:30 and jogged 2 miles before breakfast. I looked at my watch as I
1.

_____ the bus, and it was just 8:15—plenty of time to get to my 9:00 English class.
2.

In addition to English, I've also _____ for statistics this semester. It's hard, but I'm
3.

not going to _____. I'll need it for business school. The apartment has some
4.

problems, but I've been using your feng shui tips to _____ the living room. I just
5.

_____ a new computer workstation on sale, which I'm going to _____
6.   7.

this weekend. I'll need it for business school, which I _____ now. I also bought a
8.

desk lamp to help _____ my work area. More later . . .
9.

Marta

Dear Mr. Livingston:

I've just moved into apartment 4B, and I need to report some problems.

- The previous tenant _____ some furniture in front of the apartment house.
  1.

  It looks awful. Please have someone remove it.

- Before I moved in, I _____ that there was a problem with the lock on the back
  2.

  door. This is an important safety issue. A locksmith needs to _____ the lock
  3.

  and replace it if necessary.

- The tenant in 5B is very noisy. Some of the tenants would like to talk to her about this.

We hope you will _____ this plan and _____ at our next tenant's
4.   5.

meeting. If you would like to _____ to discuss these issues, please let me know.
6.

Sincerely,

Marta Nosko

Marta Nosko

3 | *Imagine that you have just moved into a new apartment building. Look at the picture of the lobby of the building. Work with a partner. Discuss the problems and make a list of the things that you want the landlord to do. Go to Appendices 18 and 19 on pages A-6 and A-8 for help.*

EXAMPLES: **A:** They really need to clean this place up. It's a mess.
   B: The first thing they could do is throw out the trash. It looks terrible.
   A: And they need to touch up the paint. It's peeling in several places.

1. *throw out the trash*   6. _____

2. *touch up the paint*   7. _____

3. _____   8. _____

4. _____   9. _____

5. _____   10. _____

4 | Work with your partner. Together, write a letter to the landlord of the building in Exercise 3. Describe the problems and ask the landlord to fix them. Try to use some more formal verbs when possible. Go to Appendices 18 and 19 on pages A-6 and A-8 for help.

EXAMPLE: Dear Ms. Bryce:

We'd like to make you aware of several problems in the lobby.
Here are some things that would improve its appearance and safety:

- Discard the trash. It looks terrible.

- Touch up the paint. It's peeling in several places.

We hope you can take care of these issues as soon as possible.
Thank you for your attention.

Sincerely,

5 | Exchange notes with another pair. Underline the verbs that suggest what the landlord should do. Then answer the following questions.

	Yes	No
1. Are there places where the writers could use more formal verbs instead of phrasal verbs?	☐	☐
2. If there are phrasal verbs with pronouns, are the pronouns in the right place?	☐	☐

6 | Discuss your editing suggestions with the other pair. Then rewrite your own letter. Make any necessary corrections.

ADJECTIVE CLAUSES

Adjective Clauses with Subject Relative Pronouns

FRIENDS AND PERSONALITY TYPES

STEP 1 GRAMMAR IN CONTEXT

Before You Read

Look at the cartoon and the caption. Discuss the questions.

1. What is the personality of an extrovert? An introvert?
2. Can people with very different personalities get along?

Read

Read the article about introverts and extroverts.

EXTROVERTS

AND

INTROVERTS

By Kurt Chattery

Extrovert: someone **who loves being in a group of people**
Introvert: someone **who avoids extroverts**

My friend Nadia, **who needs to spend several hours alone each day**, avoids large social gatherings whenever possible. She hates small talk, and at office holiday parties, **which are "must-attend" events**, she's always the first one to leave.

You probably know someone like Nadia. Maybe you're even one of those people **that nag[1] a friend like her to get out more**. If so, stop! Nadia is an introvert, and there's really nothing wrong with that. Introverts are people **that get their energy by spending time alone**. Their opposites are extroverts, people **whose energy comes from being around others**. Neither type is better than the other. However, because there are so many more extroverts than introverts, there is a lot of misunderstanding about the introverts among us.

First, most people think that all introverts are shy. Not so. Shy people fear social situations, but many introverts just try to avoid the ones **that drain[2] their energy**. Nadia, **who is great at leading big, noisy business meetings**, isn't afraid of those meetings. But she needs a lot of recovery time afterwards. Unlike extroverts, **who love the small talk at those meetings**, she prefers private conversations **that focus on feelings and ideas**.

[1] **nag:** to keep telling someone to do something in a way that is very annoying
[2] **drain:** to use too much of something so that there is not enough left

EXTROVERTS AND INTROVERTS

Secondly, people also assume that you have to be an extrovert (or act like one) in order to succeed. However, every day the news is full of examples **that contradict that belief**. Microsoft's Bill Gates is one famous introvert **who comes to mind**. Another is Avon's very successful CEO Andrea Jung. Jung, **who grew up in a traditional Chinese family**, considers herself "reserved,[3]" but not shy. A writer **who has studied the personality traits[4] of business leaders** points out that the one trait **that absolutely defines successful leaders** is creativity. Introverts are known for being creative, so it shouldn't be a surprise to find many of them at the top of their professions.

What happens when an extrovert and an introvert become friends or fall in love? Opposites attract, but can first attraction survive really big personality differences? Yes, but only if both can accept the other person's needs—and it's not always easy. Extroverts like me, **who have to talk through everything before we even know what we think**, can drive an introvert crazy. Nadia, **who always thinks before she speaks**, doesn't always understand my need to talk. On the other hand, many extroverts, **who reach for their cell phones after two minutes alone**, can't see why an introvert like Nadia requires so much time by herself. (Is that really *normal*? they wonder.) However, if both people take the time to understand the other's personality type, the results can pay off. The introvert, **who has a rich inner life**, can help the extrovert become more sensitive to feelings. And the risk-loving[5] extrovert can help the introvert develop a sense of adventure **that he or she might miss** on his or her own. As a result, each friend's personality becomes more complete.

It's important to remember that no one is a pure introvert or extrovert. In fact, we are probably all ambiverts, **people who act like introverts in some situations and extroverts in others**. Like everyone else, you have a unique personality—your own special combination of traits **that makes you *you*!**

---

[3] ***reserved:*** not talkative
[4] ***trait:*** a quality in someone's character such as honesty or cruelty
[5] ***risk-loving:*** attracted to situations that might fail or be dangerous

After You Read

A | Vocabulary: *Complete the sentences with the words from the box.*

contradict	define	personality	require	sensitive	unique

1. Megan's _____ is very outgoing. She loves to be with other people.

2. Rahul is so _____. He knows when I'm upset even when I hide my feelings.

3. Nadia hates to _____ people, even when they're obviously wrong.

4. Introverts _____ time alone. They get very unhappy without it.

5. No two people are exactly alike. Everyone is _____.

6. It's hard to _____ creativity. It's such a complicated personality trait.

B | Comprehension: *Check (✓)* **Introvert** *or* **Extrovert** *for each description.*

Who . . . ?	Introvert	Extrovert
1. gets energy from being alone	☐	☐
2. gets energy from other people	☐	☐
3. enjoys small talk	☐	☐
4. likes to talk about ideas and feelings	☐	☐
5. talks while thinking	☐	☐
6. thinks before talking	☐	☐
7. is sensitive to feelings	☐	☐
8. likes to take risks	☐	☐

STEP 2 GRAMMAR PRESENTATION

ADJECTIVE CLAUSES WITH SUBJECT RELATIVE PRONOUNS

Adjective Clauses After the Main Clause

Main Clause			Adjective Clause		
Subject	**Verb**	**Predicate Noun/Pronoun**	**Subject Relative Pronoun**	**Verb**	
I	read	a book	*that* / *which*	discusses	personality.
An introvert	is	someone	*that* / *who*	needs	time alone.
			Whose + Noun		
I	have	a friend	*whose* personality	is	like mine.

Adjective Clauses Inside the Main Clause

Main Clause	Adjective Clause			Main Clause *(cont.)*	
Subject Noun / Pronoun	**Subject Relative Pronoun**	**Verb**		**Verb**	
The book	*that* / *which*	discusses	personality	is	by Ruben.
Someone	*that* / *who*	needs	time alone	may be	an introvert.
	Whose + Noun				
My friend,	*whose* personality	is	like mine,	loves	parties.

208   UNIT 13

1 Use **adjective clauses** to **identify** or give **additional information** about **nouns** (people, places, or things).

- I have a *friend* **who avoids parties**. *(The clause* who avoids parties *identifies the friend.)*

- She lives in *Miami*, **which is my hometown**. *(The clause* which is my hometown *gives additional information about* Miami.)

Adjective clauses can also identify or describe **indefinite pronouns** such as *one*, *someone*, *somebody*, *something*, *another*, and *other(s)*.

- I'd like to meet *someone* **who is outgoing**.

2 You can think of **sentences with adjective clauses** as a <u>combination of two sentences</u>.

I have a friend. + She is an extrovert. =
- I have a friend **who is an extrovert**.

Notice that the **adjective clause**:
- **directly follows** the noun or pronoun it is identifying or describing
- comes **after** the main clause or **inside** the main clause

Lea calls often. + She lives in Rome. =
- Lea, **who lives in Rome**, calls often.

She has a son. + His name is Max. =
- She has a son **whose name is Max**.

3 Adjective clauses begin with **relative pronouns**. Relative pronouns that can be the **subject** of the clause are *who*, *that*, *which*, and *whose*.

a. Use *who* or *that* for **people**.

SUBJECT
- I have a **friend** *who* lives in Mexico. OR

SUBJECT
- I have a **friend** *that* lives in Mexico.

b. Use *which* or *that* for **places** or **things**.

SUBJECT
- The **book** *which* I bought is about friends. OR

SUBJECT
- The **book** *that* I bought is about friends.

USAGE NOTE: In conversation, we use *that* more often than *who* and *which*. It's less formal.

c. Use *whose* + **noun** to show **possession** or **relationship**.

SUBJECT
- She's the **neighbor** *whose* house is for sale.

BE CAREFUL! Do **NOT use a subject pronoun** (*I*, *you*, *he*, *she*, *it*, *we*, *they*) and a subject relative pronoun in the same adjective clause.

- Scott is someone *who* avoids parties.
  NOT: Scott is someone who ~~he~~ avoids parties.

(continued on next page)

4	**Relative pronouns** always have the **same form**. They do not change for singular and plural nouns or pronouns, or for males and females.	• That's the **person** *that* gives great parties. • Those are the **people** *that* give great parties. • That's the **man** *who* gives great parties. • That's the **woman** *who* gives great parties.
5	The **verb in the adjective clause** is singular if the subject relative pronoun refers to a singular noun or pronoun. It is plural if it refers to a plural noun or pronoun. **BE CAREFUL!** When *whose* + **noun** is the subject of an adjective clause, the verb agrees with the subject of the adjective clause.	• Ben is my **friend** *who* **lives** in Boston. • Al and Ed are my **friends** *who* **live** in Boston. • Ed is a man *whose* **friends are** like family. NOT: Ed is a man whose friends ~~is~~ like family.
6	There are two kinds of adjective clauses, **identifying** and **nonidentifying**: a. An **identifying** adjective clause is **necessary to identify** the noun it refers to. b. A **nonidentifying** adjective clause gives <u>additional information</u> about the noun it refers to. It is **NOT necessary to identify** the noun. The noun is often **already identified** with an adjective such as *first*, *last*, *best*, or *most*, or is the name of a person or place. **BE CAREFUL!** Do **NOT use** *that* to introduce nonidentifying adjective clauses. Use *who* for people and *which* for places and things.	• I have a lot of good friends. My friend **who lives in Chicago** visits me often. *(The adjective clause is necessary to identify which friend.)* • I have a lot of good friends. My **best** friend**, who lives in Chicago,** visits me often. *(The friend has already been identified as the speaker's best friend. The adjective clause gives additional information, but it isn't needed to identify the friend.)* • **Marielle,** *who* introduced us at the party, called me last night. NOT: Marielle, ~~that~~ introduced us at the party, called me last night. • **Miami,** *which* reminds me of home, is my favorite vacation spot. NOT: Miami, ~~that~~ reminds me of home, is my favorite vacation spot.
7	In **writing**, use **commas** to separate a nonidentifying adjective clause from the rest of the sentence. In **speaking**, use short **pauses** to separate the nonidentifying adjective clause. **Without commas or pauses**, an adjective clause has a <u>very different meaning</u>.	NONIDENTIFYING ADJECTIVE CLAUSE • My sister**, who lives in Seattle,** is an introvert. NONIDENTIFYING ADJECTIVE CLAUSE • My sister *(pause)* **who lives in Seattle** *(pause)* is an introvert. *(I have only one sister. She's an introvert.)* IDENTIFYING ADJECTIVE CLAUSE • My sister **who lives in Seattle** is an introvert. *(I have several sisters. This one is an introvert.)*

EXERCISE 1: Discover the Grammar

Read this article about two other personality types. Circle the relative pronouns and underline the adjective clauses. Then draw an arrow from the relative pronoun to the noun or pronoun that it refers to.

Wellness Today   September–October 2012   47

"It's half full!"   "It's half empty!"

It's All How You Look at It

Look at the photo. Do you see a glass which is half full or a glass which is half empty? For optimists, people who believe that things in the future will work out fine, the glass is half full. On the other hand, for pessimists, people who expect things to go badly, the glass is half empty.

Most of us know people who have a strong tendency[1] to be either optimistic or pessimistic. I have a friend whose life motto is "Things have a way of working out." Even when something bad happens, Cindi remains optimistic. Last year, she lost a job that was extremely important to her. She didn't get depressed; she just thought "Well, maybe I'll find a new job that's even better than this one!" But then there is the example of Monica, who always sees the dark side of every situation, even when something good happens. She recently won a lot of money in a contest. Is she happy about this windfall? Not really. She worries that she won't know how to spend the money wisely. And now she's also worried that her friend Dan, a talented web designer who is struggling to start a business, will be jealous of her.

Cindi and Monica are women whose outlooks on life are as different as day and night. But the two women are best friends! Is it true what they say?

Do opposites attract? Cindi says that their very different ways of seeing things help balance each other. Sometimes Monica has views that are more realistic than her friend's. Right after Cindi was laid off, for example, Monica persuaded her to take a temporary job. "Just until you find that dream job," she said. On the other hand, Monica admits that she's sometimes too negative, and that Cindi, whose nickname is "Miss Sunshine," often gets her to see opportunities in a difficult situation. "Why not invest in Dan's business?" Cindi suggested the other day.

Former U.S. president Harry Truman defined the two personalities well: "A pessimist is one who makes difficulties of his opportunities, and an optimist is one who makes opportunities of his difficulties." However, as Cindi and Monica are learning, we can learn to make these tendencies less extreme. Today's experts agree: Half full or half empty, you may not be able to change how much water is in your glass, but you can often change how you view the situation and how you respond to it. Optimists and pessimists may be able to help each other do this more appropriately.

---

[1] *tendency:* the way that someone usually thinks or behaves

EXERCISE 2: Relative Pronouns and Verbs

(Grammar Notes 5–7)

Complete each sentence with an appropriate relative pronoun and the correct form of the verbs in parentheses.

Personality Quiz

Do you agree with the following statements? Check (✔) **True** or **False**.

True **False**

1. People ____who____ ____talk____ a lot tire me. ☐ ☐
                  (talk)

2. On a plane, I like to speak to the stranger _____ _____ the seat next to me. ☐ ☐
                   (take)

3. At a social event, I am often the first one _____ _____. ☐ ☐
                 (leave)

4. My best friend, _____ _____ a lot, is just like me. ☐ ☐
          (talk)

5. I prefer to have conversations _____ _____ on feelings and ideas. ☐ ☐
              (focus)

6. I am someone _____ idea of a great time _____ reading a good book. ☐ ☐
                (be)

7. People can have close friends _____ personalities _____ different from theirs. ☐ ☐
                (be)

8. I'm someone _____ always _____ the glass as half full, not half empty. ☐ ☐
            (see)

9. Difficult situations are often the ones _____ _____ the best opportunities. ☐ ☐
             (provide)

10. I like people _____ _____ sensitive to others' feelings. ☐ ☐
       (be)

EXERCISE 3: Identifying Adjective Clauses

(Grammar Notes 2–7)

A | *We often use identifying adjective clauses to define words. First, match the words on the left with the descriptions on the right.*

__h__ **1.** difficulty	**a.**	This situation gives you a chance to experience something good.
_____ **2.** extrovert	**b.**	This attitude shows your ideas about your future.
_____ **3.** introvert	**c.**	This ability makes you able to produce new ideas.
_____ **4.** opportunity	**d.**	This person usually sees the bright side of situations.
_____ **5.** opposites	**e.**	This person requires a lot of time alone.
_____ **6.** optimist	**f.**	This money was unexpected.
_____ **7.** outlook	**g.**	This person usually sees the dark side of situations.
_____ **8.** pessimist	**h.**	This problem is hard to solve.
_____ **9.** creativity	**i.**	These people have completely different personalities.
_____ **10.** windfall	**j.**	This person requires a lot of time with others.

B | *Now write definitions with adjective clauses for the words on the left. Use the correct description on the right and an appropriate relative pronoun.*

1. *A difficulty is a problem that is hard to solve.* OR *A difficulty is a problem which is hard to solve.*

2. _____

3. _____

4. _____

5. _____

6. _____

7. _____

8. _____

9. _____

10. _____

EXERCISE 4: Nonidentifying Adjective Clauses

(Grammar Notes 2–7)

Combine the pairs of sentences. Make the second sentence in each pair an adjective clause. Use the correct punctuation. Make any other necessary changes.

1. I'm attending English 101. It meets three days a week.

   I'm attending English 101, which meets three days a week .

2. Sami is an optimist. He's in my English class.

   Sami, who is in my English class, is an optimist.

3. He drives to school with his sister Jena. She wants to go to law school.

   _____ .

4. Jena is always contradicting him. She loves to argue.

   _____ .

5. That never annoys cheerful Sami. He just laughs.

   _____ .

6. Jena is going to have a great career. Her personality is perfect for a lawyer.

   _____ .

7. I always look forward to the class. The class meets three days a week.

   _____ .

8. San Antonio has a lot of community colleges. San Antonio is in Texas.

   _____ .

9. My school has students from all over the world. It's one of the largest colleges in the country.

   _____ .

Adjective Clauses with Subject Relative Pronouns   **213**

EXERCISE 5: Identifying or Nonidentifying Adjective Clauses

(Grammar Notes 2–7)

Read the conversations. Then use the first and last sentences in each conversation to help you write a summary. Use adjective clauses. Remember to use commas where necessary.

1.　　**A:** This article is really interesting.

　　　B: What's it about?

　　　A: It discusses the different types of personalities.

SUMMARY: *This article, which discusses the different types of personalities, is really interesting.*

2.　　**A:** The office party is going to be at the restaurant.

　　　B: Which restaurant?

　　　A: You know the one. It's across the street from the library.

SUMMARY: _____

3.　　**A:** I liked that speaker.

　　　B: Which one? We heard several!

　　　A: I forget his name. He talked about optimists.

SUMMARY: _____

4.　　**A:** Bill and Sue aren't close friends with the Swabodas.

　　　B: No. The Swabodas' interests are very different from theirs.

SUMMARY: _____

5.　　**A:** I lent some chairs to the new neighbors.

　　　B: Why did they need chairs?

　　　A: They're having a party tonight.

SUMMARY: _____

6.　　**A:** I'm watching an old video of Jason.

　　　B: Look at that! He was telling jokes when he was five!

　　　A: I know. This totally defines his personality.

SUMMARY: _____

7.　　**A:** My boyfriend left me a lot of plants to water.

　　　B: How come?

　　　A: He's visiting Venezuela with some friends.

SUMMARY: _____

Read this student's essay about a friend. There are eleven mistakes in the use of adjective clauses and their punctuation. Each incorrectly punctuated clause counts as one mistake. (For example, "My mother who is my best friend just turned 50" needs two commas, but it counts as one mistake.) The first mistake is already corrected. Find and correct ten more.

Good Friends

A writer once said that friends are born, not made. I think he meant that friendship is like love at first sight—we become friends immediately with people who ~~they~~ are compatible with us. I have to contradict this writer. Last summer I made friends with some people who's completely different from me.

In July, I went to Mexico City to study Spanish for a month. In our group, there were five adults, which were all language teachers from our school. Two teachers stayed with friends in Mexico City, and we only saw those teachers during the day. But we saw the teachers, who stayed with us in the dormitory, both day and night. They were the ones who they helped us when we had problems. Bob Taylor who is much older than I am became a really good friend. After my first two weeks, I had a problem that was getting me down. Mexico City, that is a very exciting place, was too distracting. I'm a real extrovert—someone who wants to go out all the time—and I stopped going to my classes. But my classes required a lot of work, and my grades suffered as a result. When they got really bad, I wanted to leave. Bob, who have studied abroad a lot, was very sensitive to those feelings. But he was also a lot more optimistic about my situation. He helped me get back into my courses which were actually pretty interesting. I managed to do well after all! After the trip I kept writing to Bob, who's letters are always friendly and encouraging. Next summer, he's leading another trip what sounds great. It's a three-week trip to Spain, which is a place he knows a lot about. I hope I can go.

EXERCISE 7: Listening

A | *Some friends are at a high school reunion. They haven't seen one another for 25 years. Read the statements. Then listen to the conversation. Listen again and circle the correct words to complete the statements.*

1. People at the reunion (have) / haven't changed a lot.

2. Ann is wearing a lot of jewelry / a scarf.

3. It's the man / woman who first recognizes Kado.

4. Bob and Pat are the students who worked on the school paper / ran for class president.

5. Asha is looking at a photo / Bob.

6. Asha is the woman who married Pete Rizzo / Raza Gupta.

7. The man and woman know / don't know who is sitting between Asha and Pat.

B | *Look at the picture. Then listen again to the conversation and write the correct name next to each person.*

| Ann | Asha | ~~Bob~~ | Kado | Pat | Pete |

EXERCISE 8: Pronunciation

A | *Read and listen to the Pronunciation Note.*

> **Pronunciation Note**
>
> In **writing**, we use **commas** around **nonidentifying adjective clauses**.
>
> In **speaking**, we **pause** briefly **before and after** nonidentifying adjective clauses.
>
> **EXAMPLE:**   Marta**,** who lives across from me**,** has become a good friend. →
>
> "Marta [PAUSE] who lives across from me [PAUSE] has become a good friend."

B | *Listen to the sentences. Add commas if you hear pauses around the adjective clauses.*

1. My neighbor who is an introvert called me today.

2. My neighbor who is an introvert called me today.

3. My brother who is one year older than me is an extrovert.

4. My sister who lives in Toronto visits us every summer.

5. My friend who is in the same class as me lent me a book.

6. The book which is about personality types is really interesting.

7. The article that won a prize is in today's newspaper.

8. My boyfriend who hates parties actually agreed to go to one with me.

C | *Listen again and repeat the sentences.*

EXERCISE 9: Discussion

A | *Take the quiz in Exercise 2.*

B | *Work with a partner. Discuss your answers to the quiz. What do you think your answers show about your personality?*

> **EXAMPLE:**   **A:** Question 1. People who talk a lot tire me. That's true.
> **B:** I think that means you're probably an introvert. It wasn't true for me. I myself talk a lot, and I enjoy people who talk a lot too.

EXERCISE 10: Questionnaire

A | Complete the questionnaire. Check (✓) all the items that you believe are true. Then add your own idea.

A friend is someone who . . .

☐ 1. always tells you the truth

☐ 2. has known you for a very long time

☐ 3. cries with you

☐ 4. lends you money

☐ 5. talks to you every day

☐ 6. helps you when you are in trouble

☐ 7. listens to your problems

☐ 8. does things with you

☐ 9. respects you

☐ 10. accepts you the way you are

☐ 11. is sensitive to your feelings

☐ 12. gives you advice

☐ 13. keeps your secrets

☐ 14. never contradicts you

Other: _____

B | Now compare questionnaires with a partner. Discuss the reasons for your choices.

> **EXAMPLE:** **A:** I think a friend is someone who always tells you the truth.
> **B:** I don't agree. Sometimes the truth can hurt you.

C | After your discussion, tally the results of the whole class. Discuss the results.

EXERCISE 11: Quotable Quotes

Work in small groups. Choose three of these quotations and talk about what they mean. Give examples from your own experience to support your ideas.

1. Show me a friend who will weep[1] with me; those who will laugh with me I can find myself.
—*Slavic proverb*

> **EXAMPLE:** **A:** I think this means that it's easier to find friends for good times than for bad times.
> **B:** I agree. A true friend is someone who is there for you during good *and* bad times.
> **C:** My best friend in high school was like that. She was someone who . . .

2. An optimist is a guy that has never had much experience.
—*Don Marquis (U.S. writer, 1878–1937)*

3. A pessimist is one who has been compelled[2] to live with an optimist.
—*Elbert Hubbard (U.S. writer, 1856–1915)*

4. He is wise who can make a friend of a foe.[3]
—*Scottish proverb*

5. Very few people can congratulate without envy a friend who has succeeded.
—*Aeschylus (Greek playwright, 525–456 B.C.E)*

---

[1] **weep:** to cry

[2] **compelled:** forced

[3] **foe:** an enemy

6. A pessimist is one who makes difficulties of his opportunities and an optimist is one who makes opportunities of his difficulties.
   —*Harry Truman (33rd U.S. president, 1884–1972)*

7. Wherever you are it is your own friends who make your world.
   —*Ralph Barton Perry (U.S. philosopher, 1876–1957)*

8. Blessed[4] is the person who is too busy to worry in the daytime and too sleepy to worry at night.
   —*Author Unknown*

9. A true friend is somebody who can make us do what we can.
   —*Ralph Waldo Emerson (U.S. writer, 1803–1882)*

10. How much pain they have cost us, the evils[5] which have never happened.
    —*Thomas Jefferson (3rd U.S. president, 1743–1826)*

---

[4] **blessed:** lucky

[5] **evil:** a bad thing

EXERCISE 12: Writing

A | *Write a two-paragraph essay about a friend. You may want to begin your essay with one of the quotations from Exercise 11. Use adjective clauses with subject relative pronouns. You can use the essay in Exercise 6 as a model.*

> **EXAMPLE:**   Do friends have to be people who have the same interests or personality? I don't think so. My friend Richie and I are best friends who are complete opposites. He's an extrovert who can walk into a room that is full of strangers with no problem. In an hour, they'll all be new friends. I'm an introvert who . . .

B | *Check your work. Use the Editing Checklist.*

Editing Checklist

Did you use . . . ?
- ☐ *who* or *that* for people
- ☐ *which* or *that* for places and things
- ☐ *whose* to show possession or relationship
- ☐ the correct verb form in adjective clauses
- ☐ identifying adjective clauses to identify a noun
- ☐ nonidentifying adjective clauses to give more information about a noun
- ☐ commas to separate nonidentifying adjective clauses

A | Circle the correct words to complete the sentences.

1. I have a lot of friends who <u>is / are</u> introverts.

2. Maria is someone <u>whose / who</u> idea of a good time is staying home.

3. Ben, who always <u>think / thinks</u> carefully before he speaks, is very sensitive to people's feelings.

4. He lives in Los Angeles, <u>which / where</u> is a city I'd love to visit.

5. He wrote this book, <u>that / which</u> is very interesting, about personality types.

6. My friend <u>who / which</u> read it liked it a lot.

B | Complete each sentence with a relative pronoun and the correct form of the verb in parentheses.

1. Thinkers and Feelers are types of people _____ _____ very differently.
   (behave)

2. A Thinker, _____ _____ decisions based on facts, is a very logical person.
   (make)

3. Emotions, _____ usually _____ a Feeler, are more important than facts to
   (convince)

   this personality type.

4. A Thinker is someone _____ always _____ fairly and honestly.
   (speak)

5. A Feeler avoids saying things _____ _____ another person's feelings.
   (hurt)

6. I dislike arguments, _____ usually _____ me. I guess I'm a Feeler.
   (upset)

7. Ed, _____ personality _____ different from mine, loves to argue.
   (be)

C | Find and correct seven mistakes. Remember to check punctuation.

It's true that we are often attracted to people whose are very different from ourselves. An extrovert, which personality is very outgoing, will often connect with a romantic partner who are an introvert. They are both attracted to someone that have different strengths. My cousin Valerie who is an extreme extrovert, recently married Bill, whose idea of a party is a Scrabble game on the Internet. Can this marriage succeed? Will Bill learn the salsa, that is Valerie's favorite dance? Will Valerie start collecting unusual words? Their friends, what care about both of them, are hoping for the best.

UNIT 14

Adjective Clauses with Object Relative Pronouns or *When* and *Where*

THE IMMIGRANT EXPERIENCE

STEP 1 GRAMMAR IN CONTEXT

Before You Read

Look at the book reviews and photos. Discuss the questions.

1. Where do you think the two cities in the photographs are located? Describe them.
2. Do the cities look different from where you live now? If yes, how?
3. What do you think the title means?

Read

Read the book reviews.

TORN[1] BETWEEN TWO WORLDS

"I'm filled to the brim[2] with what I'm about to lose—images of Cracow, **which I loved as one loves a person**, of the sun-baked villages **where we had taken summer vacations**, of the hours **I spent poring over passages of music with my music teacher**, of conversations and escapades[3] with friends."

These sad words were written by Eva Hoffman, author of *Lost in Translation: A Life in a New Language* (New York: Penguin, 1989). Hoffman, an award-winning journalist[4] and author, spent her early childhood in Cracow, Poland. She moved with her family to Vancouver, Canada, when she was 13. Her autobiography[5] describes her experiences as she leaves her beloved Cracow and struggles to find herself in a new place and a new language.

In spite of her family's poverty and small, crowded apartment, Ewa Wydra (Hoffman's Polish name) loved her native Cracow.

(*continued on next page*)

[1] ***torn:*** not able to decide between two people, places, or things because you want both
[2] ***filled to the brim:*** completely filled (like a glass with water that goes to the top)
[3] ***escapade:*** an adventure
[4] ***journalist:*** a person who writes professionally for newspapers or magazines
[5] ***autobiography:*** a book a person writes about his or her own life

Hoffman remembers Cracow as a place **where life was lived intensely**. She remembers visiting the city's cafés with her father, **who she watched in lively conversations with his friends**. She also remembers neighbors, "People **between whose apartments there's constant movement with kids, sugar, eggs, and teatime visits**." As she grew up, her friendship with Marek, **whose apartment she visited almost daily**, deepened, and the two always believed that they would one day be married.

Madame Witeszczak, Hoffman's piano teacher, was the last person **she said goodbye to** before she left Poland.

"What do you think you'll miss most?" her teacher asked. "Everything. Cracow. The school … you. Everything …"

At her new school in Vancouver, Hoffman is given her English name, Eva, **which her teachers find easier to pronounce**. Hoffman, however, feels no connection to the name. In fact, she feels no real connection to the English name of anything **that she feels is important**. All her memories and feelings are still in her first language, Polish. The story of Hoffman as she grows up and comes to terms with[6] her new identity and language is fascinating and moving.[7]

---

[6] **come to terms with:** to learn to accept
[7] **moving:** causing strong feelings

Also recommended is *The Rice Room*, by Ben Fong-Torres (New York: Hyperion, 1994). Unlike Hoffman, Fong-Torres was born in the United States. However, his parents had emigrated from China, and many of the problems **that he describes** are, like Hoffman's, connected to language. Fong-Torres struggles to bring together his family's culture and his new culture. He doesn't have the language **he needs to do this** because he only knows the Chinese **that he had learned as a child**. A successful radio announcer and journalist in English, Fong-Torres cannot really talk to his parents, **for whom English is still a foreign language**.

"When we talk, it sounds like baby talk—at least my half of it.… I don't know half the words **I need**; I either never learned them, or I heard but forgot them." The language barrier[8] separated Fong-Torres and his parents "…through countless moments **when we needed to talk with each other**, about the things **parents and children usually discuss**: jobs and careers; marriage and divorce; health and finances; history, the present, and the future. This is one of the great sadnesses of my life.… I'm a journalist

and a broadcaster[9]—my job is to communicate—and I can't with the two people **with whom I want to most**."

Whether first- or second-generation immigrant, the issues are the same. These two books describe the lives of people trying to connect the worlds **that they left behind** and the worlds **that they now call home**.

---

[8] **language barrier:** problem caused by not being able to speak another person's language
[9] **broadcaster:** someone who talks professionally on radio or TV

A | **Vocabulary:** *Complete the sentences with the words from the box.*

connection	generation	immigrant	issue	poverty	translation

1. The author wrote in Spanish, but I'm reading an English _____.

2. It's always interesting to hear the older _____ talk about how life used to be.

3. My grandfather's parents were very poor. They left their country to escape from a life of

_____.

4. What's your _____ to Poland? Is your family from there?

5. At my first job, the language barrier with my boss was the biggest _____.

6. Life can be very difficult for a(n) _____, who often has to learn a lot of new

things in a very short time.

B | **Comprehension:** *Check (✓) the correct boxes. For some items, you will check both boxes.*

Who . . . ?	Hoffman	Fong-Torres
1. studied music	☐	☐
2. was a first-generation American	☐	☐
3. went to cafés with a parent	☐	☐
4. had to learn English	☐	☐
5. had a name change	☐	☐
6. had immigrant parents	☐	☐
7. has difficulty communicating with family	☐	☐
8. is a professional writer	☐	☐

ADJECTIVE CLAUSES WITH OBJECT RELATIVE PRONOUNS OR *WHEN* AND *WHERE*

Adjective Clauses After the Main Clause

Main Clause			Adjective Clause		
Subject	Verb	Predicate Noun / Pronoun	(Object Relative Pronoun)	Subject	Verb
He	read	the book	(*that*) (*which*)	she	wrote.
She	is	someone	(*who[m]*)	I	respect.
			***Whose* + Noun**		
That	is	the author	*whose* book	I	read.
			Where / (When)		
She	loves	the city	*where*	she	grew up.
They	cried	the day	(*when*)	they	left.

Adjective Clauses Inside the Main Clause

Main Clause	Adjective Clause			Main Clause (cont.)	
Subject	(Object Relative Pronoun)	Subject	Verb	Verb	
The book	(*that*) (*which*)	I	read	is	great.
Someone	(*who[m]*)	you	know	was	there.
	***Whose* + Noun**				
The man	*whose* sister	you	know	writes	books.

Main Clause	Adjective Clause			Main Clause (cont.)	
Subject	*Where / (When)*	Subject	Verb	Verb	
The library	*where*	I	work	has	videos.
The summer	(*when*)	she	left	passed	slowly.

GRAMMAR NOTES

1

In Unit 13, you learned about adjective clauses in which the **relative pronoun** was the **subject** of the clause.

SUBJ.
Eva is a writer. + *She was born in Poland.* =

SUBJ.
• Eva, *who was born in Poland*, is a writer.

A **relative pronoun** can also be the **object** of an adjective clause.

OBJ.
Eva is a writer. + *I saw her on TV.* =

OBJ.
• Eva, *who I saw on TV*, is a writer.

Notice that:

SUBJ.
• Ben, *who lives in California*, is a journalist.

a. **relative pronouns** (subject or object) come at the **beginning** of the adjective clause.

OBJ.
• Ben, *who we just met*, reports on music.

b. **relative pronouns** (subject or object) always have the **same form**. They do not change for singular and plural nouns, or for males and females.

• That's the **man** *who* I met.
• That's the **woman** *who* I met.
• Those are the **people** *who* I met.

c. the **object relative pronoun** is followed by the subject and verb of the adjective clause. The **verb in the adjective clause** is singular if the subject of the clause is singular. It is plural if the subject of the clause is plural.

SUBJ.　　VERB
• I like the **columns which** *he writes*.
• I like the **column which** *they write*.

BE CAREFUL! Do **NOT use an object pronoun** (*me, you, him, her, it, us, them*) and an object relative pronoun in the same adjective clause.

• She is the writer *who* **I saw on TV**.
Noт: She is the writer who I saw ~~her~~ on TV.

2

REMEMBER: There are two kinds of adjective clauses, **identifying** and **nonidentifying**.

IDENTIFYING:
• I read a lot of books. The book **which I just finished** was very moving.
  (The adjective clause is necessary to identify which book I mean.)

NONIDENTIFYING:
• I read a lot of books. This book**, which I just finished,** was very moving.
  (I'm pointing to the book, so the adjective clause isn't necessary to identify it. The clause gives additional information.)

In **writing**, use **commas** to separate a nonidentifying adjective clause from the rest of the sentence.
In **speaking**, use short **pauses** to separate the nonidentifying adjective clause.

You can often **leave out an object** relative pronoun in an **identifying** adjective clause.

• The book *which* **I just finished** is great. OR
• The book **I just finished** is great.

But do **NOT leave out the object** relative pronoun in a **nonidentifying** adjective clause.

Noт: ~~The book, I just finished, is great.~~

(continued on next page)

3 **Relative pronouns** that can be the **object** of the adjective clause are **who(m)**, **that**, **which**, and **whose**.

a. Use **whom**, **who**, or **that** for **people**. You can also <u>leave out</u> the relative pronoun.

USAGE NOTE: **Whom** is very formal. Most people do not use **whom** in everyday speech. **That** is less formal than **who**. In everyday speech, most people use no relative pronoun.

b. Use **which** or **that** for **things**. You can also leave out the relative pronoun.

USAGE NOTE: **That** is less formal than **which**. In everyday speech, most people use no relative pronoun.

c. Use **whose** + **noun** to show **possession** or **relationship**. You cannot leave out **whose**.

REMEMBER: Don't leave out relative pronouns in nonidentifying adjective clauses.

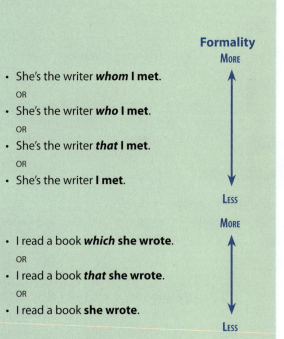

Formality

MORE

- She's the writer **whom** I met.
  OR
- She's the writer **who** I met.
  OR
- She's the writer **that** I met.
  OR
- She's the writer **I met**.

LESS

MORE

- I read a book **which** she wrote.
  OR
- I read a book **that** she wrote.
  OR
- I read a book **she wrote**.

LESS

- That's the author **whose** book I read.
  Not: That's the author ~~book I read~~.

- She remembers Marek, **who** she visited often.
  Not: She remembers Marek, ~~she visited often~~.

4 The relative pronouns **who(m)**, **that**, **which**, and **whose** can be the **object of a preposition**.

You can <u>leave out</u> **who(m)**, **that**, and **which**, but not **whose**.

USAGE NOTES:
a. In **formal English**, we put the preposition <u>at the beginning</u> of the clause. When the preposition is at the beginning, we use only **whom** (not **who** or **that**) for <u>people</u>, and **which** (not **that**) for <u>things</u>.
b. In **everyday spoken English** and in **informal writing**, we put the preposition <u>at the end</u> of the clause.

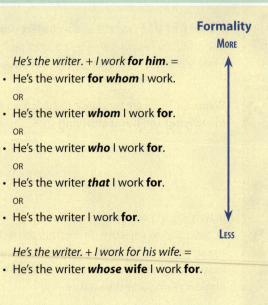

Formality

MORE

He's the writer. + I work for him. =
- He's the writer **for whom** I work.
  OR
- He's the writer **whom** I work **for**.
  OR
- He's the writer **who** I work **for**.
  OR
- He's the writer **that** I work **for**.
  OR
- He's the writer I work **for**.

LESS

He's the writer. + I work for his wife. =
- He's the writer **whose wife** I work **for**.

- He's the writer **for whom** I work.
- That's the book **about which** he spoke.

- He's the writer **who** I work **for**.
- That's the book **that** he spoke **about**.

<table>
<tr>
<td>**5**</td>
<td colspan="2">**When** and **where** can also begin adjective clauses.</td>
</tr>
<tr>
<td></td>
<td>**a.** Use **where** for a **place**.</td>
<td>• That's the library **where she works**.</td>
</tr>
<tr>
<td></td>
<td>**b.** Use **when** or **that** for a **time**.</td>
<td>• I remember the day **when I met him**.
OR
• I remember the day **that I met him**.
OR
• I remember the day **I met him**.</td>
</tr>
<tr>
<td></td>
<td>You can <u>leave out</u> **when** and **that** in identifying adjective clauses.</td>
<td></td>
</tr>
</table>

REFERENCE NOTE

For additional information about **identifying and nonidentifying adjective clauses**, see Unit 13, page 210.

STEP 3 FOCUSED PRACTICE

EXERCISE 1: Discover the Grammar

A | *This excerpt from* Lost in Translation *describes Eva Hoffman's home in Cracow. Underline the adjective clauses and circle the relative pronouns,* **when,** *and* **where.** *Then draw an arrow from each relative pronoun to the noun or pronoun that it refers to. There are both subject and object relative pronouns.*

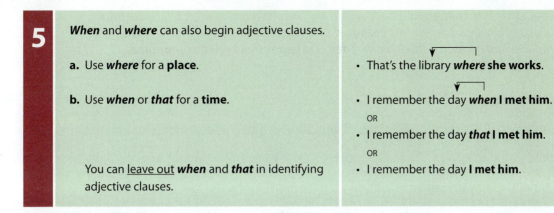

   The kitchen is usually steamy with large pots of soup cooking on the wood stove for hours, or laundry being boiled in vats[1] for greater whiteness; behind the kitchen, there's a tiny balcony, barely big enough to hold two people, on which we sometimes go out to exchange neighborly gossip[2] with people peeling vegetables, beating carpets, or just standing around on adjoining[3] balconies. Looking down, you see a paved courtyard, in which I spend many hours bouncing a ball against the wall with other kids, and a bit of garden, where I go to smell the few violets that come up each spring and climb the apple tree, and where my sister gathers the snails that live under the boysenberry bushes, to bring them proudly into the house by the bucketful. . . .

   Across the hall from us are the Twardowskis, who come to our apartment regularly . . . I particularly like the Twardowskis' daughter, Basia, who is several years older than I and who has the prettiest long braids,[4] which she sometimes coils around her head. . . .

---
[1]*vat:* a large container for liquid
[2]*gossip:* conversations or comments about other people's actions or their private lives
[3]*adjoining:* next to
[4]*braid:* a hair style where three pieces of hair are twisted like a rope

B | Read another excerpt from the same book about Hoffman's music school. There are four adjective clauses in which the relative pronouns have been left out. The first one is already underlined. Find and underline three more. Then add appropriate relative pronouns.

Pani Konek teaches at the Cracow Music School, which I've been attending for two years—ever since it has been decided that I should be trained as a professional pianist. I've always liked going to school. At the beginning of the year, I like buying smooth navy blue fabric from which our dressmaker will make my school uniform—an anonymous[1] overdress <u>*that* OR *which* we are required to wear over our regular clothes in order to erase economic and class distinctions</u>; I like the feel of the crisp, untouched notebook . . . and dipping my pen into the deep inkwell in my desk, and learning how to make oblique[2] letters. It's fun to make up stories about the eccentric characters[3] I know, or about the shapes icicles make on the winter windows, and try to outwit the teacher when I don't know something, and to give dramatic recitations of poems we've memorized. . . .

_____

[1]*anonymous:* not showing a person's identity or personality
[2]*oblique:* slanted, not straight (for example, *italicized* letters are oblique)
[3]*eccentric characters:* strange or unusual people

EXERCISE 2: Relative Pronouns and Verbs

(Grammar Notes 1–5)

*Complete the interview from a school newspaper. Use **who, that, which, when** or **where,** and the correct forms of the verbs in parentheses.*

The Grover	September 19, 2012	page 3

Meet Your Classmates

Maniya, _____*who*_____ a lot of our readers already _____*know*_____,
                                                  1. (know)
has been at Grover High for three years now. We interviewed Maniya, who is from the Philippines, about her experiences as a new immigrant in the United States.

INTERVIEWER: How did your family choose Atlanta, Maniya?

    MANIYA: My cousin, _____ we _____ with at
                                               2. (stay)
        first, lives here.

INTERVIEWER: What were your first impressions?

MANIYA: At first it was fun. We got here at the beginning of the summer, _____ there

_____ no school, so I didn't feel much pressure to speak English.
3. (be)

INTERVIEWER: What was the most difficult thing about going to school?

MANIYA: Of course, the class in _____ I _____ the biggest problems at
4. (have)

first was English. It was so hard for me to write compositions or to say the things

_____ I _____ to say. It was really a big issue for me. Now it's
5. (want)

much easier. I have a much stronger connection to English now.

INTERVIEWER: What was the biggest change for you when you got here?

MANIYA: We used to live in a big house, _____ there _____ always a lot
6. (be)

of people. We were several generations under one roof. Here I live with just my parents and

sister, _____ I _____ after school.
7. (take care of)

INTERVIEWER: How did you learn English so quickly?

MANIYA: At night, I write words and idioms on a small piece of paper _____ I

_____ in my shirt pocket. Then I study them at school whenever I have a
8. (put)

chance between classes.

INTERVIEWER: Is there anything _____ you still _____ trouble with?
9. (have)

MANIYA: One thing _____ I still _____ hard to do is to make jokes in
10. (find)

English. Some things are funny in Tagalog but not in English.

EXERCISE 3: Identifying Adjective Clauses

(Grammar Notes 2–5)

*Complete the story. Use the sentences from the box. Change them to identifying adjective
clauses and use relatives pronouns, **when,** or **where.***

I drank coffee there every day.	**I knew her sister from school.**
I had to leave Cracow then.	~~**I loved it very much.**~~
I hoped it would continue to grow.	**Many students attended it.**

Cracow is a city in Poland _____*that I loved very much*_____. My parents
1.

owned a café _____. One day I met a woman
2.

there _____. Her sister and I were in a class
3.

together _____. The woman and I felt a strong
4.

connection _____. For me it was a sad day
5.

_____.
6.

EXERCISE 4: Nonidentifying Adjective Clauses

(Grammar Notes 2–5)

Complete the information about Ben Fong-Torres. Use the sentences in parentheses to write nonidentifying adjective clauses with relative pronouns, **when**, or **where**. Add commas where necessary.

Ben Fong-Torres was born in Alameda, California, in 1945. He was the son of first-generation Chinese parents. To escape a life of poverty, his father immigrated to the Philippines and then to the United

States _, where he settled down_____.
          1. (He settled down there.)

His mother came to the United States

10 years later _____.
      2. (Their marriage was arranged by relatives then.)

Fong-Torres, along with his brother and sister, grew up in Oakland, California,

_____. His family owned a Chinese restaurant
    3. (There was a large Chinese community there.)

_____ when they were not in school. Young
    4. (All the children worked there.)

Ben was always an enthusiastic reader of cartoons and a huge fan of popular music

_____. At the age of 12, Ben went with his
    5. (He heard it on the radio.)

father to Texas _____. It was a difficult time
    6. (They opened another Chinese restaurant there.)

for Ben because he was among people who had had no previous contact with Asians.

Back in Oakland, after the failure of the Texas restaurant, Ben got jobs writing for various magazines and newspapers. His interviews with hundreds of famous musicians included the Beatles, the Rolling Stones, Grace Slick, and an interview with Ray Charles

_____. Fong-Torres was also a DJ for San
    7. (He won an award for it.)

Francisco radio station KSAN, which plays rock music, and in 1976 he won an award for broadcasting excellence.

Fong-Torres and Diane Sweet _____ still
          8. (He married her in 1976.)

live in San Francisco. He hosts many events for the Chinese community in that city, and continues to write about music for publications such as the e-zine (Internet magazine) www.AsianConnections.com.

EXERCISE 5: Identifying and Nonidentifying Adjective Clauses (Grammar Notes 1–5)

Combine the pairs of sentences. Make the second sentence in each pair an adjective clause.
Make any other necessary changes. Use relative pronouns only when necessary.

1. That's the house. I grew up in the house.

   That's the house I grew up in.

2. I lived with my parents and my siblings. You've met them.

   _____

3. I had two sisters and an older brother. I felt a close connection to my sisters.

   _____

4. My sisters and I shared a room. We spent nights talking there.

   _____

5. My brother slept on the living room couch. I hardly ever saw him.

   _____

6. It was a large old couch. My father had made the couch himself.

   _____

7. My best friend lived across the hall. I loved her family.

   _____

8. We went to the same school. We both studied English there.

   _____

9. Mr. Robinson was our English teacher. Everyone was a little afraid of Mr. Robinson.

   _____

10. After school I worked in a bakery. My aunt and uncle owned it.

    _____

11. They sold delicious bread and cake. People stood in line for hours to buy the bread and cake.

    _____

12. My brother and sisters live far away now. I miss them.

    _____

13. When we get together we like to talk about the old days. We all lived at home then.

    _____

EXERCISE 6: Editing

*Read this student's essay. There are nine mistakes in the use of adjective clauses and their punctuation. The first **two** mistakes are already corrected. Find and correct seven more.*

Tai Dong, where I grew up, is a small city on the southeast coast of Taiwan. My family moved there from Taipei the summer where I was born. I don't remember our first house, we rented from a relative, but when I was two, we moved to the house that I grew up in. I have a very clear image of it. The house, which my parents still live, is on a main street in Tai Dong. To me, this was the best place in the world. My mother had a food stand in our front courtyard whom she sold omelets early in the morning. All her customers, which I always chatted with, were very friendly to me. On the first floor, my father conducted his tea business in the front room. After school, I always went straight to the corner where he sat drinking tea with his customers. In the back was our huge kitchen with its stone floor and brick oven. I loved dinnertime because the kitchen was always full of relatives and the customers, that my father had invited to dinner. It was a fun and noisy place to be. Next to the kitchen, there was one small bedroom. My oldest cousin, whose father wanted him to learn the tea business, slept there. Our living room and bedrooms were upstairs. My two older sisters slept in one bedroom, and my older brother and I slept in the other. My younger sister shared a room with my grandmother, whose took care of her a lot of the time.

STEP 4 COMMUNICATION PRACTICE

EXERCISE 7: Listening

A | *Read the statements. Then listen to this description of an author's childhood room. Listen again and check (✓) True or False. Correct the false statements.*

	True	False
1. Maria originally wrote her book in ~~English.~~ *Spanish*	☐	☑
2. Maria has a clear image of her childhood bedroom.	☐	☐
3. She shared a room with her sister.	☐	☐
4. There was a rug under Maria's bed.	☐	☐
5. The sisters liked looking at themselves in the mirror.	☐	☐

		True	False
6.	They did their homework in the kitchen.	☐	☐
7.	Maria played the guitar.	☐	☐
8.	Maria has happy memories about her childhood.	☐	☐

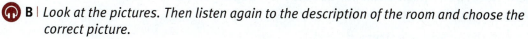

B | *Look at the pictures. Then listen again to the description of the room and choose the correct picture.*

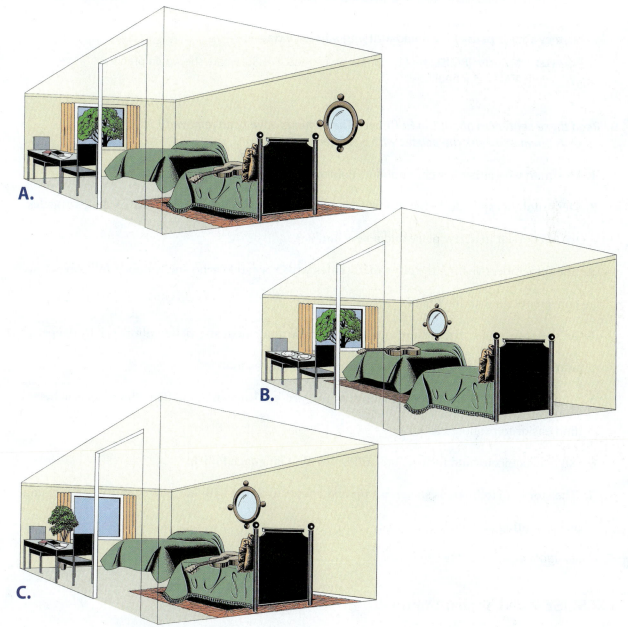

A.

B.

C.

C | *Listen again to the description and check (✓) the correct box.*

This description is in _____ English.

☐ formal

☐ informal

EXERCISE 8: Pronunciation

🎧 **A** | *Read and listen to the Pronunciation Note.*

Pronunciation Note

When we speak, we **break long sentences** into parts called **thought groups**. This makes sentences easier to say and easier to understand.

Each thought group has at least **one stressed word**.

We **pause** briefly **before a new thought group**. Not all speakers pause in the same place, but they **always pause for a nonidentifying adjective clause**.

EXAMPLE: My sister [PAUSE] kept her guitar on her bed [PAUSE] where she would practice [PAUSE] for hours.

🎧 **B** | *Read these sentences about Eva Hoffman. (The commas have been removed.) Then listen to them and mark the pauses with a slanted line (/).*

1. Hoffman who spent her childhood in Poland moved to Canada when she was 13.

2. Her autobiography describes her experiences as she leaves her beloved Cracow and struggles to find herself in a new place and a new language.

3. She remembers visiting the city's many cafés with her father who she watched in lively conversations with his friends.

4. As she grew up her friendship with Marek whose apartment she visited almost daily deepened and the two always believed that they would one day be married.

5. At her new school in Vancouver Hoffman is given her English name Eva which her teachers find easier to pronounce.

6. All her memories and feelings are still in her first language Polish.

7. The story of Hoffman as she grows up and comes to terms with her new identity and language is fascinating and moving.

🎧 **C** | *Listen again and repeat the sentences.*

EXERCISE 9: What About You?

Bring in some photos to share with your classmates. Work in small groups. Describe the people and places in your photos.

EXAMPLE: **A:** This is the street where we lived before we moved here.
B: Is that the house you grew up in?
A: Yes, it is. I lived there until I was 10.

EXERCISE 10: Quotable Quotes

Work in small groups. Choose three of these quotations and talk about what they mean. Give examples from your own experience to support your ideas.

1. Home is where the heart is.
   —*Pliny the Elder (Roman soldier and encyclopedist, 23–79)*

   EXAMPLE: **A:** I think this means that home is not necessarily a place.
   B: I agree. It's a feeling that you have.
   C: I think it can be a place or person that you love.

2. Home is where one starts from.
   —*T. S. Eliot (British poet, 1885–1905)*

3. Home is the place where you feel happy.
   —*Salman Rushdie (Indian author, 1947–)*

4. Home is a place you grow up wanting to leave, and grow old wanting to get back to.
   —*John Ed Pearce (U.S. journalist, 1917–2006)*

5. Home is not where you live but where they understand you.
   —*Christian Morgenstern (German poet, 1871–1914)*

6. Home is the place where, when you have to go there, they have to take you in.
   —*Robert Frost (U.S. poet, 1874–1963)*

EXERCISE 11: Writing

A | *Write one or two paragraphs about a place you remember from your childhood. Use adjective clauses with object relative pronouns, **when**, or **where** to help you explain where things were and why they were important. You can use the essay in Exercise 6 as a model.*

EXAMPLE: The town where I grew up was a small farming village. Living there was like living in an earlier century. We didn't lock our doors, and my friends, who lived across the street, could visit whenever they wanted to . . .

B | *Check your work. Use the Editing Checklist.*

> ### Editing Checklist
>
> Did you use the correct . . . ?
> ☐ adjective clause (identifying or nonidentifying)
> ☐ relative pronoun, ***where***, or ***when***
> ☐ verb form in the adjective clause
> ☐ punctuation for nonidentifying adjective clauses

A | *Circle the correct words to complete the sentences.*

1. Mrs. Johnson, <u>whom / whose</u> dog I walk, lives next door.

2. She lives in an old house <u>that / who</u> her father built.

3. It's right next to the park <u>where / when</u> I run every morning.

4. She has a daughter <u>which / who</u> I went to school with.

5. We became best friends in 2000 <u>where / when</u> we were in the same class.

6. Ann, <u>that / who</u> I still call every week, moved to Canada last year.

B | *Complete each sentence with a relative pronoun,* **when,** *or* **where.**

1. Today I took a trip back to Brooklyn, _____ I grew up.

2. I saw the house _____ my family lived in for more than 10 years.

3. I walked to the high school _____ I attended.

4. I saw some old neighbors _____ I remembered well.

5. Mrs. Gutkin, _____ son I used to help with his homework, still lives next door.

6. She's a very nice woman _____ I always liked.

7. Today brought back a lot of good memories _____ I had forgotten.

C | *Find and correct seven mistakes. Remember to check punctuation.*

I grew up in an apartment building who my grandparents owned. There was a small dining room when we had family meals and a kitchen in that I ate my breakfast. My aunt, uncle, and cousin, in who home I spent a lot of my time lived in an identical apartment on the fourth floor. I remember the time my parents gave me a toy phone set that we set up so I could talk to my cousin. There weren't many children in the building, but I often visited the building manager, who's son I liked. I enjoyed living in the apartment, but for me it was a happy day where we moved into our own house.

From Grammar to Writing
ADDING DETAILS WITH ADJECTIVE CLAUSES

Details help to explain what you are writing about. One way to add details is with **adjective clauses** that give more **information about** *who*, *what*, *which*, *whose*, *where*, and *when*.

EXAMPLE: She was born in Chile. ➔
She was born in Chile, *where* **her parents had emigrated after the war**.

1 | *Read this student's essay about a famous person. Underline the adjective clauses.*

Writer, Poet, Diplomat

Octavio Paz is considered one of the greatest writers <u>that the Spanish-speaking world has produced</u>. He was born in Mexico in 1914. As a child, he was exposed to writing by his grandfather and father. His childhood was hard because of his father's political activities, which forced his family into exile and poverty.

Paz began writing when he was very young. He published his first poem at age 16. He attended law school in Mexico City, where he joined a Marxist student group. Around the same time, he married his first wife, Elena Garro. Paz's literary career received a boost in his early 20s when he sent a manuscript to the Chilean poet Pablo Neruda. Neruda was impressed, and he encouraged Paz to go to Spain to attend a writing conference. Paz remained there and joined the forces that were fighting against General Franco in the Spanish Civil War. Later, he went on to become a diplomat, representing his country in France, Japan, the United States, and India.

Paz wrote both poetry and prose. He is most famous for *The Labyrinth of Solitude*, a collection of essays that deal with the character of the Mexican people. He also founded *Vuelta*. In 1990 he received the Nobel Prize for Literature. He died eight years later.

2 | *The student added details in a second draft. Read the student's notes below. Then find places in the essay to add the information. Rewrite the sentences with adjective clauses. Remember to use commas when necessary.*

> ## Additional Information
> • Both his grandfather and father were political journalists.
> • Elena Garro was also a writer.
> • Pablo Neruda was already famous in Spain and Latin America.
> • Vuelta was one of Latin America's most famous literary magazines.

1. _As a child, he was exposed to writing by his grandfather and father, who were both political journalists._

2. _____

3. _____

4. _____

3 | *Before you write . . .*

1. Choose a famous person to write about. Do some research in the library or on the Internet. Take notes about the main events in this person's life.

2. Exchange notes with a partner. Write a question mark (**?**) next to items you would like your partner to add more details about.

4 | *Write your essay. Answer your partner's questions using adjective clauses to add details.*

5 | *Exchange essays with a different partner. Underline the adjective clauses. Write a question mark (**?**) where you would like more information. Then answer the following questions.*

	Yes	No
1. Did the writer use adjective clauses?	☐	☐
2. Did the writer use the correct relative pronoun for each adjective clause?	☐	☐
3. Did the writer punctuate the adjective clauses correctly?	☐	☐
4. Did the writer give enough details?	☐	☐

6 | *Work with your partner. Discuss each other's editing questions from Exercise 5. Then rewrite your essay and make any necessary corrections.*

APPENDICES

1 Irregular Verbs

BASE FORM	SIMPLE PAST	PAST PARTICIPLE
arise	arose	arisen
awake	awoke	awoken
be	was/were	been
beat	beat	beaten/beat
become	became	become
begin	began	begun
bend	bent	bent
bet	bet	bet
bite	bit	bitten
bleed	bled	bled
blow	blew	blown
break	broke	broken
bring	brought	brought
build	built	built
burn	burned/burnt	burned/burnt
burst	burst	burst
buy	bought	bought
catch	caught	caught
choose	chose	chosen
cling	clung	clung
come	came	come
cost	cost	cost
creep	crept	crept
cut	cut	cut
deal	dealt	dealt
dig	dug	dug
dive	dived/dove	dived
do	did	done
draw	drew	drawn
dream	dreamed/dreamt	dreamed/dreamt
drink	drank	drunk
drive	drove	driven
eat	ate	eaten
fall	fell	fallen
feed	fed	fed
feel	felt	felt
fight	fought	fought
find	found	found
fit	fit/fitted	fit
flee	fled	fled
fling	flung	flung
fly	flew	flown
forbid	forbade/forbid	forbidden
forget	forgot	forgotten
forgive	forgave	forgiven
freeze	froze	frozen
get	got	gotten/got
give	gave	given
go	went	gone
grind	ground	ground
grow	grew	grown

BASE FORM	SIMPLE PAST	PAST PARTICIPLE
hang	hung*/hanged**	hung*/hanged**
have	had	had
hear	heard	heard
hide	hid	hidden
hit	hit	hit
hold	held	held
hurt	hurt	hurt
keep	kept	kept
kneel	knelt/kneeled	knelt/kneeled
knit	knit/knitted	knit/knitted
know	knew	known
lay	laid	laid
lead	led	led
leap	leaped/leapt	leaped/leapt
leave	left	left
lend	lent	lent
let	let	let
lie (*lie down*)	lay	lain
light	lit/lighted	lit/lighted
lose	lost	lost
make	made	made
mean	meant	meant
meet	met	met
pay	paid	paid
prove	proved	proved/proven
put	put	put
quit	quit	quit
read /rid/	read /rɛd/	read /rɛd/
ride	rode	ridden
ring	rang	rung
rise	rose	risen
run	ran	run
say	said	said
see	saw	seen
seek	sought	sought
sell	sold	sold
send	sent	sent
set	set	set
sew	sewed	sewn/sewed
shake	shook	shaken
shave	shaved	shaved/shaven
shine (*intransitive*)	shone/shined	shone/shined
shoot	shot	shot
show	showed	shown
shrink	shrank/shrunk	shrunk/shrunken
shut	shut	shut
sing	sang	sung
sink	sank/sunk	sunk

* hung = *hung an object*
** hanged = *executed by hanging*

(continued on next page)

Base Form	Simple Past	Past Participle	Base Form	Simple Past	Past Participle
sit	sat	sat	swim	swam	swum
sleep	slept	slept	swing	swung	swung
slide	slid	slid	take	took	taken
speak	spoke	spoken	teach	taught	taught
speed	sped/speeded	sped/speeded	tear	tore	torn
spend	spent	spent	tell	told	told
spill	spilled/spilt	spilled/spilt	think	thought	thought
spin	spun	spun	throw	threw	thrown
spit	spit/spat	spat	understand	understood	understood
split	split	split	upset	upset	upset
spread	spread	spread	wake	woke	woken
spring	sprang	sprung	wear	wore	worn
stand	stood	stood	weave	wove/weaved	woven/weaved
steal	stole	stolen	weep	wept	wept
stick	stuck	stuck	win	won	won
sting	stung	stung	wind	wound	wound
stink	stank/stunk	stunk	withdraw	withdrew	withdrawn
strike	struck	struck/stricken	wring	wrung	wrung
swear	swore	sworn	write	wrote	written
sweep	swept	swept			

2 Non-Action Verbs

EMOTIONS	MENTAL STATES		WANTS AND PREFERENCES	SENSES AND PERCEPTION	APPEARANCE AND VALUE	POSSESSION AND RELATIONSHIP
admire	agree	imagine	desire	feel	appear	belong
adore	assume	know	hope	hear	be	come from (*origin*)
appreciate	believe	mean	need	notice	cost	contain
care	consider	mind	prefer	observe	equal	have
detest	disagree	presume	want	perceive	look (*seem*)	own
dislike	disbelieve	realize	wish	see	matter	possess
doubt	estimate	recognize		smell	represent	
envy	expect	remember		sound	resemble	
fear	feel (*believe*)	see (*understand*)		taste	seem	
hate	find (*believe*)	suppose			signify	
like	forget	suspect			weigh	
love	guess	think (*believe*)				
miss	hesitate	understand				
regret	hope	wonder				
respect						
trust						

3 Verbs Followed by Gerunds (Base Form of Verb + *-ing*)

acknowledge	celebrate	endure	give up (*stop*)	permit	quit	resist
admit	consider	enjoy	go	postpone	recall	risk
advise	delay	escape	imagine	practice	recommend	suggest
allow	deny	excuse	justify	prevent	regret	support
appreciate	detest	explain	keep (*continue*)	prohibit	report	tolerate
avoid	discontinue	feel like	mention	propose	resent	understand
ban	discuss	finish	mind (*object to*)			
can't help	dislike	forgive	miss			

A-2

4 Verbs Followed by Infinitives (*To* + Base Form of Verb)

afford	can('t) afford	expect	hurry	neglect	promise	volunteer
agree	can't wait	fail	intend	offer	refuse	wait
appear	choose	grow	learn	pay	request	want
arrange	consent	help	manage	plan	seem	wish
ask	decide	hesitate	mean (*intend*)	prepare	struggle	would like
attempt	deserve	hope	need	pretend	swear	yearn

5 Verbs Followed by Object + Infinitive

advise	challenge	encourage	help*	order	remind	urge
allow	choose*	expect*	hire	pay*	request	want*
ask*	convince	forbid	instruct	permit	require	warn
beg*	dare*	force	invite	persuade	teach	wish*
cause	enable	get*	need*	promise*	tell	would like*

*These verbs can also be followed by an infinitive without an object (EXAMPLE: *ask to leave* or *ask someone to leave*).

6 Verbs Followed by Gerunds or Infinitives

begin	forget*	love	start
can't stand	hate	prefer	stop*
continue	like	remember*	try

*These verbs can also be followed by either a gerund or an infinitive, but there is a big difference in meaning.

7 Verb + Preposition Combinations

admit to	choose between	feel like/about	pay for	talk about
advise against	complain about	go along with	plan on	thank s.o. for
apologize for	deal with	insist on	rely on	think about
approve of	decide on	look forward to	resort to	wonder about
believe in	dream about/of	object to	succeed in	worry about

8 Adjective + Preposition Combinations

accustomed to	awful at	concerned about	fed up with	known for	sad about	sorry for/about
afraid of	bad at	content with	fond of	nervous about	safe from	surprised at/about/by
amazed at/by	bored with/by	curious about	glad about	opposed to	satisfied with	terrible at
angry at	capable of	different from	good at	pleased about	shocked at/by	tired of
ashamed of	careful of	excited about	happy about	ready for	sick of	used to
aware of	certain about	famous for	interested in	responsible for	slow at/in	worried about

9 Adjectives Followed by Infinitives

afraid	ashamed	difficult	easy	glad	pleased	reluctant	surprised
alarmed	curious	disappointed	embarrassed	happy	prepared	right	touched
amazed	delighted	distressed	encouraged	hesitant	proud	sad	upset
angry	depressed	disturbed	excited	likely	ready	shocked	willing
anxious	determined	eager	fortunate	lucky	relieved	sorry	wrong

10 Nouns Followed by Infinitives

attempt	desire	offer	price	right
chance	dream	opportunity	promise	time
choice	failure	permission	reason	trouble
decision	need	plan	request	way

11 Irregular Comparisons of Adjectives, Adverbs, and Quantifiers

ADJECTIVE	ADVERB	COMPARATIVE	SUPERLATIVE
bad	badly	worse	the worst
far	far	farther/further	the farthest/furthest
good	well	better	the best
little	little	less	the least
many/a lot of	—	more	the most
much*/a lot of	much*/a lot	more	the most

*Much is usually only used in questions and negative statements.

12 Adjectives that Form the Comparative and Superlative in Two Ways

ADJECTIVE	COMPARATIVE	SUPERLATIVE
common	commoner/more common	commonest/most common
cruel	crueler/more cruel	cruelest/most cruel
deadly	deadlier/more deadly	deadliest/most deadly
friendly	friendlier/more friendly	friendliest/most friendly
handsome	handsomer/more handsome	handsomest/most handsome
happy	happier/more happy	happiest/most happy
likely	likelier/more likely	likeliest/most likely
lively	livelier/more lively	liveliest/most lively
lonely	lonelier/more lonely	loneliest/most lonely
lovely	lovelier/more lovely	loveliest/most lovely
narrow	narrower/more narrow	narrowest/most narrow
pleasant	pleasanter/more pleasant	pleasantest/most pleasant
polite	politer/more polite	politest/most polite
quiet	quieter/more quiet	quietest/most quiet
shallow	shallower/more shallow	shallowest/most shallow
sincere	sincerer/more sincere	sincerest/most sincere
stupid	stupider/more stupid	stupidest/most stupid
true	truer/more true	truest/most true

13 Participial Adjectives

-ed	-ing	-ed	-ing	-ed	-ing
alarmed	alarming	disturbed	disturbing	moved	moving
amazed	amazing	embarrassed	embarrassing	paralyzed	paralyzing
amused	amusing	entertained	entertaining	pleased	pleasing
annoyed	annoying	excited	exciting	relaxed	relaxing
astonished	astonishing	exhausted	exhausting	satisfied	satisfying
bored	boring	fascinated	fascinating	shocked	shocking
confused	confusing	frightened	frightening	surprised	surprising
depressed	depressing	horrified	horrifying	terrified	terrifying
disappointed	disappointing	inspired	inspiring	tired	tiring
disgusted	disgusting	interested	interesting	touched	touching
distressed	distressing	irritated	irritating	troubled	troubling

14 Reporting Verbs

STATEMENTS

acknowledge	complain	note	state
add	conclude	observe	suggest
admit	confess	promise	tell
announce	declare	remark	warn
answer	deny	repeat	whisper
argue	exclaim	reply	write
assert	explain	report	yell
believe	indicate	respond	
claim	maintain	say	
comment	mean	shout	

INSTRUCTIONS, COMMANDS, REQUESTS, AND INVITATIONS

advise	invite
ask	order
caution	say
command	tell
demand	urge
instruct	warn

QUESTIONS

ask
inquire
question
want to know
wonder

15 Time Word Changes in Indirect Speech

DIRECT SPEECH		INDIRECT SPEECH
now	→	then
today	→	that day
tomorrow	→	the next day OR the following day OR the day after
yesterday	→	the day before OR the previous day
this week/month/year	→	that week/month/year
last week/month/year	→	the week/month/year before
next week/month/year	→	the following week/month/year

16 Phrases Introducing Embedded Questions

I don't know . . .	I'd like to know . . .	Do you know . . . ?
I don't understand . . .	I want to understand . . .	Do you understand . . . ?
I wonder . . .	I'd like to find out . . .	Can you tell me . . . ?
I'm not sure . . .	We need to find out . . .	Could you explain . . . ?
I can't remember . . .	Let's ask . . .	Can you remember . . . ?
I can't imagine . . .		Would you show me . . . ?
It doesn't say . . .		Who knows . . . ?

17 Verbs and Expressions Used Reflexively

allow yourself	be proud of yourself	enjoy yourself	keep yourself (busy)	remind yourself
amuse yourself	behave yourself	feel sorry for yourself	kill yourself	see yourself
ask yourself	believe in yourself	forgive yourself	look after yourself	take care of yourself
avail yourself of	blame yourself	help yourself	look at yourself	talk to yourself
be hard on yourself	cut yourself	hurt yourself	prepare yourself	teach yourself
be yourself	deprive yourself of	imagine yourself	pride yourself on	tell yourself
be pleased with yourself	dry yourself	introduce yourself	push yourself	treat yourself

18 Transitive Phrasal Verbs

(s.o. = someone   s.t. = something)
- **Separable phrasal verbs** show the object between the verb and the particle: **call** s.o. **up**.
- **Verbs that must be separated** have an asterisk (*): **do** s.t. **over***
- **Inseparable phrasal verbs** show the object after the particle: **carry on** s.t.

REMEMBER: You can put a **noun object** between the verb and the particle of **separable** two-word verbs (*call Jan up* OR *call up Jan*). You <u>must</u> put a **pronoun object** between the verb and the particle of separable verbs (*call her up* NOT ~~call up her~~).

PHRASAL VERB	MEANING	PHRASAL VERB	MEANING
ask s.o. **over***	*invite to one's home*	**draw** s.t. **together**	*unite*
block s.t. **out**	*stop from passing through (light/ noise)*	**dream** s.t. **up**	*invent*
		drink s.t. **up**	*drink completely*
blow s.t. **out**	*stop burning by blowing air on it*	**drop** s.o. or s.t. **off**	*take someplace*
blow s.t. **up**	1. *make explode*	**drop out of** s.t.	*quit*
	2. *fill with air (a balloon)*	**empty** s.t. **out**	*empty completely*
	3. *make something larger (a photo)*	**end up with** s.t.	*have an unexpected result*
bring s.t. **about**	*make happen*	**fall for** s.o.	*feel romantic love for*
bring s.o. or s.t. **back**	*return*	**fall for** s.t.	*be tricked by, believe*
bring s.o. **down***	*depress*	**figure** s.o. or s.t. **out**	*understand (after thinking about)*
bring s.t. **out**	*introduce (a new product/book)*	**fill** s.t. **in**	*complete with information*
bring s.o. **up**	*raise (children)*	**fill** s.t. **out**	*complete (a form)*
bring s.t. **up**	*bring attention to*	**fill** s.t. **up**	*fill completely*
build s.t. **up**	*increase*	**find** s.t. **out**	*learn information*
burn s.t. **down**	*burn completely*	**fix** s.t. **up**	*redecorate (a home)*
call s.o. **back***	*return a phone call*	**follow through with** s.t.	*complete*
call s.o. **in**	*ask for help with a problem*	**get** s.t. **across**	*get people to understand an idea*
call s.t. **off**	*cancel*	**get off** s.t.	*leave (a bus/a train)*
call s.o. **up**	*contact by phone*	**get on** s.t.	*board (a bus/a train)*
carry on s.t.	*continue*	**get out of** s.t.	*leave (a car/taxi)*
carry s.t. **out**	*conduct (an experiment/a plan)*	**get** s.t. **out of** s.t.*	*benefit from*
cash in on s.t.	*profit from*	**get through with** s.t.	*finish*
charge s.t. **up**	*charge with electricity*	**get to** s.o. or s.t.	1. *reach s.o. or s.t.*
check s.t. **out**	*examine*		2. *upset s.o.*
cheer s.o. **up**	*cause to feel happier*	**get together with** s.o.	*meet*
clean s.o. or s.t. **up**	*clean completely*	**give** s.t. **away**	*give without charging money*
clear s.t. **up**	*explain*	**give** s.t. **back**	*return*
close s.t. **down**	*close by force*	**give** s.t. **out**	*distribute*
come off s.t.	*become unattached*	**give** s.t. **up**	*quit, abandon*
come up with s.t.	*invent*	**go after** s.o. or s.t.	*try to get or win, pursue*
count on s.o. or s.t.	*depend on*	**go along with** s.t.	*support*
cover s.o. or s.t. **up**	*cover completely*	**go over** s.t.	*review*
cross s.t. **out**	*draw a line through*	**hand** s.t. **in**	*submit, give work (to a boss/teacher)*
cut s.t. **down**	1. *bring down by cutting (a tree)*		
	2. *reduce*	**hand** s.t. **out**	*distribute*
cut s.t. **off**	1. *stop the supply of*	**hang** s.t. **up**	*put on a hook or hanger*
	2. *remove by cutting*	**help** s.o. **out**	*assist*
cut s.t. **out**	*remove by cutting*	**hold** s.t. **on**	*keep attached*
cut s.t. **up**	*cut into small pieces*	**keep** s.o. or s.t. **away**	*cause to stay at a distance*
do s.t. **over***	*do again*	**keep** s.t. **on***	*not remove (a piece of clothing/jewelry)*
do s.o. or s.t. **up**	*make more beautiful*		

PHRASAL VERB	**MEANING**	**PHRASAL VERB**	**MEANING**
keep s.o. or s.t. **out**	prevent from entering	**show up on** s.t.	appear
keep up with s.o. or s.t.	go as fast as	**shut** s.t. **off**	stop (a machine/light)
lay s.o. **off**	end employment	**sign** s.o. **up** (for s.t.)	register
lay s.t. **out**	1. arrange according to a plan	**start** s.t. **over***	start again
	2. spend money	**stick with/to** s.o. or s.t.	not quit, not leave, persevere
leave s.t. **on**	1. not turn off (a light/radio)	**straighten** s.t. **up**	make neat
	2. not remove (a piece of clothing/jewelry)	**switch** s.t. **on**	start (a machine/light)
		take s.t. **away**	remove
leave s.t. **out**	omit, not include	**take** s.o. or s.t. **back**	return
let s.o. **down**	disappoint	**take** s.t. **down**	remove
let s.o. or s.t. **in**	allow to enter	**take** s.t. **in**	1. notice, understand, and remember
let s.o. **off**	1. allow to leave (a bus/car)		2. earn (money)
	2. not punish	**take** s.t. **off**	remove
let s.o. or s.t. **out**	allow to leave	**take** s.o. **on**	hire
light s.t. **up**	illuminate	**take** s.t. **on**	agree to do
look after s.o. or s.t.	take care of	**take** s.t. **out**	borrow from a library
look into s.t.	research	**take** s.t. **up**	begin a job or activity
look s.o. or s.t. **over**	examine	**talk** s.o. **into***	persuade
look s.t. **up**	try to find (in a book/on the Internet)	**talk** s.t. **over**	discuss
		team up with s.o.	start to work with
make s.t. **up**	create	**tear** s.t. **down**	destroy
miss out on s.t.	lose the chance for something good	**tear** s.t. **up**	tear into small pieces
		think back on s.o. or s.t.	remember
move s.t. **around***	change the location	**think** s.t. **over**	consider
pass s.t. **out**	distribute	**think** s.t. **up**	invent
pass s.o. or s.t. **up**	decide not to use	**throw** s.t. **away/out**	discard, put in the trash
pay s.o. or s.t. **back**	repay	**touch** s.t. **up**	improve by making small changes
pick s.o. or s.t. **out**	1. choose		
	2. identify	**try** s.t. **on**	put clothing on to see if it fits
pick s.o. or s.t. **up**	lift	**try** s.t. **out**	use to see if it works
pick s.t. **up**	1. buy, purchase	**turn** s.t. **around***	change the direction so the front is at the back
	2. get (an idea/an interest)		
	3. answer the phone	**turn** s.o. **down**	reject
point s.o. or s.t. **out**	indicate	**turn** s.t. **down**	1. lower the volume (a TV/radio)
put s.t. **away**	put in an appropriate place		2. reject (a job/an idea)
put s.t. **back**	return to its original place	**turn** s.t. **in**	submit, give work (to a boss/teacher)
put s.o. or s.t. **down**	stop holding		
put s.o. **off**	discourage	**turn** s.o. or s.t. **into***	change from one form to another
put s.t. **off**	delay	**turn** s.o. **off***	[slang] destroy interest
put s.t. **on**	cover the body (with clothes or jewelry)	**turn** s.t. **off**	stop (a machine), extinguish (a light)
put s.t. **together**	assemble		
put s.t. **up**	erect	**turn** s.t. **on**	start (a machine/light)
run into s.o.	meet accidentally	**turn** s.t. **over**	turn something so the top side is at the bottom
see s.t. **through***	complete		
send s.t. **back**	return	**turn** s.t. **up**	make louder (a TV/radio)
send s.t. **out**	mail	**use** s.t. **up**	use completely, consume
set s.t. **off**	cause to explode	**wake** s.o. **up**	awaken
set s.t. **up**	1. prepare for use	**watch out for** s.o. or s.t.	be careful about
	2. establish (a business/an organization)	**work** s.t. **off**	remove by work or activity
		work s.t. **out**	solve, understand
settle on s.t.	choose s.t. after thinking about many possibilities	**write** s.t. **down**	write on a piece of paper
		write s.t. **up**	write in a finished form
show s.o. or s.t. **off**	display the best qualities		

Phrasal Verb	Meaning
act up	cause problems
blow up	explode
break down	stop working (a machine)
break out	happen suddenly
burn down	burn completely
call back	return a phone call
catch on	1. become popular
	2. understand
cheer up	make happier
clean up	clean completely
clear up	become clear
close down	stop operating
come about	happen
come along	come with, accompany
come around	happen
come back	return
come down	become less (price)
come in	enter
come off	become unattached
come out	appear
come up	arise
dress up	wear special clothes
drop in	visit by surprise
drop out	quit
eat out	eat in a restaurant
empty out	empty completely
end up	1. do something unexpected or unintended
	2. reach a final place or condition
fall off	become detached
find out	learn information
follow through	complete
fool around	act playful
get ahead	make progress, succeed
get along	have a good relationship
get back	return
get by	survive
get off	1. leave (a bus, the Internet)
	2. end a phone conversation
get on	enter, board (a bus, a train)
get through	finish
get together	meet
get up	rise from bed, arise
give up	quit

Phrasal Verb	Meaning
go away	leave a place or person
go back	return
go down	become less (price, number), decrease
go off	explode (a gun/fireworks)
go on	continue
go out	leave
go over	succeed with an audience
go up	1. be built
	2. become more (price, number), increase
grow up	become an adult
hang up	end a phone call
hold on	1. wait
	2. not hang up the phone
keep away	stay at a distance
keep on	continue
keep out	not enter
keep up	go as fast as
lie down	recline
light up	illuminate
look out	be careful
make up	end a disagreement, reconcile
miss out	lose the chance for something good
pay off	be worthwhile
pick up	improve
play around	have fun
run out	not have enough of
show up	appear
sign up	register
sit down	take a seat
slip up	make a mistake
stand up	rise
start over	start again
stay up	remain awake
straighten up	make neat
take off	depart (a plane)
turn out	have a particular result
turn up	appear
wake up	stop sleeping
watch out	be careful
work out	1. be resolved
	2. exercise

A. SOCIAL MODALS AND EXPRESSIONS

FUNCTION	MODAL OR EXPRESSION	TIME	EXAMPLES
Ability	can can't	Present	• Sam **can swim**. • He **can't skate**.
	could couldn't	Past	• We **could swim** last year. • We **couldn't skate**.
	be able to* not be able to*	All Verb Forms	• Lea **is able to run** fast. • She **wasn't able to run** fast last year.
Advice	should shouldn't ought to had better** had better not**	Present or Future	• You **should study** more. • You **shouldn't miss** class. • We **ought to leave**. • We**'d better go**. • We**'d better not stay**.
Advisability in the Past and **Regret or Blame**	should have shouldn't have ought to have could have might have	Past	• I **should have become** a doctor. • I **shouldn't have wasted** time. • He **ought to have told** me. • She **could have gone** to college. • You **might have called**. I waited for hours.
Necessity	have to* not have to*	All Verb Forms	• He **has to go** now. • He **doesn't have to go** yet. • I **had to go** yesterday. • I **will have to go** soon.
	have got to* must	Present or Future	• He**'s got** to leave! • You **must use** a pen for the test.
Permission	can can't could may may not	Present or Future	• **Can** I **sit** here? • **Can** I **call** tomorrow? • Yes, you **can**. • No, you **can't**. Sorry. • **Could** he **leave** now? • **May** I **borrow** your pen? • Yes, you **may**. • No, you **may not**. Sorry.
Prohibition	must not can't	Present or Future	• You **must not drive** without a license. • You **can't drive** without a license.
Requests	can can't could will would	Present or Future	• **Can** you **close** the door, please? • Sure, I **can**. • Sorry, I **can't**. • **Could** you please **answer** the phone? • **Will** you **wash** the dishes, please? • **Would** you please **mail** this letter?

*The meaning of this expression is similar to the meaning of a modal. Unlike a modal, it has *-s* for third-person singular.

**The meaning of this expression is similar to the meaning of a modal. Like a modal, it has no *-s* for third-person singular.

B. LOGICAL MODALS AND EXPRESSIONS

FUNCTION	MODAL OR EXPRESSION	TIME	EXAMPLES
Conclusions and Possibility	must must not have to* have got to*	Present	• This **must be** her house. Her name is on the door. • She **must not be** home. I don't see her car. • She **has to know** him. They went to school together. • He's **got to be** guilty. We saw him do it.
	may may not might might not could	Present or Future	• She **may be** home now. • It **may not rain** tomorrow. • Lee **might be sick** today. • He **might not come** to class. • They **could be** at the library. • It **could rain** tomorrow.
	may have may not have might have might not have could have	Past	• They **may have left** already. I don't see them. • They **may not have arrived** yet. • He **might have called.** I'll check my phone messages. • He **might not have left** a message. • She **could have forgotten** to mail the letter.
Impossibility	can't	Present or Future	• That **can't be** Ana. She left for France yesterday. • It **can't snow** tomorrow. It's going to be too warm.
	couldn't	Present	• He **couldn't be** guilty. He wasn't in town when the crime occurred. • The teacher **couldn't give** the test tomorrow. Tomorrow's Saturday.
	couldn't have	Past	• You **couldn't have failed**. You studied so hard.

*The meaning of this expression is similar to the meaning of a modal. Unlike a modal, it has -s for third-person singular.

21 Irregular Plural Nouns

SINGULAR	PLURAL	SINGULAR	PLURAL	SINGULAR	PLURAL	SINGULAR	PLURAL
analysis	analyses	half	halves	person	people	deer	deer
basis	bases	knife	knives	man	men	fish	fish
crisis	crises	leaf	leaves	woman	women	sheep	sheep
hypothesis	hypotheses	life	lives	child	children		
		loaf	loaves	foot	feet		
		shelf	shelves	tooth	teeth		
		wife	wives	goose	geese		
				mouse	mice		

22   Spelling Rules for the Simple Present: Third-Person Singular (*He, She, It*)

1. Add *-s* for most verbs.

work	work**s**
buy	buy**s**
ride	ride**s**
return	return**s**

2. Add *-es* for verbs that end in *-ch*, *-s*, *-sh*, *-x*, or *-z*.

watch	watch**es**
pass	pass**es**
rush	rush**es**
relax	relax**es**
buzz	buzz**es**

3. Change the *y* to *i* and add *-es* when the base form ends in a **consonant** + *y*.

study	stud**ies**
hurry	hurr**ies**
dry	dr**ies**

   Do not change the *y* when the base form ends in a vowel + *y*. Add *-s*.

play	play**s**
enjoy	enjoy**s**

4. A few verbs are irregular.

be	**is**
do	**does**
go	**goes**
have	**has**

23   Spelling Rules for Base Form of Verb + *-ing* (Progressive and Gerund)

1. Add *-ing* to the base form of the verb.

read	read**ing**
stand	stand**ing**

2. If the verb ends in a silent *-e*, drop the final *-e* and add *-ing*.

leave	leav**ing**
take	tak**ing**

3. In **one-syllable verbs**, if the last three letters are a consonant-vowel-consonant combination (CVC), double the last consonant and add *-ing*.

   C V C
   ↓ ↓ ↓
   s i t   sit**ting**

   C V C
   ↓ ↓ ↓
   p l a n   plan**ning**

4. In verbs of **two or more syllables** that end in a consonant-vowel-consonant combination, double the last consonant only if the last syllable is stressed.*

admít	admít**ting**	*(The last syllable is stressed.)*
whísper	whisper**ing**	*(The last syllable is not stressed, so don't double the **-r**.)*

5. If the verb ends in *-ie*, change the *ie* to *y* before adding *-ing*.

die	d**ying**
lie	l**ying**

   ---

   *The symbol ′ shows main stress.

   Do not double the last consonant in verbs that end in *-w*, *-x*, or *-y*.

sew	sew**ing**
fix	fix**ing**
play	play**ing**

24 Spelling Rules for Base Form of Verb + -ed (Simple Past and Past Participle of Regular Verbs)

1. If the verb ends in a consonant, add -ed.

return	return**ed**
help	help**ed**

2. If the verb ends in -e, add -d.

live	live**d**
create	create**d**
die	die**d**

3. In **one-syllable verbs**, if the last three letters are a consonant-vowel-consonant combination (CVC), double the last consonant before adding -ed.

   C V C
   ↓ ↓ ↓
   h o p   hop**ped**

   C V C
   ↓ ↓ ↓
   p l a n   plan**ned**

   Do not double the last consonant of one-syllable words ending in -**w**, -**x**, or -**y**.

bow	bow**ed**
mix	mix**ed**
play	play**ed**

4. In verbs of **two or more syllables** that end in a consonant-vowel-consonant combination, double the last consonant only if the last syllable is stressed.*

pre′fer	prefer**red**	*(The last syllable is stressed, so double the r.)*
′visit	visit**ed**	*(The last syllable is not stressed, don't double the -**t**.)*

5. If the verb ends in **consonant** + **y**, change the y to *i* and add -ed.

worry	worr**ied**
carry	carr**ied**

6. If the verb ends in **vowel** + **y**, add -ed. (Do not change the y to *i*.)

play	play**ed**
annoy	annoy**ed**
EXCEPTIONS:	pay—p**aid**
	lay—l**aid**
	say—s**aid**

   *The symbol ′ shows main stress.

25 Spelling Rules for the Comparative (-er) and Superlative (-est) of Adjectives

1. With **one-syllable** adjectives add -**er** to form the comparative. Add -**est** to form the superlative.

cheap	cheap**er**	cheap**est**
bright	bright**er**	bright**est**

2. If the adjective ends in -**e**, add -**r** or -**st**.

nice	nice**r**	nice**st**

3. If the adjective ends in a **consonant** + **y**, change **y** to i before you add -**er** or -**est**.

pretty	prett**ier**	prett**iest**

   EXCEPTION:

shy	shy**er**	shy**est**

4. In one-syllable adjectives, if the last three letters are a consonant-vowel-consonant combination (CVC), double the last consonant before adding -**er** or -**est**.

   C V C
   ↓ ↓ ↓
   b i g   big**ger**   big**gest**

   Do not double the consonant in words ending in -**w** or -**y**.

slow	slow**er**	slow**est**
gray	gray**er**	gray**est**

26   Spelling Rules for Adverbs Ending in *-ly*

1. Add *-ly* to the corresponding adjective.

nice	nice**ly**
quiet	quiet**ly**
beautiful	beautiful**ly**

2. If the adjective ends in **consonant** + *y*, change the *y* to *i* before adding *-ly*.

easy	eas**ily**

3. If the adjective ends in *-le*, drop the *e* and add *-y*.

possible	possib**ly**

Do not drop the *e* for other adjectives ending in *-e*.

extreme	extreme**ly**

EXCEPTION:

true	tru**ly**

4. If the adjective ends in *-ic*, add *-ally*.

basic	basic**ally**
fantastic	fantastic**ally**

27   Direct Speech: Punctuation Rules

Direct speech may either follow or come before the reporting verb.

When direct speech follows the reporting verb:

a. Put a comma after the reporting verb.

b. Use opening quotation marks (") before the first word of the direct speech.

c. Begin the quotation with a capital letter.

d. Use the appropriate end punctuation for the direct speech. It may be a period (.), a question mark (**?**), or an exclamation point (**!**).

e. Put closing quotation marks (") after the end punctuation of the quotation.

> **EXAMPLES:**   He said, "I had a good time."
> She asked, "Where's the party**?**"
> They shouted, "Be careful**!**"

When direct speech comes before the reporting verb:

a. Begin the sentence with opening quotation marks (").

b. Use the appropriate end punctuation for the direct speech.
If the direct speech is a statement, use a comma (**,**).
If the direct speech is a question, use a question mark (**?**).
If the direct speech is an exclamation, use an exclamation point (**!**).

c. Use closing quotation marks after the end punctuation for the direct speech (").

d. Begin the reporting clause with a lowercase letter.

e. Use a period at the end of the main sentence (**.**).

> **EXAMPLES:**   "I had a good time," he said.
> "Where's the party**?**" she asked.
> "Be careful**!**" they shouted.

28 Pronunciation Table

These are the pronunciation symbols used in this text. Listen to the pronunciation of the key words.

	VOWELS				CONSONANTS		
Symbol	Key Word	Symbol	Key Word	Symbol	Key Word	Symbol	Key Word
i	beat, feed	ə	banana, among	p	pack, happy	ʃ	ship, machine, station,
ɪ	bit, did	ɚ	shirt, murder	b	back, rubber		special, discussion
eɪ	date, paid	aɪ	bite, cry, buy, eye	t	tie	ʒ	measure, vision
ɛ	bet, bed	aʊ	about, how	d	die	h	hot, who
æ	bat, bad	ɔɪ	voice, boy	k	came, key, quick	m	men, some
ɑ	box, odd, father	ɪr	beer	g	game, guest	n	sun, know, pneumonia
ɔ	bought, dog	ɛr	bare	tʃ	church, nature, watch	ŋ	sung, ringing
oʊ	boat, road	ɑr	bar	dʒ	judge, general, major	w	wet, white
ʊ	book, good	ɔr	door	f	fan, photograph	l	light, long
u	boot, food, student	ʊr	tour	v	van	r	right, wrong
ʌ	but, mud, mother			θ	thing, breath	y	yes, use, music
				ð	then, breathe	t̮	butter, bottle
				s	sip, city, psychology		
				z	zip, please, goes		

29 Pronunciation Rules for the Simple Present: Third-Person Singular (He, She, It)

1. The third-person singular in the simple present always ends in the letter -s. There are three different pronunciations for the final sound of the third-person singular.

/s/	/z/	/ɪz/
talks	loves	dances

2. The final sound is pronounced /s/ after the voiceless sounds /p/, /t/, /k/, and /f/.

top	tops
get	gets
take	takes
laugh	laughs

3. The final sound is pronounced /z/ after the voiced sounds /b/, /d/, /g/, /v/, /m/, /n/, /ŋ/, /l/, /r/, and /ð/.

describe	describes
spend	spends
hug	hugs
live	lives
bathe	bathes
seem	seems
remain	remains
sing	sings
tell	tells
lower	lowers

4. The final sound is pronounced /z/ after all **vowel sounds**.

agree	agrees
try	tries
stay	stays
know	knows

5. The final sound is pronounced /ɪz/ after the sounds /s/, /z/, /ʃ/, /ʒ/, and /tʃ/. /dʒ/ adds a syllable to the verb.

relax	relaxes
freeze	freezes
rush	rushes
massage	massages
watch	watches
judge	judges

6. *Do* and *say* have a change in vowel sound.

do	/du/	does	/dʌz/
say	/seɪ/	says	/sɛz/

30 Pronunciation Rules for the Simple Past and Past Participle of Regular Verbs

1. The regular simple past and past participle always ends in the letter *-d*. There are three different pronunciations for the final sound of the regular simple past and past participle.

/t/	/d/	/ɪd/
raced	lived	attended

2. The final sound is pronounced /t/ after the voiceless sounds /p/, /k/, /f/, /s/, /ʃ/, and /tʃ/.

hop	hopped
work	worked
laugh	laughed
address	addressed
publish	published
watch	watched

3. The final sound is pronounced /d/ after the voiced sounds /b/, /g/, /v/, /z/, /ʒ/, /dʒ/, /m/, /n/, /ŋ/, /l/, /r/, and /ð/.

rub	rubbed
hug	hugged
live	lived
surprise	surprised
massage	massaged
change	changed
rhyme	rhymed
return	returned
bang	banged
enroll	enrolled
appear	appeared
bathe	bathed

4. The final sound is pronounced /d/ after all **vowel sounds**.

agree	agreed
play	played
die	died
enjoy	enjoyed
row	rowed

5. The final sound is pronounced /ɪd/ after /t/ and /d/. /ɪd/ adds a syllable to the verb.

start	started
decide	decided

	USE FOR . . .	**EXAMPLES**
capital letter	• the pronoun *I* • proper nouns • the first word of a sentence	Tomorrow **I** will be here at 2:00. His name is **Karl**. He lives in **Germany**. **When** does the train leave? **At** 2:00.
apostrophe (')	• possessive nouns • contractions	Is that **Marta's** coat? **That's** not hers. **It's** mine.
comma (,)	• after items in a list • before sentence connectors *and*, *but*, *or*, and *so* • after the first part of a sentence that begins with *because* • after the first part of a sentence that begins with a preposition • after the first part of a sentence that begins with a time clause or an *if* clause • before and after a non-identifying adjective clause in the middle of a sentence. • before a non-identifying adjective clause at the end of a sentence	He bought **apples, pears, oranges,** and **bananas**. They watched TV, **and** she played video games. **Because it's raining**, we're not walking to work. **Across from the post office**, there's a good restaurant. **After he arrived**, we ate dinner. **If it rains**, we won't go. Tony, **who lives in Paris**, emails me every day. I get emails every day from Tony, **who lives in Paris**.
exclamation mark (!)	• at the end of a sentence to show surprise or a strong feeling	You're here! That's great! Stop! A car is coming!
period (.)	• at the end of a statement	Today is Wednesday.
question mark (?)	• at the end of a question	What day is today?

GLOSSARY OF GRAMMAR TERMS

action verb A verb that describes an action.
- *Alicia **ran** home.*

active sentence A sentence that focuses on the agent (the person or thing doing the action).
- ***Ari kicked** the ball.*

addition A clause or a short sentence that follows a statement and expresses similarity or contrast with the information in the statement.
- *Pedro is tall, **and so is Alex**.*
- *Trish doesn't like sports. **Neither does her sister**.*

adjective A word that describes a noun or pronoun.
- *It's a **good** plan, and it's not **difficult**.*

adjective clause A clause that identifies or gives additional information about a noun.
- *The woman **who called you** didn't leave her name.*
- *Samir, **who you met yesterday**, works in the lab.*

adverb A word that describes a verb, an adjective, or another adverb.
- *She drives **carefully**.*
- *She's a **very** good driver.*
- *She drives **really** well.*

affirmative A statement or answer meaning *Yes*.
- *He **works**. (affirmative statement)*
- ***Yes**, he **does**. (affirmative short answer)*

agent The person or thing doing the action in a sentence. In passive sentences, the word *by* is used before the agent.
- *This magazine is published **by National Geographic**.*

article A word that goes before a noun. The **indefinite** articles are ***a*** and ***an***.
- *I ate **a** sandwich and **an** apple.*

The **definite** article is ***the***.
- *I didn't like **the** sandwich. **The** apple was good.*

auxiliary verb (also called **helping verb**) A verb used with a main verb. *Be, do,* and *have* are often auxiliary verbs. Modals (*can, should, may, must . . .*) are also auxiliary verbs.
- *I **am** exercising right now.*
- *I **should** exercise every day.*
- ***Do** you like to exercise?*

base form The simple form of a verb without any endings (*-s, -ed, -ing*) or other changes.
- ***be, have, go, drive***

clause A group of words that has a subject and a verb. A sentence can have one or more clauses.
- ***We are leaving now.** (one clause)*
- ***If it rains, we won't go.** (two clauses)*

common noun A word for a person, place, or thing (but not the name of the person, place, or thing).
- *Teresa lives in a **house** near the **beach**.*

comparative The form of an adjective or adverb that shows the difference between two people, places, or things.
- *Alain is **shorter** than Brendan. (adjective)*
- *Brendan runs **faster** than Alain. (adverb)*

conditional sentence A sentence that describes a condition and its result. The sentence can be about the past, the present, or the future. The condition and result can be real or unreal.
- *If it **rains**, I **won't go**. (future, real)*
- *If it **had rained**, I **wouldn't have gone**. (past, unreal)*

continuous See **progressive**.

contraction A short form of a word or words. An apostrophe (') replaces the missing letter or letters.
- ***she's** = she is*
- ***can't** = cannot*

count noun A noun that you can count. It has a singular and a plural form.
- *one **book**, two **books***

definite article *the* This article goes before a noun that refers to a specific person, place, or thing.

- *Please bring me **the book** on **the table**. I'm almost finished reading it.*

dependent clause (also called **subordinate clause**) A clause that needs a main clause for its meaning.

- ***If I get home early**, I'll call you.*

direct object A noun or pronoun that receives the action of a verb.

- *Marta kicked **the ball**. I saw **her**.*

direct speech Language that gives the exact words a speaker used. In writing, quotation marks come before and after the speaker's words.

- *"**I saw Bob yesterday**," she said.*
- *"**Is he in school?**"*

embedded question A question that is inside another sentence.

- *I don't know **where the restaurant is**.*
- *Do you know **if it's on Tenth Street**?*

formal Language used in business situations or with adults you do not know.

- *Good afternoon, Mr. Rivera. Please have a seat.*

gerund A noun formed with verb + *-ing* that can be used as a subject or an object.

- ***Swimming** is great exercise.*
- *I enjoy **swimming**.*

helping verb See **auxiliary verb**.

identifying adjective clause A clause that identifies which member of a group the sentence is about.

- *There are 10 students in the class. The student **who sits in front of me** is from Russia.*

***if* clause** The clause that states the condition in a conditional sentence.

- ***If I had known you were here**, I would have called you.*

imperative A sentence that gives a command or instructions.

- ***Hurry!***
- ***Turn left on Main Street.***

indefinite article *a or an* These articles go before a noun that does not refer to a specific person, place, or thing.

- *Can you bring me **a book**? I'm looking for something to read.*

indefinite pronoun A pronoun such as *someone, something, anyone, anything, anywhere, no one, nothing, nowhere, everyone,* and *everything.* An indefinite pronoun does not refer to a specific person, place, or thing.

- ***Someone** called you last night.*
- *Did **anything** happen?*

indirect object A noun or pronoun (often a person) that receives something as the result of the action of the verb.

- *I told **John** the story.*
- *He gave **me** some good advice.*

indirect speech Language that reports what a speaker said without using the exact words.

- *Ann said **she had seen Bob the day before**.*
- *She asked **if he was in school**.*

infinitive *to* + base form of the verb.

- *I want **to leave** now.*

infinitive of purpose *(in order) to* + base form. This form gives the reason for an action.

- *I go to school **(in order) to learn** English.*

informal Language used with family, friends, and children.

- *Hi, Pete. Sit down.*

information question See ***wh-* question**.

inseparable phrasal verb A phrasal verb whose parts must stay together.

- *We **ran into** Tomás at the supermarket. (Nοτ: We ran Tomás into . . .)*

intransitive verb A verb that does not have an object.

- *She **paints**.*
- *We **fell**.*

irregular A word that does not change its form in the usual way.

- *good → well*
- *bad → worse*
- *go → went*

main clause   A clause that can stand alone as a sentence.
- *I called my friend Tom, who lives in Chicago.*

main verb   A verb that describes an action or state. It is often used with an auxiliary verb.
- *Jared is **calling**.*
- *Does he **call** every day?*

modal   A type of auxiliary verb. It goes before a main verb or stands alone as a short answer. It expresses ideas such as ability, advice, permission, and possibility. *Can, could, will, would, may, might, should,* and *must* are modals.
- ***Can** you swim?*
- *Yes, I **can**.*
- *You really **should** learn to swim.*

negative   A statement or answer meaning *No*.
- *He **doesn't** work. (negative statement)*
- ***No**, he **doesn't**. (negative short answer)*

non-action verb   (also called **stative verb**). A verb that does not describe an action. It describes such things as thoughts, feelings, and senses.
- *I **remember** that word.*
- *Chris **loves** ice cream.*
- *It **tastes** great.*

non-count noun   A noun you usually do not count (*air, water, rice, love . . .*). It has only a singular form.
- *The **rice** is delicious.*

nonidentifying adjective clause   (also called **nonrestrictive adjective clause**) A clause that gives additional information about the noun it refers to. The information is not necessary to identify the noun.
- *My sister Diana, **who usually hates sports**, recently started tennis lessons.*

nonrestrictive adjective clause   See **nonidentifying adjective clause**.

noun   A word for a person, place, or thing.
- *My **sister**, **Anne**, works in an **office**.*
- *She uses a **computer**.*

object   A noun or a pronoun that receives the action of a verb. Sometimes a verb has two objects.
- *Layla threw **the ball**.*
- *She threw **it** to **Tom**.*
- *She threw **him** the ball.*

object pronoun   A pronoun (*me, you, him, her, it, us, them*) that receives the action of the verb.
- *I gave **her** a book.*
- *I gave **it** to **her**.*

object relative pronoun   A relative pronoun that is an object in an adjective clause.
- *I'm reading a book **that** I really like.*

paragraph   A group of sentences, usually about one topic.

particle   A word that looks like a preposition and combines with a main verb to form a phrasal verb. It often changes the meaning of the main verb.
- *He looked the word **up**. (He looked for the meaning of the word in the dictionary.)*

passive causative   A sentence formed with *have* or *get* + object + past participle. It is used to talk about services that you arrange for someone to do for you.
- *She **had the car checked** at the service station.*
- *He's going to **get his hair cut** by André.*

passive sentence   A sentence that focuses on the object (the person or thing receiving the action). The passive is formed with *be* + past participle.
- *The **ball was kicked** by Ari.*

past participle   A verb form (verb + *-ed*). It can also be irregular. It is used to form the present perfect, past perfect, and future perfect. It can also be an adjective.
- *We've **lived** here since April.*
- *They had **spoken** before.*
- *She's **interested** in math.*

phrasal verb   (also called two-word verb) A verb that has two parts (verb + particle). The meaning is often different from the meaning of its separate parts.
- *He **grew up** in Texas. (became an adult)*
- *His parents **brought** him **up** to be honest. (raised)*

phrase   A group of words that forms a unit but does not have a main verb. Many phrases give information about time or place.
- ***Last year**, we were living **in Canada**.*

plural   A form that means *two or more*.
- *There **are** three **people** in the restaurant.*
- ***They are** eating dinner.*
- ***We** saw **them**.*

possessive Nouns, pronouns, or adjectives that show a relationship or show that someone owns something.

- *Zach is **Megan's** brother.* (possessive noun)
- *Is that car **his**?* (possessive pronoun)
- *That's **his** car.* (possessive adjective)

predicate The part of a sentence that has the main verb. It tells what the subject is doing or describes the subject.

- *My sister **works for a travel agency**.*

preposition A word that goes before a noun or a pronoun to show time, place, or direction.

- *I went **to** the bank **on** Monday. It's **next to** my office.*

progressive (also called **continuous**) The verb form *be* + verb + *-ing*. It focuses on the continuation (not the completion) of an action.

- *She**'s reading** the paper.*
- *We **were watching** TV when you called.*

pronoun A word used in place of a noun.

- *That's my brother. You met **him** at my party.*

proper noun A noun that is the name of a person, place, or thing. It begins with a capital letter.

- ***Maria** goes to **Central High School**.*
- *It's on **High Street**.*

punctuation Marks used in writing (period, comma, . . .) that make the meaning clear. For example, a period **(.)** shows the end of a sentence. It also shows that the sentence is a statement, not a question.

quantifier A word or phrase that shows an amount (but not an exact amount). It often comes before a noun.

- *Josh bought **a lot of** books last year.*
- *He doesn't have **much** money.*

question See **yes / no question** and **wh- question**.

question word See **wh- word**.

quoted speech See **direct speech**.

real conditional sentence A sentence that talks about general truths, habits, or things that happen again and again. It can also talk about things that will happen in the future under certain circumstances.

- *If it rains, he takes the bus.*
- *If it rains tomorrow, we'll take the bus with him.*

regular A word that changes its form in the usual way.

- *play → played*
- *fast → faster*
- *quick → quickly*

relative pronoun A word that connects an adjective clause to a noun in the main clause.

- *He's the man **who** lives next door.*
- *I'm reading a book **that** I really like.*

reported speech See **indirect speech**.

reporting verb A verb such as *said, told,* or *asked*. It introduces direct and indirect speech. It can also come after the quotation in direct speech.

- *She **said**, "I'm going to be late." OR "I'm going to be late," she **said**.*
- *She **told** me that she was going to be late.*

restrictive adjective clause See **identifying adjective clause**.

result clause The clause in a conditional sentence that talks about what happens if the condition occurs.

- *If it rains, **I'll stay home**.*
- *If I had a million dollars, **I would travel**.*
- *If I had had your phone number, **I would have called you**.*

sentence A group of words that has a subject and a main verb.

- ***Computers are** very useful.*

separable phrasal verb A phrasal verb whose parts can separate.

- *Tom **looked** the word **up** in a dictionary.*
- *He **looked** it **up**.*

short answer An answer to a *yes / no* question.

   A: *Did you call me last night?*
   B: *No, I didn't. OR No.*

singular A form that means *one*.

- *They have **a sister**.*
- *She works in **a hospital**.*

statement A sentence that gives information. In writing, it ends in a period.

- *Today is Monday.*

stative verb See **non-action verb**.

subject The person, place, or thing that the sentence is about.

- **Ms. Chen** *teaches English.*
- **Her class** *is interesting.*

subject pronoun A pronoun that shows the person (*I, you, he, she, it, we, they*) that the sentence is about.

- **I** *read a lot.*
- **She** *reads a lot too.*

subject relative pronoun A relative pronoun that is the subject of an adjective clause.

- *He's the man* **who** *lives next door.*

subordinate clause See **dependent clause**.

superlative The form of an adjective or adverb that is used to compare a person, place, or thing to a group of people, places, or things.

- *Cindi is* **the shortest** *player on the team.* (adjective)
- *She dances* **the most gracefully**. (adverb)

tag question A statement + tag. The **tag** is a short question at the end of the statement. Tag questions check information or comment on a situation.

- *You're Jack Thompson,* **aren't you?**
- *It's a nice day,* **isn't it?**

tense The form of a verb that shows the time of the action.

- **simple present**: *Fabio* **talks** *to his friend every day.*
- **simple past**: *Fabio* **talked** *to his teacher yesterday.*

third-person singular The pronouns *he, she,* and *it* or a singular noun. In the simple present, the third-person-singular verb ends in -*s*.

- *Tomás* **works** *in an office.* (Tomás = he)

three-word verb A phrasal verb + preposition.

- *Slow down! I can't* **keep up with** *you.*

time clause A clause that begins with a time word such as *when, before, after, while,* or *as soon as*.

- *I'll call you* **when I get home**.

transitive verb A verb that has an object.

- *She* **likes** *apples.*

two-word verb See **phrasal verb**.

unreal conditional sentence A sentence that talks about unreal conditions and their unreal results. The condition and its result can be untrue, imagined, or impossible.

- *If I were a bird, I would fly around the world.*
- *If you had called, I would have invited you to the party.*

verb A word that describes what the subject of the sentence does, thinks, feels, senses, or owns.

- *They* **run** *two miles every day.*
- *She* **loved** *that movie.*
- *He* **has** *a new camera.*

wh- question (also called **information question**) A question that begins with a *wh-* word. You answer a *wh-* question with information.

- **A:** **Where** *are you going?*
- **B:** *To the store.*

wh- word A question word such as *who, what, when, where, which, why, how,* and *how much*. It can begin a *wh-* question or an embedded question.

- **Who** *is that?*
- **What** *did you see?*
- **When** *does the movie usually start?*
- *I don't know* **how much** *it costs.*

yes/no question A question that begins with a form of *be* or an auxiliary verb. You can answer a *yes/no* question with *yes* or *no*.

- **A:** **Are** *you a student?*
- **B:** **Yes**, *I am.* OR **No**, *I'm not.*

UNIT REVIEW ANSWER KEY

Note: In this answer key, where a short or contracted form is given, the full or long form is also correct (unless the purpose of the exercise is to practice the short or contracted forms).

UNIT 1

A
1. helps
2. is working
3. Do
4. understand
5. usually go

B
1. 'm looking for
2. think
3. isn't carrying
4. need
5. see
6. 's standing
7. 's waiting
8. sounds
9. don't believe
10. wants

C Hi Leda,

How ~~do you do~~ *are you doing* these days? We're all fine. I'm writing to tell you that we ~~not~~ *aren't* living in California anymore. We just moved to Oregon. Also, we ~~expect~~ *'re expecting* a baby! We're looking for an interesting name for our new daughter. Do you have any ideas? Right now, we're thinking about *Gabriella* because it ~~'s having~~ *has* good nicknames. For example, *Gabby*, *Bree*, and *Ella* all seem good to us. How ~~are~~ *do* those nicknames sound to you? We hope you'll write soon and tell us your news.
Love,
Samantha

UNIT 2

A
1. met
2. was working
3. saw
4. had
5. When
6. was thinking
7. gave

B
1. were . . . doing
2. met
3. were waiting
4. met
5. were studying
6. noticed
7. entered

C It was 2005. I ~~studied~~ *was studying* French in Paris ~~while~~ *when* I met Paul. Like me, Paul was from California. We were both taking the same 9:00 A.M. conversation class.

After class we always ~~were going~~ *went* to a café with some of our classmates. One day, while we ~~was~~ *were* drinking café au lait, Paul ~~was asking~~ *asked* me to go to a movie with him. After that, we started to spend most of our free time together. We really got to know each other well, and we discovered that we had a lot of similar interests. When the course was over, we left Paris and ~~were going~~ *went* back to California together. The next year we got married!

UNIT 3

A
1. got
2. has been living
3. since
4. read
5. been playing
6. has
7. 've been studying

B
1. has been working OR has worked
2. discovered
3. didn't know
4. found out
5. did OR 'd done
6. 's gone OR 's been going
7. hasn't found
8. 's had OR 's been having

C A: How long ~~did~~ *have* you been doing adventure sports?

B: I've ~~gotten~~ *got* interested five years ago, and I haven't stopped since then.

A: You're lucky to live here in Colorado. It's a great place for adventure sports. *Have you lived* OR *Have you been living* ~~Did you live~~ here long?

B: No, not long. I moved here last year. Before that, I ~~'ve been living~~ *lived* in Alaska.

A: I haven't ~~go~~ *been* there yet, but I've heard it's great.

B: It *is* great. When you go, be sure to visit Denali National Park.

UNIT 4

A
1. had gotten
2. had been studying
3. had graduated
4. moved
5. hadn't given

B
1. had . . . been playing
2. joined
3. 'd decided
4. 'd been practicing
5. 'd taught
6. Had . . . come
7. 'd . . . moved
8. 'd been living
9. hadn't expected

C When five-year-old Sarah Chang enrolled in the Juilliard School of Music, she ~~has~~ *had* already been playing the violin for more than a year. Her parents, both musicians, had ~~been moving~~ *moved* from Korea to further their careers. They had ~~gave~~ *given* their daughter a violin as a fourth birthday present, and Sarah had

                    practicing   *had*
been ~~practiced~~ hard since then. By seven, she
already performed with several local orchestras. A
child prodigy, Sarah became the youngest person to
receive the Hollywood Bowl's Hall of Fame Award.

                        received
She had already ~~been receiving~~ several awards
including the Nan Pa Award—South Korea's highest
prize for musical talent.

UNIT 5

A 1. turn   5. is going to
   2. Are   6. 're
   3. doing   7. finishes
   4. is

B 1. will . . . be doing OR are . . . going to be doing

   2. is going to be leaving OR will be leaving

   3. 'll be sitting OR 'm going to be sitting

   4. won't be coming OR 're not going to be coming

   5. Is . . . going to cause OR Will . . . cause

   6. No . . . isn't. OR No . . . won't.

   7. 's going to be OR 'll be

   8. 'll see

                              be
C A: How long are you going to ^ staying in Beijing?

   B: I'm not sure. I'll let you know just as soon as I ~~I'll~~
      find out, OK?

   A: OK. It's going to be a long flight. What will you
      do OR *be doing*
      ~~did~~ to pass the time?

                  working
   B: I'll be ~~work~~ a lot of the time. And I'm going to
      try to sleep.

                                      'll email
   A: Good idea. Have fun, and I'~~m emailing~~ you all
      the office news. I promise.

UNIT 6

A 1. have saved   4. 'll have read
   2. get   5. By
   3. have been exercising

B 1. 'll have been living   5. 'll have found
   2. 'll have been studying   6. 'll have made
   3. 'll have graduated   7. 'll have saved
   4. graduate

C I'm so excited about your news! By the time you
                                moved
read this, you'll have already ~~moving~~ into your new
house! And I have some good news too. By the
                        have saved
end of this month, I will ~~have been saving~~ $3,000.
That's enough for me to buy a used car! And that
                                  'll have driven
means that by this time next year, I ~~drive~~ to
California to visit you! I have more news too. By the
time I ~~will~~ graduate, I will have ~~been~~ started my new
part-time job. I hope that by this time next year, I'll
      have
also ~~had~~ paid off some of my loans.

It's hard to believe that in June, we will have been
~~being~~ friends for 10 years. Time sure flies! And we'll
have ~~been~~ stayed friends even though we live 3,000
miles apart. Isn't the Internet a great thing?

UNIT 7

A 1. isn't   3. 've   5. Hasn't   7. Shouldn't
   2. Didn't   4. it   6. she

B 1. haven't   5. Yes, I am
   2. No, I haven't   6. won't
   3. Can't   7. Yes, you will
   4. are

                                                    he
C A: Ken hasn't come back from Korea yet, has ~~Ken~~?
        Yes
   B: ~~No~~, he has. He got back last week. Didn't he
      call you when he got back?

   A: No, he didn't. He's probably busy. There are a
                                      aren't there
      lot of things to do when you move, ~~isn't it~~?
                                           will want
   B: Definitely. And I guess his family ~~wanted~~ to
      spend a lot of time with him, won't they?

   A: I'm sure they will. You know, I think I'll just
                                        don't
      call him. You have his phone number, ~~have~~
      you?

   B: Yes, I do. Could you wait while I get it off my
                                      are
      computer? You're not in a hurry, ~~aren't~~ you?

UNIT 8

A 1. does   3. isn't either   5. doesn't
   2. So   4. but   6. too

B 1. I speak Spanish, and so does my brother. OR
      . . . and my brother does too.

   2. Jaime lives in Chicago, but his brother doesn't.

   3. Chicago is an exciting city, and so is New York.
      OR . . . and New York is too.

   4. Chen doesn't play tennis, but his sister does.

   5. Diego doesn't eat meat, and neither does Lila.
      OR . . . and Lila doesn't either.

C My friend Alicia and I have a lot in common. She
                                    do I
comes from Los Angeles, and so ~~I do~~. She speaks
                  do OR *I speak Spanish*
Spanish. I ~~speak~~ too. Her parents are both teachers,
and
~~but~~ mine are too. (My mother teaches math, and her
              does
father ~~do~~ too.) I don't have any brothers or sisters.
Neither
~~Either~~ does she. There are some differences too.
                                    but
Alicia is very outgoing, ~~and~~ I'm not. I like to spend
more time alone. I don't enjoy sports, but she
    does   *I'm not*
~~doesn't~~. She's on several school teams, but ~~not I'm~~.

UR-2

I just think our differences make things more

interesting, and so ~~my friend does~~! _does my friend_

UNIT 9

A 1. to use
2. (in order) to save
3. ordering
4. to relax
5. to study OR study
6. preparing
7. Stopping
8. to eat
9. having
10. Cooking

B 1. doesn't OR didn't remember eating

2. wants OR wanted him to take

3. wonders OR wondered about Chu's OR Chu eating

4. didn't stop to have OR is going to stop to have

5. forgot to mail

C **A:** I was happy to hear that the cafeteria is serving

salads now. I'm eager ~~trying~~ them. _to try_

B: Me too. Someone recommended eating more

salads in order ~~for losing~~ weight. _to lose_

A: It was that TV doctor, right? He's always urging

~~we~~ to exercise more too. _us_

B: That's the one. He's actually convinced me to

stop ~~to eat~~ meat. _eating_

A: Interesting! It would be a hard decision for us

~~making~~, though. We love to barbecue. _to make_

UNIT 10

A 1. helped
2. had
3. made
4. let
5. got

B 1. didn't OR wouldn't let me have

2. got them to give

3. made me walk

4. had me feed

5. didn't OR wouldn't help me take / to take

6. got him to give

7. let them have

C Lately I've been thinking a lot about all the people

who helped me ~~adjusting~~ to moving here when I was _adjust OR to adjust_

a kid. My parents got me ˄ join some school clubs so _to_

that I met other kids. Then my dad helped me

~~improves~~ my soccer game so I could join the team. _improve OR to improve_

And my mom never let me ✕ stay home. She made

me ✕ get out and do things. My parents also spoke

to my new teacher, and they had her ~~called~~ on me a _call_

lot so the other kids got to know me quickly. The

---

neighbors helped too. They got ~~I~~ to walk their dog _me_

Red, and Red introduced me to all her human

friends! The fact that so many people wanted to

help me made me ✕ realize that I was not alone.

Before long I felt part of my new school, my new

neighborhood, and my new life.

UNIT 11

A 1. off
2. it down
3. ahead
4. up
5. away
6. back
7. it up

B 1. take down
2. touch up
3. settle on
4. figure . . . out
5. show up
6. find out
7. left . . . on
8. turn . . . off

C **A:** This apartment is bringing me down. Let's do

~~over it~~. _it over_

B: It *is* depressing. Let's put ~~around~~ a list and _together_

figure out what to do first.

A: OK. Write this down: Pick ~~on~~ new paint colors. _out_

We can look at some online.

B: The new streetlight shines into the bedroom.

We need to block ~~up~~ the light somehow. _out_

A: We could put ~~on~~ some dark curtains in that _up_

room. That should take care of the problem.

UNIT 12

A 1. f   3. a   5. b   7. g
2. e   4. c   6. d

B 1. woke Jason up
2. pick it up
3. count on her
4. call me back
5. got off the phone
6. put my nightshirt on
7. turned the lights off

C I'm so tired of telemarketers calling me up as

soon as I get ~~from work back~~ or just when I sit ~~up~~ for _back from work_   _down_

a relaxing dinner! It's gotten to the point that I've

stopped picking ˄ the phone when it rings between _up_

6:00 to 8:00 P.M. ˄~~up~~. I know I can count on it being a

telemarketer who will try to talk me into spending

money on something I don't want. But it's still

annoying to hear the phone ring, so sometimes I

turn ~~off it~~. Then, of course, I worry that it may be _it off_

someone important. So I end up checking caller ID

to find out. I think the Do Not Call list is a great idea.

Who thought ~~up it~~? I'm going to sign ~~for it up~~ _it up_   _up for it_

tomorrow!

UNIT 13

A 1. are   3. thinks   5. which
       2. whose   4. which   6. who

B 1. who OR that behave   5. that OR which hurt
       2. who makes   6. which . . . upset
       3. which . . . convince   7. whose . . . is
       4. who OR that . . . speaks

C It's true that we are often attracted to people
who OR *that*
~~whose~~ are very different from ourselves. An
                    whose
extrovert, ~~which~~ personality is very outgoing, will
                                              is
often connect with a romantic partner who ~~are~~ an
introvert. They are both attracted to someone that
has
~~have~~ different strengths. My cousin Valerie, who is an
extreme extrovert, recently married Bill, whose idea
of a party is a Scrabble game on the Internet. Can
this marriage succeed? Will Bill learn the salsa,
which
~~that~~ is Valerie's favorite dance? Will Valerie start
                                          who
collecting unusual words? Their friends, ~~what~~ care
about both of them, are hoping for the best.

UNIT 14

A 1. whose   3. where   5. when
       2. that   4. who   6. who

B 1. where   5. whose
       2. that OR which   6. who(m)
       3. that OR which   7. that OR which
       4. who(m) OR that

C I grew up in an apartment building ~~who~~ my
                                  that OR *which*
grandparents owned. There was a small dining room
where OR *in which*   *in which* OR *where*
~~when~~ we had family meals and a kitchen ~~in that~~ I ate
                                          whose
my breakfast. My aunt, uncle, and cousin, in ~~who~~

home I spent a lot of my time, lived in an identical
apartment on the fourth floor. I remember the time
my parents gave me a toy phone set that we set up
so I could talk to my cousin. There weren't many
children in the building, but I often visited the
                        whose
building manager, ~~who's~~ son I liked. I enjoyed living
in the apartment, but for me it was a happy day
when OR *that*
~~where~~ we moved into our own house.

UNIT 15

A 1. get   4. can't   7. post
       2. may   5. help   8. must not
       3. 've got   6. might   9. be able to

B 1. 'd better not OR shouldn't OR ought not to give
       2. 'd better OR 've got to OR must register
       3. must not be

4. has got to OR must get

5. can't OR must not eat

6. may OR might OR could come

C 1. Could that ~~being~~ Amelie in this photograph?
                be

2. No, that's impossible. It doesn't look anything
                    can't OR *couldn't*
like Amelie. It ~~doesn't have to~~ be her.

3. I don't know this person. I guess I'd ~~not better~~
                                    better not
accept him as a friend on my Facebook page.

4. With MySpace, I ~~must not~~ call to keep in touch
                   don't have to
with friends. It's just not necessary.
     Will
5. ~~May~~ hi5 be as popular as Facebook someday?

UNIT 16

A 1. have   3. could   5. shouldn't
       2. ought   4. given   6. should I

B 1. I should've studied for the math test.

       2. You could've shown me your class notes.

       3. I shouldn't have stayed up so late the night
          before the test.

       4. John ought to have called you.

       5. You might've invited me to join the study
          group.

C I shouldn't have ~~stay~~ up so late. I overslept and
                       stayed
                                              to
missed my bus. I ought ^ have asked Erik for a ride. I
got to the office late, and my boss said, "You might
have   *should*
~~had~~ called." She was right. I ~~shouldn't~~ have called. At
lunch my co-workers went out together. They really
         have   *I have*
could ~~of~~ invited me to join them. Should ~~have I~~ said
something to them? Then, after lunch, my mother
called. She said, "Yesterday was Aunt Em's birthday.
                    sent
You could've ~~sending~~ her a card!" I really think my
                   have
mother might ~~has~~ reminded me. Not a good day! I
              should've
~~shouldn't have~~ just stayed in bed.

UNIT 17

A 1. must   5. may
       2. might not have   6. have
       3. have   7. couldn't
       4. taken

B 1. might OR may not have gotten my message

       2. must not have studied

       3. couldn't OR can't have forgotten our date

       4. may OR might OR could have been at the movies

       5. must have forgotten

       6. must not have seen me

C Why did the Aztecs build their capital city in the middle of a lake? Could they ~~had~~ *have* wanted the protection of the water? They might have ~~been~~. Or the location may ~~has~~ *have* helped them to control nearby societies. At first it must have ~~being~~ *been* an awful place, full of mosquitoes and fog. But it must ~~no~~ *not* have been a bad idea—the island city became the center of a very powerful empire. To succeed, the Aztecs had to have ~~became~~ *become* fantastic engineers quite quickly. When the Spanish arrived, they couldn't have ~~expect~~ *expected* the amazing palaces, floating gardens, and well-built canals. Unfortunately, they destroyed the city anyway.

A
1. Spanish is spoken in Bolivia.
2. They play soccer in Bolivia.
3. Reza Deghati took the photo.
4. The articles were translated into Spanish.
5. Quinoa is grown in the mountains.
6. They named the main street El Prado.

B
1. was discovered
2. is spoken
3. is grown
4. is exported
5. are OR have been employed
6. was made
7. has been performed
8. is attended

C Photojournalist Alexandra Avakian was born and ~~raise~~ *raised* in New York. Since she began her career, she has covered many of the world's most important stories. Her work ~~have~~ *has* been published in many newspapers and magazines including *National Geographic*, and her photographs have ~~being~~ *been* exhibited around the world. Avakian has also written a book, *Window of the Soul: My Journey in the Muslim World*, which was ~~been~~ published in 2008. It has not yet been translated ~~by translators~~ into other languages, but the chapter titles appear in both English and Arabic. Avakian's book ~~have be~~ *has been* discussed on international TV, radio, and numerous websites.

A
1. done
2. be replaced
3. could
4. had
5. be
6. won't
7. has
8. are

B
1. should be trained
2. have to be given
3. must . . . be tested
4. can be experienced
5. will be provided
6. may be sent
7. could . . . be developed

C The new spacesuits are going to be ~~testing~~ *tested* underwater today. They've got to ~~been~~ *be* improved before they can be used on the Moon or Mars. Two astronauts are going to be wearing them while they're working, and they'll ∧*be* watched by the engineers. This morning communication was lost with the Earth's surface, and all decisions had to be ~~make~~ *made* by the astronauts themselves. It was a very realistic situation. This crew ~~will got~~ *will have* OR *has got* to be very well prepared for space travel. They're going to the Moon in a few years.

A
1. have it cut
2. done
3. get
4. your house painted
5. by

B
1. have OR get it repaired
2. have OR get them cleaned
3. have OR get them shortened
4. have OR get it colored
5. have OR get it fixed
6. had OR got it removed
7. have OR get it renewed
8. 'll have OR get OR 'm going to have OR 'm having OR getting it checked

C I'm going on vacation next week. I'd like to have ~~done some work~~ *some work done* in my office, and this seems like a good time for it. Please have my carpet ~~clean~~ *cleaned* while I'm gone. And could you have my computer and printer looked at? It's been quite a while since they've been serviced. Ted wants to have my office painted ~~by a painter~~ while I'm gone. Please tell him any color is fine except pink! Last week, I ~~had designed some new brochures~~ *had some new brochures designed* by Perfect Print. Please call the printer and have them delivered directly to the sales reps. And could you ~~get made up more business cards~~ *get more business cards made up* too? When I get back, it'll be time to plan the holiday party. I think we should have it catered this year ~~from~~ *by* a professional. While I'm gone, why don't you call around and get some estimates from

caterers? ~~Has~~ *Have* the estimates sent to Ted. Thanks.

UNIT 21

A 1. do . . . do   6. doesn't stay
2. are   7. closes
3. is   8. go
4. shop   9. feel
5. happens   10. think

B 1. When OR If it's 7:00 A.M. in Honolulu, what time is it in Mumbai?

2. If you love jewelry, you should visit an international jewelry show.

3. A tourist might have more fun if she tries bargaining.

4. If OR When you're shopping at an outdoor market, you can always bargain for a good price.

5. But don't try to bargain if OR when you're shopping in a big department store.

C 1. If I don't like something I bought online, then I ~~returned~~ *return* it.

2. Don't buy from an online site, if you don't know anything about the company.

3. When he shops online, Frank always saves a lot of time.

4. I always ~~fell~~ *fall* asleep if I fly at night. It happens every time.

5. Isabel always has a wonderful time, when she visits Istanbul.

UNIT 22

A 1. d   3. a   5. b
2. f   4. c   6. e

B 1. take

2. 'll be OR 'm going to be

3. will . . . do OR are . . . going to do

4. don't get

5. 'll stay OR 'm going to stay

6. get

7. pass

8. 'll celebrate OR 'm going to celebrate

C It's been a hard week, and I'm looking forward to

the weekend. If the weather ~~will be~~ *is* nice tomorrow, Marco and I are going to go to the beach. The ocean is usually too cold for swimming at this time of year, so I probably ~~don't~~ *won't* go in the water unless it's really hot outside. But I love walking along the beach and breathing in the fresh sea air.

If Marco has time, he might ~~makes~~ *make* some sandwiches to bring along. Otherwise, we'll just get some pizza. I hope it'll be a nice day. I just listened to the weather report, and there may be some rain in

the afternoon. ~~Unless~~ *If* it rains, we'*ll* probably go to the movies instead. That's our Plan B. But I really want to go to the beach, so I'm keeping my fingers crossed!

UNIT 23

A 1. 'd feel   5. could
2. were   6. weren't
3. could   7. 'd
4. found

B 1. would . . . do   5. would become
2. found   6. put
3. Would . . . take   7. made
4. knew   8. would learn

C 1. Pablo wishes he ~~can~~ *could* speak German.

2. If he had the time, he'*d* study in Germany. But he doesn't have the time right now.

3. He could get a promotion ~~when~~ *if* he spoke another language.

4. His company ~~may~~ *might* pay the tuition if he took a course.

5. What would you do if you ~~are~~ *were* in Pablo's situation?

UNIT 24

A 1. hadn't told   4. If
2. had   5. gone
3. would have been

B 1. would've been

2. hadn't missed

3. had been

4. wouldn't have discovered

5. hadn't accepted

6. had taken

7. wouldn't have met

8. hadn't seen

9. wouldn't have believed

C Tonight we watched the movie *Back to the Future*

starring Michael J. Fox. I might never ~~had~~ *have* seen it if I hadn't read his autobiography, *Lucky Man*. His book was so good that I wanted to see his most famous

movie. Now I wish I ~~saw~~ *had seen* it in the theater when it first came out, but I hadn't even been born yet! It would

have been better if we ~~would have~~ *had* watched it on a big screen. Fox was great. He looked really young—

just like a teenager. But I would have recognized him

even ~~when~~ *if* I hadn't known he was in the film.
In real life, when Fox was a teenager, he was too
small to become a professional hockey player. But if

he hadn't looked so young, he ~~can't~~ *couldn't* OR *wouldn't* have gotten his
role in the TV hit series *Family Ties*. In Hollywood,
he had to sell his furniture to pay his bills, but he

kept trying to find an acting job. If he ~~wouldn't have~~ *hadn't*,
he might never have become a star.

UNIT 25

A
1. says
2. "I'd love to."
3. planned
4. he
5. 'd
6. told
7. had been
8. his

B
1. (that) she always gets OR got up early.
2. (that) water boils OR boiled at 100 degrees Celsius.
3. (that) he liked OR likes my haircut.
4. (that) she loved OR 'd loved the pasta.
5. (that) it was OR is his own recipe.
6. (that) she mailed OR 'd mailed him the check.
7. (that) his boss had liked OR liked his work.

C
1. A psychologist I know often tells me ✗ that people today tell hundreds of lies every day. ✗
2. Yesterday Marcia's boyfriend ~~said her~~ *said* OR *told her* that he liked her new dress.
3. When she heard that, Marcia said she didn't really believe ~~you~~ *him*.
4. I didn't think that was so bad. I said that her boyfriend ~~tells~~ *had told* OR *told* her a white lie.
5. But Marcia hates lying. She said that to ~~me~~ *her*, all lies are wrong.

UNIT 26

A
1. was
2. I
3. take
4. might
5. today
6. would
7. could
8. there

B
1. (that) it was going to rain
2. (that) it could be the worst storm this year
3. (that) it was going to start soon
4. (that) they should buy water
5. (that) they had to leave right then
6. (that) she would call me the next day

C What a storm! They ~~told~~ *said* it ~~is~~ *was* going to be bad, but
it was terrible. They said it ~~will~~ *would* last two days, but it
lasted four. On the first day of the storm, my mother

called and told me that we should ~~have left~~ *leave* the house

right ~~now~~ *then*. (I still can hear her exact words: "You
should leave the house *right now*!") We should have
listened to her! We just didn't believe it was going to
be so serious. I told her last night that if we had

known, we would ~~had~~ *have* left right away. We're lucky we
survived. I just listened to the weather forecast. Good
news! They said tomorrow should be sunny.

UNIT 27

A
1. . [*period*]
2. give
3. "Please sit down."
4. not to
5. say
6. told
7. invited

B
1. He told OR asked her to show him her license.
2. She advised OR told him to get more exercise.
3. She invited OR asked them to come to the English Department party.
4. He asked her to turn on the light.
5. She invited OR asked them to hang out at her house.

C My teacher, Mr. Wong, ~~told~~ *said* OR *told us* to sleep well before

the test. He said ~~to don't~~ *not to* stay up late studying. He

always invites ~~we~~ *us* to ask him questions. He says,

"~~Not to~~ *Don't* be shy." I'm glad my friend Tom advised me
~~taking~~ *to take* his class. He ~~said me~~ *said* OR *told me* to register early, and he
warned me ✗ that the class filled up fast every

semester. ✗ I told him ~~don't~~ *not* to worry. I said I'd already
registered.

UNIT 28

A
1. . [*period*]
2. if
3. their office was
4. I lived
5. I had

B
1. who the company had hired.
2. if OR whether I had taken the job.
3. if OR whether I liked my present job.
4. who my boss was.
5. how many employees worked there.
6. why I wanted to change jobs.
7. what the starting salary was.
8. if OR whether I could start soon.

C They asked me so many questions! They asked me
where ~~did I work~~ *I worked*. They asked who ~~was my boss~~ *my boss was*.
They asked why I ~~did want~~ *wanted* to change jobs. They
asked how much money I made. They ~~ask~~ *asked* me who I
~~have~~ *had* voted for in the last election. They even asked
me what my favorite color was͵ Finally, I asked
myself whether or ~~no~~ *not* I really wanted that job!

UNIT 29

A
1. we should
2. our server is
3. . [*period*]
4. to
5. I should
6. ? [*question mark*]
7. whether

B
1. where the restaurant is?
2. if OR whether the subway goes to the museum.
3. if OR whether we should tip the porter.
4. why we didn't buy the book on tipping.
5. how much we should tip the tour guide.
6. if OR whether you have any travel books.
7. what this sign says?

C **A:** Hi. Is this a good time to call? I wasn't sure

what time you have dinner͵

B: This is fine. I didn't know ~~were you~~ *if OR whether you were* back from
your trip.

A: We got back two days ago. I can't remember
~~did I email~~ *if OR whether I emailed* you some photographs.

B: Yes. They were great. Can you tell me where
~~took you~~ *you took* that picture of the lake? I want to go!

A: Hmm. I'm not sure which one ~~was that~~ *that was*. We
saw a lot of lakes in Switzerland.

B: I'll show it to you. I'd really like to find out
where ~~is it~~ *it is*.

INDEX

This index is for the full and split editions. All entries are in the full book. Entries for Volume A of the split edition are in black. Entries for Volume B are in red.

CREDITS